KAMANDAKIYA NITISARA

KAMANDAKIYA NITISARA

OR

THE ELEMENTS OF POLITY

(IN ENGLISH)

EDITED AND PUBLISHED BY

MANMATHA NATH DUTT, M. A., M. R. A. S.

GYAN

Published by

Gyan Publishing House
5, Ansari Road
Daryaganj, New Delhi-110002
Phone: 011-47034999, 9811692060
E-mail: books@gyanbooks.com

Distribution Network
gyanbooks.com
India, USA, Canada, UK, Australia, France

ISBN: 978-81-212-7971-0 (PB)
First Published, 1896

2nd Impression 2023

Printed at: Gyan Press, Delhi.

KAMANDAKIYA NITISARA
Editor: MANMATHA NATH DUTT

KAMANDAKIYA NITISARA

OR

THE ELEMENTS OF POLITY

(IN ENGLISH.)

EDITED AND PUBLISHED BY

MANMATHA NATH DUTT, M.A., M.R.A.S.

RECTOR, KESHUB ACADEMY;

Author of the English Translations of the Ramayana, Śrimadbhaga-vatam, Vishnupuranam, Mahabharata, Bhagavat-Gita and other works.

CALCUTTA:

PRINTED BY H. C. DASS,

ELYSIUM PRESS, 65/2 BEADON STREET.

1896.

INTRODUCTION.

—:o:—

The science of Polity: its origin.

THE superiority of the ancient Hindus in metaphysical and theological disquisitions has been established beyond all doubts. Our literature abounds in treatises, which, for philosophical discussions, sound reasonings and subtle inferences regarding many momentous problems of existence, have not been beaten down by the modern age of culture and enlightenment. The world has all along been considered by the ancient Hindu writers as a flood-gate of miseries of existence, and the *summum bonum* of human existence is, in their view, the unification of the humanity with the divinity. The chief aim of all the ancient writers of India has been to solve the mighty problem, namely, the cessation of miseries of existence and the attainment of the God-head. Admitting their exalted superiority in matters of philosophical and theological speculation, some people of the present generation boldly launch the theory that our literature lacks in works which may serve as a guidance of practical life. To disabuse the popular mind of this perilous misconception, we might safely assert that Hindu writers paid no less attention to practical morals and politics. We find a very beautiful account of the Science of Polity in the Rajdharma section of the great Epic, the Mahabharata.

Formerly for the protection of creatures Brahma wrote the science of Polity in ten million chapters. Siva obtained this from Brahma and epitomised it in ten thousand chapters. His work is called *Vaishalakshya* from his name (*Vishalaksha* or large-eyed). Indra made an abridgement of it in five thousand chapters. Vrihaspati converted it into three thousand chapters, and Sukra into one thousand. Thus it was gradually abridged by various sages having in view the shortened life of the people around them.

It was Chanakya, the Machæval of India who first reformed this Science at the end of the age of Rishis. His work consisting of a hundred verses is a well-known brochure which even the school boys of India get by rote. The author, of the work which is the subject of our translation, was a disciple of Chanakya who raised the first Mauriya king Chandra Gupta on the throne of Pataliputra (B. C. 319.)

Tradition fully corroborates this date. From a report submitted

Date.

by Dr. Frederich to the Batavian Society of arts and Sciences on the Sanskrita literature of Bali, it appears that the most popular work in that Island on Polity is entitled *Kamandakiya Nitisára*, and all the Sanskrita books there extant are acknowledged to be the counterparts of purely Indian originals. The researches of Sir Stamford Raffles and Crawfurd shew that the predominance of Buddhism in the island of Java obliged the Hindu inhabitants of that place to retire in the fourth century of the Christian era, with their household gods and their sacred scriptures to the island of Bali, where they and their descendants have, ever since, most carefully preserved the authenticity of their literature and their religion. It has also been shewn by the same authorities that since the period of their exile, they have not had any religious intercourse with India; it would therefore follow that the Sanskrita works now available in Bali, including the *Kamandakiya Niti*, are of a date anterior to the 4th century. The contents, however, of the Balenese code of morals, are unknown, and it would be premature, from the similarity of names, to infer its identity with the work now presented to the public; yet the fact that the people of Bali themselves acknowledge all their Sanskrita literature to have been obtained from India, would argue the existence of at least a *Kamandakiya Nitisàra* at the time when that literature was imported from the shores of Bharatavarsha.

An internal evidence of some moment is in favour of the antiquity which tradition has ascribed to this work. It is dedicated to Chandragupta, and the author, a Buddhist, apparently with a view not to offend the feelings of his Hindu patron with the name of a Buddhist deity, has thought fit to forego the usual invocation at the commencement of his work—a circumstance which has been made the theme of much erudite disquisition by the author of the Siddhanta Muktavali.

Although written in verse, its style is peculiarly unpoetical, and in its rude simplicity approaches the older Smritis. The work has not, however, any of the antiquated grammatical forms and obsolete expressions which are so freely met with in Manu and occasionally in the other Smritis, and its versification is unexceptionable. Indeed, had it to be judged by its metres alone they would have justified the inference that its origin is due to a much later age than that of Kalidasa.

It has been observed by some that the use of the word *horá* in this work is fatal to its claim to antiquity, that word having been shown, in a paper published in the Journal of the Asiatic Society (Vol. p.), to be of Arabic origin, and to have been borrowed by the Brahmanas in the 10th century. Mr. Ravenshaw's speculations, however, have not yet obtained that confirmation which would justify our rejecting the testimony of the dedication, and infer the date of the work from the use of a single word which may after all be the result of an interpolation or a mislection.

Style.

The style is condensed and pithy like that of proverbs. The essential characteristics are its gravity and sententiousness. In the early state of society concise rules and flashing proverbs " the condensed conclusions of experience " form better guides of life and are therefore more frequently resorted to than lengthy ratiocinations in search of general truths. Wise men of old from Solomon downwards all preferred this method of communicating their ideas.

Sources.

Apologue or fable was also adopted as a form in which moral counsel could be successfully imparted. Probably apologues followed proverbs and essays succeeded them next. Hitapodesha the most celebrated work of moral counsels is in the shape of apologues; some scholars hold that Hitopodesha is the model which Kamandaka followed. They base their arguments on the theory that apologue was the earliest form of literary productions. We however hold that *Kamandakiya Nitisára* is the earlier work, proverbs in our view, preceding the apologues as the form of literary compositions. Even looking to the Mahabharata which is anterior to both we see maxims in the very words as in this work. Agnipuran has a section in which

Kamandaki has been freely quoted though not by name. Thus we see that these and similar maxims were among the Hindus as the heir-looms of remote antiquity.

Moral tone.

Some critics are of opinion that the moral tone of the state-policy is not worthy of a descendant of the ancient Rishis. Its corner stone is cunning and artifice intended to favor arbitrary power and its main object is to put down party opposition. Chanakya, the preceptor of the author, was always on the alert to over-throw his powerful rival Rakshasa. For this he took recourse to one eternal round of stratagems and artifices from which forgery, perjury and even poisoning were not excluded. His disciple Kamandaka could not shake off the influence of his powerful teacher. But this defect is confined entirely to the sections on deplomacy and does not affect at all his rules regarding the general conduct of kings and their officers. Herein we find an earnest advocacy of truth, justice and honesty which stands a favourable comparison with works of much higher pretensions.

The Synopsis of the work.

The maxims of Kamandaki are arranged under nineteen different heads, and embrace almost all the subjects that may be fairly included under the term polity, besides some which have only the voucher of Hindu writers to appear in this work. The first chapter is devoted to the inculcation, in princes, of the necessity of study and of controlling their passions. The second has for its subjects the division of learning, the duties of the different castes and the importance of criminal jurisprudence. In the third occurs an exposition of the duty of princes to their subjects, of the necessity of impartial justice, and the impropriety of tyrannising over their people. The fourth affords a description of the essential constituents of a good government. The duties of masters and servants engross the whole of the fifth chapter, and the mode of removing difficulties or rather of punishing the wicked, forms the subject of the sixth. The seventh is devoted to the duty of guarding the persons of kings and crown princes, and includes a variety of expedients against surprises, poisoning, the infidelity of servants, wives and relatives, and the dishonesty of medical attendants. The mode of consolidating a kingdom by providing it with the necessary officers of state, and including within it a number of dependencies and subordinate chiefs, forms the subject of the next chapter. Then follow a series of rules regarding negotiations and disputes with foreign powers, conferences, embassies and spies, which take up the whole of the 9th, 10th, 11th and the 12th chapter. The 13th opens with an exhortation in favour of constant activity and attention to business, and the evils which attend idleness and vicious propensities. The latter are indicated by the term *vyásana*, and include a number of vices and frailties—such as over-fondness for hunting and gambling, sleeping in the day, calumny, concupiscence, dancing, singing, playing, idleness, drinking, general depravity, violence, injury, envy, malice, pride, and tyranny. The term is very comprehensive, and when applied to other than men, is made to imply "defects" generally, and the subsequent chapter particularises the various defects to which the seven members of a government are frequently liable. It is followed by a dissertation on military expeditions. The 16th chapter has fortification, entrenchment and encamping of armies for its subjects, and, though short, is highly interesting, for the rules it contains on matters in which the modern Hindus are so entirely ignorant. The different expedients for overcoming enemies such as reconciliation, wealth, show of military power, domestic discord, diplomacy, feigning, and stratagem, are detailed in the following chapter, and those failing, a king is recommended to enter into actual warfare, and on the mode of carrying it on, including surprises, guerilla fights, pitched battles, and military stratagies; the uses of the different members of an army, such as the infantry, cavalry and elephants; the arrays of soldiers into columns, lines, squares &c.; the duties of commanders, and the principle of selecting one's ground; the two subsequent chapters contain the most curious details.

Our object.

We have undertaken to translate into English this great work of Kamandaka for it stands pre-eminently high among works dealing with the science of Polity. It is thorougly representative in its character and the precepts, of the great sage, we are sure, will prove a profitable reading to the general public and more so to many Hindu princes who govern over the destiny of a vast section of the Indian population. Now that it has pleased the Gracious Providence to link the destinies of India with those of England this work is likely to give some idea to our rulers as to how the ancient Hindu kings ruled their subjects. In India we have glorious traditions of loyalty. In India loyalty is the very back-bone of the Indian races by whom a king is regarded as a god-head. It will not be therefore useless both for the rulers and the ruled to know how the ancient Hindu kings swayed over the vast millions and what was the key-note of the loving fidelity of these latter to their king.

KAMANDAKIYA NITISARA.

SECTION I.

SALUTATION unto the Glorious Ganesha.

1. *May that lord of the earth be ever attended with victory over his internal and external enemies, through whose Regal power† this world is stationed in the paths of rectitude; who is rich in his wealth of learning‡ and is

* It was customary with Sanskrit writers of yore to eulogise, in the first instance, the central character that would figure in their respective treatises. In accordance with this time-honored custom the author here salutes the 'lords of the earth' for whose guidance he is going to lay down maxims of practical politics. The first Sloka also contains an allusion to the Mauriya king Chandragupta (B. C. 319) who had been installed on the throne of Pátaliputra by the preceptor of the writer of this brochure. The reader will see, that immediately after the author salutes his renowned and well-known teacher, the celebrated Chánakya the Machiavel of India.

† *Prabháva.*—Is here synonymous with *Sakti* (Regal power), which has three parts or elements, viz (1) *Prabhusakti* which means 'majesty or pre-eminent position of the king himself.' (2) *Mantrasakti* which means 'the power of good counsel.' (3) *Utsáhasakti*, which means, 'the power of energy.' *c.f.* '*Rájayam náma saktitrayáyattam.*' The essential requisites for a monarchy are the possession of these three *Saktis*.

‡ *Sriman.*—Ordinarly translated would mean 'attended with *Sri* or prosperity'. The commentator takes *Sri* to mean 'knowledge of the *Shástras*, prudence, wisdom &c.'

god-like* (in prosperity); and (lastly) who (equitably) inflicts punishment† (on those deserving it).

2—6. Salutation unto the highly intelligent Vishnugupta,‡ who sprang from an extensive and illustrious dynasty the descendants of which lived like the Rishis§ accepting alms from nobody; unto him whose renown became world-wide; unto him who was effulgent like the (highly blazing) fire;|| unto that most artful and cunning one, the foremost of those conversant with *Paramártha*,¶ who mastered the four Vedas as if they were only one. Salutation unto that one whose fire of energy was like the flash of lightning, and through whose magical powers,** that resembled in potency and in fury the thunder-bolt itself, the wide-spread, renowned, powerful and mountain-like dynasty of Nanda†† was

---

* *Deva.*—All the qualities indicated by the root are only possible in a celestial, hence the word has ordinarily come to mean a deity. A king is held in as high and sacred an estimation as a deity, and is said to possess all the attributes in common with a god.

† *Dandadhára.*—May have two meanings, both of which may be accepted here; the first word of this compound means 'a sceptre' as well as 'punishment'; and the second word means 'to hold' as well as 'to deal out.' So the compound may have two significations (1) holding the sceptre as a symbol of authority (2) dealing out punishments.

‡ *Vishnugupta.*—Another name of Chánakya. He had many other designations such as *Droumina, Koutilya, Amsoola* &c.

§ *Rishi.*—A seer.

|| *Játaveda.*—Is one of the diverse designations of fire; it is so called as it is supposed to know all beings born on the face of the earth. The reference is here to one of the sacred ceremonies of the Hindus, according to which a fire is to be kindled in the lying-in-room of a new born babe.

¶ *Vedavidám.*—*Veda* here means *Paramártha*, that is, the highest or most sublime truth, true spiritual knowledge about *Brahman* or the Supreme Spirit.

***Avichára vajram.*—*Avichára* signifies 'employment of magical spells for malevolent purposes.'

†† *Suparva.*—The *parva* of a mountain is its peak. *Nandaparvata.*—The dynasty of Nanda was dethroned through the machinations and

eradicated for good.* Salutation unto him who resembled the god Saktidhara† himself (in prowess) and who, single-handed, by means of his *Mantrasakti* and *Utsâhasakti*,‡ brought the entire earth under the thorough control of Chandragupta, the foremost of sovereigns. Salutation unto that wisest of counselors who collated the nectar-like *Niti-Shâstras* from the mighty main of the *Arthashâstras*.§

7—8. Culling from the Code of that one of pure intelligence who had reached the end of (mastered) the different branches of learning, we shall inculcate, out of our love for the Science of Polity, a series of short and significant lessons to the kings, directing them regarding the acquirement and preservation of territory; whatever, we shall say, will be in perfect harmony with the views of those well-versed in the science of politics.||

9. The king is the cause of the prosperity and progress of this world, and is held in high estimation even by grown

---

intrigues of Chánakya. The dynasty is here compared to a mountain owing to its various branches and offshoots.

* *Mulata.*—The commentator explains it as 'not to rise again; fallen for good.' We have accepted this meaning. For *Papâta Mulata*, some read *papâtâmulata*;

† *Saktidhara.*—Is another name for Kártikeya, the son of Siva. He is the Mars or the god of war of the Hindu mythology.

‡ *Mantrasakti and Utsâhasakti.*—Vide note † to sloka (1).

§ *Nitishâstra* and *Arthashâstra.*—In sanskrit literature *Niti* has a diversity of meaning which is quite puzzling; for instance it means, ethics, politics, morality, policy, decorum &c. But in this connection it is easy to find out its true signification which is politics. *Shástra* means science here. In the same manner, *Arthashástra* may have various meanings, of which we accept the following, viz 'the science of practical life.'

|| *Rájvidyávidám.*—The author alludes to *Vrihaspati*, the preceptor of the celestials, and to *Usanas*, the preceptor of the Asuras; both these are known as writers on civil and religious law, and are accepted as authorities on civil polity.

up people; he affords delight to the eyes of men, even as the moon affords delight unto the (mighty) ocean.*

10. If a ruler of men does not lead his subjects to the paths of rectitude, then are these latter (hopelessly) tossed about in the ocean of existence, even as a (frail) bark, having none to steer her through, is tossed about in a rough sea.

11. A righteous king, protecting his subjects to the best of his resources and having the power of capturing hostile cities, should be held in as high a regard as the Lord *Prajápati*† himself.

12. The sovereign should protect his subjects (by the equitable distribution of rewards and punishments). The subjects should increase the prosperity of the sovereign (by yielding taxes and tributes in the shape of agricultural products). Preservation of good order is preferable to a seeming increase of prosperity, for when all order is lost,‡ then prosperity, though present, is of no use.

13. A sovereign discharging his duties according to the rules of Polity soon secures *Trivarga*§ for himself and for his subjects; acting otherwise he is sure to ruin himself and his subjects.

14. Following the paths of rectitude king Vaijavana‖

---

* The rising and swelling of the waters of the ocean (flood-tide) occasioned by the influence of the moon was to the eye of the Sanskrit poets an indication of the ocean's delight.

† An epithet of the ten lords of created beings first created by *Brahmá.* Some times the word means *Brahmá* himself.

‡ '*Tadabhávai.*'—Another reading is accepted '*Tannásai*'; but this makes no difference in meaning.

§ The three objects of worldly existence, for the attainment of which all beings strive; these are *Dharma* or religious merit, *Artha* or wealth and *Káma* or objects of desire.

‖ The allusion is as follows:—King Indrasena sprang from the dynasty of Sagara. For having held sexual intercourse with his wife during her period of menstruation, he was on the point of being devoured by a Rákshasa, who only consented to relent provided the king would

governed this earth for a long period, whilst king Nahusa,* treading evil ways, was condemned to dwell in the nether regions (hell).

15. For this reason, always keeping equity in view, a king should exert himself for securing prosperity (in the shape of territorial aggrandisement &c). Through equitable dealings, an empire increases in territorial wealth; and the delicious fruit of this increase of territory is all-round prosperity.

16. King, minister, kingdom, castle, treasury, army and allies, are known to form the seven constituents of government; good sense and unebbing energy are its primary stay.

17. Depending upon his unmitigating energy and discerning through his prudence the right path to be adopted, a king should always vigorously endeavour to establish a government having those seven constituents.

18. The acquirement of wealth by equitable means, its preservation and augmentation, and its bestowal on deserving recepients—these are said to be the four duties of a sovereign.

---

never direct or allow his subjects to be engaged in pious deeds. Indrasena agreed; and his iniquity speedily brought about his destruction. Several of his descendants, following the path of their predecessor, met with ruin. Descended from this doomed line of kings Vaijavana directed the performance of virtuous acts by his subjects, and himself performed them. Thus his virtue saved him, and he continued to rule over his subjects for a long time.

* The allusion is this.—Descended from the lunar race of kings, Nahusa was a very wise and powerful king; and when Indra lay concealed under waters to expiate for the sin of having killed Vritra, a Bráhmana, he was asked to occupy Indra's seat. While there, he thought of winning the love of Indrani and caused the seven celestial sages to convey him in a palanquin to her house. On his way, he asked them to be quick using the words *Sarpa, Sarpa* (move on), when one of the sages cursed him to be a *Sarpa* (serpent). He fell down from the sky, and remained in that wretched state till he was relieved by Yudhisthira.

19. Possessing courage, a perfect knowledge of political economy, and full of energy, a king should devise expedients for attaining prosperity. Humility is the means of acquiring knowledge of political economy; and humility again is bred by a knowledge of the *Shástras.*

20. Humility is synonymous with a thorough control over the senses. Any one possessing it becomes learned in the *Shástras.* To one practising humility the mysterious meanings of the *Shástras* reveal themselves.

21—22. Knowledge of polity, wise judgment, contentment, skilfulness, absence of cowardice, (ready) power of comprehension, energy, eloquence, firmness of purpose, patience for putting up with turmoils and troubles, *Prabhâva,** purity of intention, friendliness to all beings, bestowal of wealth on worthy recipients, truthfulness, gratefulness, high lineage, good conduct, and restraint of the passions,—these and other such qualities are the sources of all prosperity.

23. In the first instance, a king should himself practise self-restraint, thereafter, he should direct his ministers, and then his dependents, and then his sons and then his subjects, to do the same.

24. A self-controlled king, whose subjects are devoted to him and who is careful in protecting his subjects, earns great prosperity for himself.

25. One should bring under his control, by striking with the goad of knowledge, the rampant elephant identified with the senses, coursing wildly in the vast wilderness of sensual enjoyments.

26. The soul inspires the mind† with activity in order that the latter may earn wealth; volition is engendered by a union of the soul and the mind.†

---

* That idea of power and superiority which is so indissolubly connected with the conception of a monarch and which we have before rendered as 'Regal power.'

† Sanskrit philosophers draw a very subtle distinction between the

27. The mind, out of a morbid desire for the objects of sensual enjoyments which are compared to most palatable dishes of meat, goads the senses after their search; this (perverse) inclination of the mind should be assiduously suppressed; and when one's mind is conquered (by himself), he is styled self-controlled.

28. *Vijnâna* (means for realising diverse kinds of knowledge), *Hridaya* (the heart), *Chittwa* (the receptacle of consciousness), *Manas* (the mind), and *Buddhi* (the intelligence), —all these are said to convey the same meaning. With the assistance of any one of these, the soul, incased inside this body, discriminates between what ought to be done and what ought not to be done.

29. Pious and impious deeds, sensations pleasurable and otherwise, the presence and absence of desire, so also human effort, the perception of sense-objects and the remembrance of the impressions of an antecedent birth,* these are said to be the signs that go to prove the existence of the soul.

30. The impossibility of the concomitance of perceptions

---

soul and the mind, which it is difficult to explain to the uninitiated. The idea seems to be that, the soul is the only living principle that retains the power of invigorating the subsidiary faculties, which latter, but for the former's help, would have been as inert as matter itself. In the Nyáya philosophy mind or *Manas* is regarded as a *Dravya* or substance; it is held to be distinct from the *Atman* or soul. It is defined as the internal organ of perception and congnition, the instrument by which the objects of the senses affect the soul or *Atman*.

* *Samskára.*—It means the faculty that retains and reproduces impressions. But the word is more often used to signify the impressions received in a previous life, which the soul is said to bring with it when it is born anew. The absolute truth of this philosophical maxim has gone out of date; and it is against modern philosophical conceptions. As a matter of fact none of us can ever remember what had been his condition in an antecedent life, even if the doctrine of transmigration of souls be accepted as true.

is said to be the sign that proves the existence of the mind.* The formation of the conceptions of various things and sense-objects is said to be the action of the mind.

31. The auditory, the tactile, the visual, the gustatory and the olfactory organs, these five and the anus, the penis, the arms, the legs, and the organ of speech, constitute what is called a conglomeration of sense-organs.

32. The perception of sound, touch, form, taste, and smell, and the acts of discharging (excretions, urine &c), feeling pleasure, taking up, moving and speaking, are said to be the respective functions of these several organs.

33. The soul and the mind are styled to be the 'internal senses' by those who are conversant with the workings of these two. By a conjoint effort of these two, volition is engendered.

34. The soul, the mind, the sense-organs, and the sense-objects, all these are said to be included under the category of 'external sense.'† Volition and muscular movement are the means of pleasurable sensations of the soul.

35. The (connecting) medium between the 'internal and the external sense' seems to be a conscious effort. Therefore

---

† *Jnanasyáyugapatbhava*—is a compound formed of *Jnana* or perception and *Ayugapatbhava* or non-concomitance. In Sanskrit philosophy there is a difference of opinion regarding the process of perception. According to some writers simultaneous perceptions are impossible while according to others they are not so. The author sides with the latter class of philosophers. So he defines 'mind' as the link connecting the distinct perceptions received at different times.

‡ An apparent contradiction is involved in Slokas 33rd and 34th where mind and soul have been defined both to be internal and external sense. But the author must be understood as taking two different phases. Mind and Soul are internal organs in respect of internal workings as introspection, thinking &c.,—they are external senses when they deal with outward objects.

suppressing this conscious effort one may try to become the master of his own mind.*

36. In this way, a king conversant with notions of justice and injustice, having subdued his mind already powerless through the suppression of the senses,† should exert himself for realising his own good.

37. How can one, who is not capable enough of subjugating his own one mind, hope to subjugate this (extensive) earth bounded by the oceans themselves?

---

* The Sloka needs illucidation. What the writer means is this; when any action is done, the 'internal senses' supply the desire and the motive only; the 'external senses' then perform what more is needed for the completion of the act. Between the desire and the actual carrying out of the action, there is another step. The writer calls that step to be *Yatna* or *Pravritti*. Modern philosophers also accept an analysis of voluntary action somewhat akin to this one. We shall quote professor Sully:—'The initial stage is the rise of some desire. This desire is accompanied by the representation of some movement (motor representation) which is recognised as subserving the realisation of the object. The recognition of the casual relation of the action to the result involves a germ of belief in the attainability of the object of desire, or in the efficacy of the action. Finally we have the carrying out of the action thus represented.' What is known as 'motor representation' seems to be the *yatna* of the present author. The first part of the Sloka being understood the latter does not present any difficulty. When one can suppress this 'motor representation' which again is the result of experience or association, no action becomes possible. In the absence of action, the soul is not brought into contact with the sense-objects and is not plunged headlong into worldliness.

† For *Karansámarthyát* we have read *Karanasamrodhát* which gives a reasonable meaning.

There is a supplement to this Sloka, which in the text from which we are translating is omitted. The Sloka undoubtedly is an interpolation as it does not occur in the original text. We subjoin its translation.

"As in this earth, one is never satiated with enjoying any of the following viz, rice (food), gold (wealth), cattle and women, so one should ever put down an excessive longing for the enjoyment of any one of these."

2

38. Like unto an elephant falling in a trap, a king falls in danger whenever his heart is ensnared by the (seemingly) beautiful objects of (sensual) enjoyment, the charm of which vanishes as soon as the enjoyment is over.

39. A king, delighting in the perpetration of vile acts and having his eyes (of knowledge and reason) blinded by the objects of (sensual) enjoyment, brings terrible catastrophe upon his own head.

40. Sound, touch, form, taste and smell, every one of these five sense-objects is capable of bringing about the ruin (of a created being).*

41. Living upon fresh grass and sprouts and capable of bounding over wide chasms, the deer seeks its own destruction from the hunter, being tempted by the latter's charming song.

42. Huge-bodied like the peak of a mountain, capable of up-rooting mighty trees in sport, a male-elephant, stupified with the touch of the female-elephant, submits to be bound by chains.

43. An insect reaps death by suddenly throwing itself, out of doubt, on the blazing flame of a lamp that attracts its attention.

44. Staying away from human sight, and swimming underneath an unfathomable depth of water, a fish tastes the iron-hook furnished with meat (bait) in order to bring about its own destruction.

45. A bee, tempted with the sweet odour of the ichor, and athirst for drinking it, receives for all its troubles, lashes from the elephant's ears that are moved with great difficulty.†

46. Each of these five poison-like sense-objects is enough to destroy a man separately. How then can that

---

* The author in the next five Slokas proceeds to illustrate his remark by examples.

† For *Sukhasamchárám* of the text the commentary reads *Asukhasamchárám*.

person expect to reap good, who is enslaved simultaneously to these five.*

47. A self-controlled person should enjoy in proper season the sense-objects being unattached to them. Happiness is the fruit of prosperity; therefore, in the absence of happiness prosperity is useless.

48. The youth and the prosperity, of kings over-powered by an extreme fondness for gazing at the countenance of their wives, dwindle away, inspite of their shedding profuse useless tears.†

49. From a strict observance of the injunctions and interdictions of the *Shâstras* wealth is acquired; from wealth proceeds desire; and the fruition of desires brings about happiness. He, that does not indulge in the reasonable enjoyment of these three objects, (wealth, desire and happiness); destroys these three as also his own self to boot.

50. Even the very name of a woman fills the frame with a joyous thrill, and bewilders the reason; not to speak of a sight of her with arching eye-brows sparkling with sensuality!

51. What fond person is not intoxicated with lust for women, skilful in amorous tricks in secret, soft and sweet spoken and beautified with coppery eyes.

52. Women can surely kindle desire in the hearts of

---

* There is a Sloka in the Mahabharata that may be cited as a parallel to Slokas 40—46. It is this:

Kuranga-mâtanga-patanga-vringas, Meenas hatása panchabhirêva pancha
Ekas pramâdi sha katham na hanyatê, Ya shêvatê panchbhirêva pancha.

† The construction of the Sloka would also allow another rendering save what we have given. The meaning as explained by a commentator seems to be as follows:—'A king, who is always fondly attached to his wife, neglects his royal duties to enjoy her company. Then his enemies opportunely attack his kingdom, and for his lethargy he is defeated and dethroned. He retires to the forest, and there with his wife he passes his youth in shedding useless tears.'

sages, even as evening twilight can enhance the beauty of the charming moon shedding silvery beams.

53. Even illustrious persons are pierced by (the charms of) women that enrapture and intoxicate the mind, even as rocks are pierced by drops of water.

54. (Excessive indulgence in) hunting, gambling at dice, and drinking,—these are condemnable when found in a ruler of the earth. Behold the catastrophe that befell the king Pandu, the king of the Nishadhas and the descendants of Vrishni, through indulgence in each of these respectively.*

55. Lust, anger, avarice, fiendish delight in doing injury, morbid desire for honor, and arrogance, these six passions should be victimized.

56—57. Subjecting themselves to these six inimical passions, the following kings were ruined, namely, king Dandaka

---

* *Pandu.*—To the readers of the Mahábharata the allusion contained in this line is evident. Once during a hunting excursion king Pandu was very much disappointed for not having lighted on any game for a long time. At last to his great joy he found within an arrow-shot a pair of consorting deer and he instantly pierced them with his shaft. To his horror he found that it was a *Rishi* who had been copulating with his spouse in the form of a deer. Provoked by the king's untimely interruption, the *Rishi* cursed the monarch saying that he should never more know sexual pleasure on pain of death. After a period the king died for having passionately embraced his junior wife, in accordance with the curse of the Rishi.

Naiṣhadha.—The history of Nala is too well-known. He was possessed by *Kali* who induced him to play at dice with his brother Puskara. In the game Nala lost all he had, his kingdom and wealth. He was then driven to forest with his wife, where he forsook her. After a prolonged separation, during which each of them had to undergo various troubles and calamities, they were re-united and Nala was set free from the evil influence of *Kali*. He regained his kingdom and ruled for a long time.

Vrishnis.—The descendants of Vrishni indulging over-much in intoxicating drink lost all their senses, and for a trifle quarreling with each other fell to slaying each other and thus ruined their own line of kings. This history is also related in the latter part of thc Mahabharata.

met with destruction through lust, Janamejaya through anger, the royal sage Aila through avarice, the Asura Vātāpi through fiendish delight in doing injury, the Rākshasa Poulasta through desire for honor, and king Dambhodbhava through arrogance.*

58. Renouncing these six inimical passions, Jāmadagnya† became the master of his senses, and Amvarisa‡ of eminent parts enjoyed the sovereignty of the world for a long period.§

---

* *Dandaka.*—One day when out hunting, this king affected with lust forcibly ravished the daughter of the sage Vrigu, through whose anger he was killed with his friends by a shower of dust.

Janamejaya.—When engaged in the celebration of the Horse-sacrifice, he found marks of recent copulation on his wife; this exasperated him, and thinking that the sacrificial priests, had committed adultery with her, he assaulted them. He met his death through the imprecation of these latter.

Aila.—This monarch used to persecute and oppress his subjects for money, who unable to brook his tyranny at last pelted him to death.

Vátápi.—This demon together with another named Ilvala used to invite innocent sages to dine with them. One of them would then assume the form of an animal and would be sacrificed by the other; his meat would then be eaten by the sages. When inside the stomach, the eaten up demon would be revived by the *Sanjívani Mantra* and would kill the sages by tearing open their abdomen. They thus delighted in killing innocent people. At last the great sage Agasthya ate this *Vátápi* up and digested him.

Poulasta.—Ravana the ten-headed demon of the Ramayana whose history we need not recount here.

Dambhodbhava—This great demon who defeated many of the celestials in battle was very much puffed up with arrogance. Finding none equal to him in single combat, he one day challenged the sage Nara to show him a combatant that would be a match for him; the sage then himself killed him with a blade of grass.

† A son of Jamadagni a pious sage deeply engaged in study and said to have obtained entire possession of the *Vedas*. His mother was *Renuká*.

‡ A king of the solar race celebrated as a worshipper of Vishnu.

§ There is a supplement to this Sloka; it is this:—' In order to increase his religious merit and worldly prosperity—which are eagerly

59. Association with a preceptor bestows knowledge of the *Shâstras*; the knowledge of the *Shâstras* increases humility. A king, modest through the effects of culture, never sinks under troubles.

60. A king, serving the elderly people, is held in high respect by the pious; though induced by persons of evil character, he does not commit vile deeds.

61. A king, everyday receiving lessons in the different arts from his preceptor, increases in prosperity, like the moon increasing in her digits during the light half of every month.

62. The prosperity of a monarch, who keeps his passions under his thorough control and who follows the path chalked out in the science of Polity, blazes forth every day; his fame also reaches the heavens.

63. Thus a monarch, well-versed in Polity, practising self-control, very soon attains to that shining pitch of prosperity which had been attained by other divine monarchs and which is as high as the highest peak of *Mahâratnagiri* *

64. Naturally the ways of exalted sovereignty are different from those of the world. Therefore through sheer force, a preceptor should coach it in self-control. And self-control goes before the successful observance of the maxims of Polity.

65. A self-controlled king receives the highest of homàges. Self-control is the ornament of kings. A self-controlled king appears as beautiful as a gentle elephant shedding ichor and moving its trunk slowly.

66. A preceptor is worshipped for the acquisition of learning. Learning, which has been mastered, becomes instrumental in enhancing the prudence of the illustrious. The

---

sought after by the pious—a person controlling his senses should devote himself to the services of his preceptor.'

* Sumeru or a fabulous mountain round which all the planets are said to revolve; it is also said to consist of gems and gold. Hence its present epithet. *Mahán* great, *Ratná* gem, and *Giri* mountain.

habit of doing acts according to the dictates of prudence is sure to lead to prosperity.

67. A pure-souled person, ever ready to serve others, attains to prosperity by serving his learned and skilful preceptor. Practising self-control, he becomes worthy of the royal throne and capable of securing peace.

68. A powerful monarch, without practising self-control, is subjugated by his enemies without the least difficulty; while a weak monarch, practising self-control and observing the injunctions of the *Shâstras*, never meets with defeat.

Thus ends the first section, the means of self-coutrol and association with the old, in the Nitisâra of Kâmandaka.

—:o:—

SECTION II.

1. A KING, after having controlled his senses, should direct his attention to (the cultivation of) the following four branches of learning, namely *Anvikshikee*, *Trayee*, *Vârtâ* and *Dandaniti*, in co-operation with men versed in them and acting according to their precepts.*

2. *Anvikshikee, Trayee, Vârtâ* and *Dandaniti*,—these and these only are the four eternal divisions of knowledge, that pave the way of corporeal beings to happiness.

3. The descendants of Manu† (men) hold that there are

* As the italicised words have been explained by the author himself in the 11th, 12th, 13th, 14th and 15th Sloka of this section, we need not anticipate him.

† *Manu*.—The name of a celebrated personage regarded as the representative man and the father of the human race, and classed with divine beings. The word is particularly applied to the fourteen successive

only three divisions of learning (namely), *Trayee, Vártá,* and *Dandaniti;* in their opinion, what is known as *Anvikshikee,* is to be regarded as a mere sub-division of *Trayee.*

4. The disciples of the celestial priest (*Vrihaspati*)* postulate the existence of two divisions only, namely, *Vártá,* and *Dandaniti,* as these only can help people in the acquisition of *Artha.*†

5. According to the school of *Usanas*‡ there is only one division of learning, namely, *Dandaniti*; and it has been said, that the origin of all other kinds of learning lies in this one.

6. But the theory of our own preceptor is, that there are four kinds of learning, on which this world is settled, for the realisation of different objects.§

7. *Anvikshikee* deals with the knowledge of the self, *Trayee* with piety and impiety, *Vártá* with gain and loss of wealth, and *Dandaniti* with justice and injustice.

---

progenitors or sovereigns of the earth mentioned in *Manusmriti.* I. 63. The first of these known as *Sváyambhuvamanu* is supposed to be a sort of secondary creator who produced the ten *Prajápatis* (vide note to Sloka IIth, Sec. I.) and to whom the code of laws called *Manusmriti* is ascribed. The seventh *Manu* called *Vaivasvata* being supposed to be born from the sun (*Vivasvan*) is regarded as the progenitor of the present race of human beings; he is also regarded as the founder of the solar dynasty of kings who ruled at Ayodhyá (modern Oudh). The names of the fourteen *Manus* are (1) *Sváyambhuva* (2) *Svarochis* (3) *Auttami* (4) *Támasa* (5) *Raivata* (6) *Chákshusa* (7) *Vaivasvata* (8) *Sávarni* (9) *Dakshsávarni* (10) *Brahmasávarni* (11) *Dharmasávarni* (12) *Rudrasávarni* (13) *Rouchya-deva-sávarni* (14) *Indrasávarni.*

* Vide note to Sloka 8th Sec. I.

† One of the three objects of existence (*Trivarga*) meaning, wealth or property. Vide note to Sloka 13th Sec. I.

‡ The preceptor of the Asuras or demons. Vide note to Sloka 8th Sec. I.

§ That is, these kinds of knowledge supply us with the means for realising the different objects.

8. *Anvikshikee, Trayee* and *Vârtâ* are considered to be the most excellent* of all knowledge. But their presence is of no avail where *Dandaniti* is neglected.†

9. When a great leader of men attains proficiency in *Dandaniti*, he becomes the master of the other remaining branches of knowledge.

10. The *Varnas*‡ and the *Asramas*,§ find their primary support in these kinds of knowledge. For this reason, a king, superintending and securing the means for the cultivation of these kinds of knowledge, becomes a sharer‖ in the religious merit earned by the different castes in their different modes of existence.

11. *Anvikshikee*¶ is the science of spiritual knowledge, for

---

* For, says the commentator, they serve as means for the acquirement of wealth and religious merit.

† The text lit: translated would be 'where a mistake is committed with regard to *Dandaniti*.' What the author means, seems to be this :—'The transgression of the rules of Political science by a king is so disastrous that it cannot be remedied even by all his learning and ingenuity.'

‡ *Varna*—means a tribe or a caste, specially applied to the four castes, namely :—*Bráhmana* (the spiritual class), *Kshatriya* (governing class), *Vaisya*, (trading and cultivating class), and *Sudra* (serving class). These classes are said to have been born respectively from the mouth (signifying intelligence), the arms (signifying strength), the abdomen (signifying hunger), and the legs (signifying servitude) of the *Purusha* or Supreme Spirit.

§ *Asrama*—or the mode of living in different periods of existence of these castes or classes ; these are four, namely :—(1) *Brahmacharyya*, or religious studentship, the life of celibacy passed by a *Bráhmana* boy in studying the Vedas. This is the first stage of life. (2) *Gárhasthya* or the order of life of a *Grihasthya* or house-holder. This is the second stage. (3) *Vánaprastha* or the religious life of an anchorite. This is the third stage. (4) *Sannyása* or the complete renunciation of the world and its possessions and attachments. The first three classes can enter upon these four stages ; but the *Sudras* are disallowed to do so.

‖ His share has been specified to be one-sixth only.

¶ Modern *Metaphysics*.

it investigates the nature of weal and woe of mankind; through its assistance the real nature of things being seen persons renounce both joy and grief.*

12. The three *Vedas*† called *Rik*, *Yajus* and *Sáma* are meant by *Trayee*. A person, living in perfect obedience to the injunctions and interdictions of *Trayee*, prospers in this as well as in the next world.

13. Sometimes, the *Angas*,‡ the four *Vedas*, the *Mimánsás*,§ the diverse sections of *Nyâya*,|| the

---

* Joy for their gain and grief for their loss.

† *Vedas*—the scriptures of the Hindus; originally there were only three *Vedas*, the *Rik*, the *Yajus* and the *Sáma*, which are collectively called *Trayee* or the sacred triad. To these three the *Artharvan* was subsequently added. The orthodox Hindu theory, regarding the composition of the *Vedas*, is that they are 'not human compositions.' They are supposed to have been directly revealed by the Supreme Being.

‡ These are certain classes of works regarded as auxiliary to the *Vedas*, designed to aid in their correct pronunciation and interpretation and the right employment of the *Mantras* in ceremonials. These are six in number *(a) Siksha* or the Science of proper articulation and pronunciation, *(b) Chandas* or the Science of Prosody, *(c) Vyákarana* or Grammar, *(d) Nirukta*, or Etymological explanation of difficult words occurring in the *Vedas*, *(e) Jyotis* or Astronomy and *(f) Kalpa*, or ritual.

§ *Mimânsá*—is the name of one of the six chief systems of Indian philosophy. It was originally divided into two systems, the *Purva-Mimânsâ* founded by Jaimini and the *Uttara-Mimânsá* founded by Vádaráyana. The two systems have very little in common between them; the first concerning itself chiefly with the correct interpretation of the rituals of the *Vedas* and the settlement of dubious points in regard to *Vedic* texts; the latter chiefly dealing with the nature of the Supreme Entity. The *Purva-Mimânsâ* is therefore rightly styled *Mimânsâ* or 'investigation and settlement.' Another name for the *Uttara-Mimânsá* is *Vedánta*, which being hardly a sequel to Jaimini's compilation is now ranked separately.

|| *Nyâya*.—A system of Hindu philosophy founded by Goutama. It is sometimes synonymous with logical philosophy. The several maxims of the *Nyâya* philosophy are referred to here.

*Dharmashâstras** and the *Purânas*† are all included under *Trayee*.

14. The occupation of those who live by rearing cattle, and by cultivation and trade is called *Vârtâ*. Well-up in *Vârtâ* a man has nothing to be afraid of in a revolution.‡

15. *Danda* is known to signify subjection. A king is also figuratively called *Danda*, for from him all punishments proceed; the system, that deals with the just infliction of punishments, is called *Dandaniti*. It is called a *Niti* as it guides kings in the right administration of justice.§

16. By the right administration of justice, a king should protect himself, and encourage the (cultivation of the) other branches of knowledge. This branch of knowledge (*Dandaniti*) directly benefits mankind, and the king is its preserver.

17. When a clever and generous-minded monarch realises *Chaturvarga*‖ by means of these branches of learning, then only is his proficiency, in these to be recognised; the root *vid* is said to mean 'to know.'

18. ¶The celebration of sacrifices, the study of the *Vedas*** and the act of giving wealth to others according to the rules of the *Shâstras*——these are considered to be

---

* *Dharmashâstras.*—The codes of morals and laws compiled by *Manu* (vide *Supra* note to Sloka 3rd), and *Yâjnavalkya* and other *Rishis* of yore.

† *Purânas*—these are supposed to have been composed by *Vyâsa*, and contain the whole body of Hindu mythology. They are eighteen in number.

‡ The reading in the text is vicious; so the commentary supplies *Avritté* for *Vritté*.

§ *Niti*—from *Ni* to guide or direct and *kti* suffix.

‖ *Chaturvarga*—Is *Trivarga* plus *Moksha* or salvation; for *Trivarga* vide note to Sloka 13th Sec. I.

¶ Having finished his dissertation on the divisions of learning, the author now proceeds to determine the duties of the various sects in the different stages of their life.

** Vide *Supra* note to Sloka 12th.

the common customary observances of the three sects, the *Brâhmanas*, the *Kshatriyas* and the *Vaisyas*.*

19. The holy acts of teaching, of conducting sacrifices on others' behalf, and of accepting alms from the pious, these have been enumerated by the sages to be the means of livelihood for those belonging to the superior sect (*Brâhmana*).

20. A king† should live by his weapons and by protecting his subjects.‡ The means of subsistence of a *Vaisya* are cattle-rearing, cultivation and trade.

21. The duty of a *Sudra* is to serve the twice-born sects§ one after the other; his unblamable means of living are the fine arts and the occupation of a ministrel.

22—23. The duties of a *Brahmachârin*|| are to live in the family of his preceptor, to worship the sacred fires,¶ to study the *Vedas* and their auxiliaries,** to observe vows, to perform ablutions during the three periods of the day (in the morning, at noon, and in the evening),†† to beg and to live for life with his spiritual guide. In the absence of a preceptor, he should live with his (preceptor's) son or with one of his

---

* Vide *Supra* note to Sloka 16th.

† Is here representative of the whole 'ruling class' or *Kshatriyas*.

‡ The subjects living under the fostering care of a protecting sovereign increase in prosperity and they willingly pay taxes by which the latter maintains himself.

§ The *Brâhmanas*, the *Kshatriyas* and the *Vaisyas* are so called because they are supposed to be born anew at the time of their investiture with the sacred thread.

|| One living in the *Brahmacharyya Asrama* (for which vide *Supra* note to Sloka 10th.

¶ These fires are three in number namely :— (1) *Gárhapatya* or domestic fire. (2) *Ahavaniya* or sacrificial fire, derived from the domestic fire ; it is sometimes called the Eastern fire. (3) *Dakshina* or the Southern fire so called because it is placed southwards.

**The *Angas* are referred to, for which vide *Supra* note to Sloka 13th.

†† Technically called *Sandhyá*. These are the three essential and daily ceremonies performed by the Brahmanas, at what are known as the *Sandhis* or joinings of the day.

fellow *Brahmachârin*; or he may, if he likes, adopt another mode of existence.

24. During the whole period of his pupilage, he should wear a *Mekhalâ** along with his sacred thread, bear matted hair or a shaved-head, carry a *Dânda*† and live with his preceptor. Afterwards, at his own will, he may choose any other mode of life.

25. The duties of a house-holder are to celebrate the *Agnihotra*‡ sacrifice, to live by the profession prescribed (for his sect) and to avoid sexual intercourse during the *Parvas.*§

26. The duties, of those who have married and settled down, are to worship the gods, the ancestral manes and the guests, to show mercy to the poor and the wretched, and to live according to the precepts of the *Srutis*‖ and the *Smritis.*¶

27—28. The duties of those who have resorted to the forest$ are, to keep matted hair,** to perform *Agnihotra*††

---

* The triple girdle worn by the first three classes; the girdle of the *Brâhmana* should be of the fibres of *Manju* or of *Kuça* grass, that of the *Kshatriya* of a *Murva* or bow-string, and of the *Vaisya* of a thread of the *Sana.*

† The staff given to a twice-born one at the time of the investiture with the sacred thread. It is made ordinarily of the branches of the *Vilva* tree (Ægle mermelos) and a species of bamboo.

‡ It is the sacrifice, the principle rite of which is the consecration and maintenance of the Sacred fires by the offering of oblations.

§ *Parva.*—The days of the four changes of the moon *i.e.* the eighth and fourteenth day of each month, and the days of the full-moon and the new moon.

‖ Are the same as *Vedas.* From *sru* to hear and *kti, i.e.* which are revealed (vide *Supra* note to Sloka 12th).

¶ *Smriti.*—From *smri* to remember and *kti, i.e.* which are remembered. Vide *Supra* note to Sloka 3rd.

$ Technically, who have entered upon the *Vânaprastha Asrama* (vide *Supra* note to Sloka 13th).

** The text reads *Jadatvam* for which the commentary supplies *Jatitvam.* What can the former mean?

†† Vide *Supra* note to Sloka 25th.

sacrifices, to sleep on the bare earth, to wear black deer skin, to live in solitary places, to sustain themselves on water, esculent roots, *Nivâra** crop, and fruits, to refuse to accept alms, to bathe thrice in the day,† to observe vows, and to adore the gods and the guests.

29—31. The duties of the wandering mendicants‡ are, to renounce all actions, to live upon what is obtained by begging, to dwell under the shelter of a tree, to refuse smallest gifts,§ to do no harm to other created beings and to maintain an equality of attitude towards them, to be indifferent‖ alike to friends and enemies, to be unmoved by joy or grief, to be purified in mind and in body,¶ to curb the speech,$ to observe vows, to retract the senses from their objects, to keep the mind always collected, to be absorbed in contemplation and to purify their intentions.

32. Harmlessness, the speaking of sweet and salutary words, truthfulness, purification of the mind and the body, and mercy and forbearance, these are said to be the common duties of all the sects in all their different modes of life.

33. These are the duties of all the sects in all their modes of existence, (the observance of) which can secure paradise and salvation for them. The neglect of these

---

* *Nivâra* is rice growing wild or without cultivation.

† Supply 'after which they should perform their *Sandhyâs*, or morning, noon and evening prayers. Vide *Supra* note to Sloka 22nd.

‡ Or who have entered upon the *Sannyâsa Asrama* (vide *Supra* note to Sloka 10th).

§ 'Even,' goes on the commentator, 'pieces of rags for binding their religious Manuscripts *(Punthi)*.'

‖ The word in the text gives no signification; and so the commentary reads '*priyâpriyâparisanga*' in its place.

¶ 'The body' says the commentator, 'is purified by rubbing and washing with earth and water, and the mind by cherishing kindness for all creatures.'

$ For *Vákmano-brahmachárità* of the text the commentary reads *Vágyamo Vratachárità*. The latter reading surely yields a better meaning.

duties results in the spread of mixed castes and thus brings about the ruin of this world.

34. The king is the lawful promoter of all these righteous practices;* therefore in the absence of a king all righteousness is lost and at the loss of righteousness, this world also meets with destruction.

35. A king, protecting the various *Varnas* and *Asramas*,† and living according to their usages and knowing the duties prescribed for each of them, becomes worthy of a place in the regions of Sakra.‡

36. §As a self-controlled|| king holds the key to the worldly as well as spiritual advancement of his own self as also of his subjects, therefore he should deal out punishments as impartially as does *Dandi*¶ himself.

37. Inflicting extraordinarily heavy punishments a king frightens his subjects, and inflicting extraordinarily light ones he is not feared by them. Therefore that king is praise-worthy who deals out punishments proportionate to the offences.

38. Punishments, dealt out proportionately to the offences, speedily increase the *Trivarga* of a king, while dispro-

---

* Another interpretation is possible, namely, 'A king is to encourage these righteous practices, not transgressing the limits of law.'

† Vide *Supra* note to Sloka 10th.

‡ *Sarvalokavag* should be read as *Sakralokavac*, which is the reading given in the commentary. Sakra or Indra is the Jupiter Pluvius of the Indian Aryans. Of all the paradises, his paradise is the most magnificent and is fraught with all sorts of pleasures, he being notorious for his incontinence and lasciviency.

§ The author now proceeds to impress upon the minds of monarchs, the necessity of the right administration of justice.

|| For *Atmata* of the text read *Atmavân* which gives a good sense. Here also we follow the commentary.

¶ *Dandi*—another appellation for the god of death, who is so called for his holding the sceptre of sway (*Danda*). One of the duties of his office is to deal out rewards and punishments to the souls of the departed according to their merits and de-merits accruing from worldly acts.

portionately inflicted, they excite anger even in those who have retired to the forest.

39. Punishments countenanced by society and the *Shâstras* ought only to be inflicted on the offender. Persecution can never bring about prosperity, as it breeds sin through which a monarch meets with his fall.

40. In this world, where beings are related to one another as food and consumer, when proper chastisements are withheld, the exertions, of a king to keep his subjects under control, become as futile as those of an angler trying to catch fish without the help of a rod.*

41. A king, by the right infliction of punishments, upholds this stayless world, that is being forcibly drowned into the lake of sin by lust and cupidity and other such passions.

42. This world is by nature enslaved to the pleasures of the senses and is ardently longing to enjoy wealth and women. Agitated by the fear of punishments, it only keeps to the eternal ways of rectitude followed by the pious.

43. Upright conduct is scarce in this slavish world of ours; but as it is, men only attend to their prescribed duties through fear of punishments; even as a respectable woman serves her lean or poor or deformed or diseased husband through fear of the sanctions specified in the codes of morality.

44. Thus, like rivers, that flow through right courses, falling into the sea, all prosperity devolves—and never dwindles away—upon a king who knowing the good and evil of

---

* Another interpretation is possible, the gist of which is as follows:—'In this world where beings stand in the relation of food and consumer, when just chastisements are withheld, the destructive Mátsya is seen to hold good. The difficulty in annotating the sloka lies in the phrase *Mâtsya Nyâya*, the exact signification of which no lexicographer has vouchsafed; no doubt it is a maxim of the *Nyâya* philosophy. The reference perhaps is to the fact of fishes devouring one another.

the infliction of punishments and following the path chalked out in the *Vedas*,* frames rules of conduct for his subects.

Thus ends the second Section, the division of learning, the duties of the Varnas and Asramas, and the necessity of punishments, in the Nitisâra of Kâmandaka.

—:o:—

SECTION III.

1. A RULER of earth, impartially inflicting punishments on his subjects like *Dandi*† himself, should treat them mercifully even as *Prajâpati*‡ does.

2. Sweet and truthful speech, kindness, charity, protection of the oppressed seeking refuge, and association with the virtuous,—these are the praiseworthy practices of a pious person.

3. A man should extricate a distressed person out of his difficulties, being actuated by tenderest compassion and moved by the heavy weight of the latter's grief that had touched his heart.

4. There is no one more pious, in respect to the performance of meritorious acts, than those who save the distressed sunk in the mire of grief.

5. Nursing tenderest compassion in his heart, and without deviating from the path of duty, a king should wipe away the tears of the oppressed and the helpless.

---

* For *Prâptamârga* of the text, the commentary gives *Shâstramârga*, which latter we have adopted.

† Vide note to Sloka 36th Sec. II.

‡ *Prajâpati*.—Another name of Brahmá the creator, who naturally is very kind to beings of his creation.

6. That kindness (harmlessness) is the highest of all virtues, is the unanimous opinion* of all animate beings. Therefore with feelings of kindness, a king should protect his poor subjects.

7. In order to secure his own happiness, a king should not persecute a poor and helpless person; a poor man, persecuted by the king, kills the latter by means of his grief.†

8. Born of a high family, what man tempted by an iota of happiness, ever oppresses beings of puny might without even judging what their faults are?

9. What prudent person ever perpetrates unrighteous deeds for the benefit of his body that is liable to suffer from mental and physical ills and that is sure to be destroyed this day or to-morrow?

10. This clayey tenement that is rendered agreeable with difficulty through artificial means,‡ is evanescent like a shadow and vanishes§ even as a bubble of water.||

11. Are ever high-souled persons enslaved by the

---

* For *Yata* in the text, the commentary suggests *Mata* which we accept.

† What the writer means is this :—'When persecuted by a powerful king, a poor man, finding all earthly assistance unavailing, daily sends up fervent prayers to the Almighty, invoking His curse on the head of the oppressor. Heaven responds to his prayers and the king duly meets his end.'

‡ Such as, perfumes, unguents, garments, ornaments, &c.

§ For *Pasyait* read *Nasyait*, which would give a good signification.

|| The homily of the author on the shortness of life reminds us of a passage in Adam's 'Secret of Success' which we can not withstand the temptation of quoting here.

'Of all the trite themes touched by moralists and poets, the tritest is the shortness of life. Life, we are told, is a bubble, a shifting dream, a thing of nought, evanescent as a morning mist, uncertain as a young maid's promise, brittle as a reed; and yet men proceed to deal with it, as if it were as inexhaustible as the widow's curse of oil, as if it were as sure and stable as the foundations of the everlasting hills.'

pleasures of the senses, which are as shifting as patches of clouds rolled to and fro by a violent storm?

12. The life of corporeal creatures is as unsteady as the reflection of the moon in water;* knowing it to be so, a man should always do what is good and just.

13. Looking upon this world as a mirage and knowing it to be very transient, a person should act, in co-operation with the pious,† to secure happiness and religious merit.

14. A noble person attended upon by the virtuous is a charming sight like a magnificient and recently white-washed mansion flooded by the silvery beams of the moon.

15. Neither the moon of cooling beams, nor the full-blown lotus, can so gladden our hearts as do the deeds of the virtuous.

16. The company of the wicked should be shunned like a dreary, naked, and arid desert, burning with the scorching rays of the summer sun.‡

17. A wicked man, having secured the confidence of the pious and the good-natured, ruins them without any reason whatever, like fire burning down a withered tree.

18. Rather live with serpents having mouths ashy with the fume of the fire-like venom emitted with every breath, than associate with the wicked.

19. The wicked, like the cat, cut off the very hand with which unsuspecting and guileless persons offer palatable food to them.

20. A wicked person is like a serpent; and like it he bears two tongues in his head, with which he pours out the

---

* Supply 'which is disturbed by the slightest movement of the water.'

† For *Swajana* read *Sujana* and for *sangata* read *sangatam*. This latter change of reading also changes the meaning, which in this case will be, 'associate with the pious.'

‡ The author now proceeds to caution kings against keeping company with the wicked.

virulent poison of his speech, the baneful effects of which cannot be counteracted by the best remedial measures.

21. A person, seeking his own good, should fold his palms to the wicked, with humility even greater than that with which he does so before his worshipful kinsmen.

22. With a view to completely steal the hearts of men, a wicked person, simulating friendship for every one, speaks charming words agreeable to men and manners.*

23. A man should always please the world with respectful words; for, a man, speaking cruel words, hurts people's feelings, even though he may give them money.

24. Even though he might be sorely oppressed, yet an intelligent person should never utter such words which would afflict men piercing them to their hearts.

25. Like sharp weapons, stinging and torturing language, uttered by ill-mannered persons, cuts people to the very quick.

26. Sweet words should always be spoken equally to friends and foes; for, by whom is not a sweet-spoken man loved like the peacock uttering the sweet *kekâ* †?

27. Peacocks are ornamented by their sweet and charming *kekâ*; men of culture are ornamented by their mellifluous speech.

28. The utterances of intoxicated swans and cuckoos and peacocks are not so charming as are those of a man of culture.

---

* In rendering this Sloka we have followed the commentary. But this meaning does not suit the text, whereas the subjoined translation will be appropriate. 'With a view to soften the heart of the wicked a person should show the greatest friendship for them and speak to them words that impart delight to all.'

† It is the cry of the peacock which to the Sanskrit Poets was very musical. It is said to resemble the *Sadja* or the fourth (according to some authorities the first) of the seven primary notes of the Hindu gamut. It is also curious to note, that the 'tuneful cry' the 'animated nail' of the peacock which is so much appreciated in India, is said to be the voice of the Demon in Italy.

29. A person strictly redeeming all his promises and appreciating the good qualities* of others and cherishing respect and kindly feelings† for them, should spend his wealth in the performance of pious deeds; and he should always speak sweet and pleasing words.

30. Those, who speak sweet words and offer hospitality to all, are surely gods under human form, ever prosperous and stainless in character.

31. Unsullied in mind and in body and with a soul purified by a belief in the contents of the *Shâstras*, a person should always worship the gods and should regard his elders as gods, and his relatives as his own self.

32. For his own welfare, a man should please his venerable elders by bowing down unto them; and he should please the virtuous by his modest behaviour; and he should propitiate the deities by acts of piety.

33. A person should please his friends by his (affable) manners, his kinsmen by his friendliness, and his wife and servants by his love and liberality respectively; and he should please persons other than these by his kind treatment to them.

34—36. To find no fault with the actions of others, to observe their own duties, to show compassion for the distressed, to address sweet words to all, to serve faithful friends at the cost of their own lives, to welcome their enemies coming to their house, to practise charities proportionate to their resources, to bear up against all sufferings, to reconciliate estranged friends, to offer good treatment to their kinsmen and to comply with their requests—these are the characteristic features of the high-minded.

37. This is the path of life prescribed for the householders that undeviatingly follow the eternal ways of the

---

* The commentator adds 'of those worthy of receiving gifts.'

† The commentator explains 'believing that charity is the best of all religious performances.'

illustrious. Treading this path, they attain prosperity in this and in the next world.

38. Even the foes of a king become his friends, if he strictly observes the above mode of life. That king can subjugate the world by his modest qualities, who is free from all feelings of animosity.

39. How vast is the difference between the kings and their myriad subjects*. How rare is a king who condescends to please his subjects with sweet words. The subjects of the king who captivates them at first with strings of sweet words, and then cherishes them, never deviate one step from the course of rectitude.

Thus ends the third Section, the determination of duties, in the Nitisára of Kámandaka.

—:o:—

SECTION IV.

1-2 KING, minister, kingdom, castle, treasury, army and allies are known to form the seven constituents of a government. They contribute to one another's weal, and the loss of even a single one of them renders the whole imperfeet; he who wishes to keep a government perfect should study well† their nature.

3. The first desideratum for a king is to attain royal qualities, and having attained them, he should look for them in others.

4. A flourishing sovereignty cannot well be obtained by the wor hless; he only, who has qualified himself, is fit to wield the sceptre.

* *Samgraha* may also mean 'welfare,' 'advancement.'

† For *Shuparikshanam* the commentary gives *Asuparikshanam*.

5. Royal prosperity so difficult to attain and more so to retain, and which entirely depends on the good will of the multitude, rests steadily only on moral purity like water in a (fixed) vessel.

6—8. Nobility of birth, equanimity, youthfulness,* good character, benevolence, activity, consistency,† veracity, respectful behaviour towards those older in age and in knowledge, gratefulness, good-fatedness,‡ keen reasoning power, relationship with the great,§ ability to conquer his enemies, unshaken reverence, far-sightedness, energy, purity, ambitious aims, modesty and piety—these are the qualities, the presence of which in a king renders him acceptable as a refuge to the people.

9. A king, possessed of these qualities, is always resorted to by his subjects seeking protection. He should act in such a way as to secure the esteem of his people.

10. A ruler of earth, desiring his own welfare, should keep a retinue consisting of descendants from illustrious families, pure, upright, and obliging in character.

11. People seek protection even from a wicked king if his counselors be good. A king with a wicked counsel is seldom approached (for protection) like a sandal tree begirt with snakes.

12. Prohibiting the access of the good to the king, his wicked counselors exhaust his treasury.|| It is for this

---

* The word in the text is *Vayas,* which the commentator explains as 'youthfulness;' but we think it to mean 'old age' which will be more suited to the text. A youthful king is scarcely resorted to as a refuge.

† The commentary reads *Avisamvádità* for *Asamvivádità* and explains the former as 'absence of contradiction in speech.'

‡ Or 'on whom fortune ever smiles.'

§ For *Akshudraparichárità* of the text the commentary reads *Akshudraparivárata,* which reading we accept.

|| The word in the text lit: translated will be 'eat up;' but the commentary very properly gives the meaning we have embodied.

reason (if not for any other), that a king should have pious and good counselors.

13. Having obtained a flourishing prosperity, a king should dedicate* it to the enjoyment of the pious. For prosperity avails nothing, if it is not participated in by the pious.

14. The wealth and prosperity of the wicked are enjoyed only by others of the same nature. Only crows and no other birds taste the fruit of the *Kimpâka* tree.†

15—19. Eloquence, self-confidence,‡ accuracy of memory, stateliness of stature, superior might,§ self-control, ingenuity for inventing various means and instruments of torture,|| perfection in all the arts, ability of easily reclaiming men treading evil ways,¶ the power of sustaining an assault of the enemy, knowledge of all the remedies against danger, promptness in detecting the weak points of an enemy, familiarity with the nature of war and peace,$ strict observance of secrecy regarding all consultations and actions, proficiency in turning into account the advantages of place and time, collection of money (from the people) and its proper expenditure, a deep insight into the nature of the dependents, freedom from anger, covetousness, fear, malice, obstinacy and fickleness, avoidance of tyranny, depravity, animosity, jealousy, and

---

* For *Vrajet* the commentary reads *Nayait.*

† *Kimpâka*—A cucurbitaceous plant (Trichosanthes palmata, also Cucumis colocynthus). In the following five Slokas, the author enumerates the necessary qualifications of a monarch.

‡ The commentator explains, 'audacity of refuting even the words of god-like people.'

§ Like that of the hero *Bhima* of the Mahabharata.

|| For *Nipuna* of the text the commentary gives *Nipunam.*

¶ For *Suvigraha* read *Svavagraha*; this reading is also suggested by the commentator.

$ By war and peace here, the author means all the six expedients to be used by a king in foreign politics. The expedients are (*a*) peace or alliance, (*b*) war, (*c*) march or expedition, (*d*) halt, (*e*) seeking shelter, and (*f*) duplicity.

falsehood, compliance with the advices of those older in age and in learning, energy, amiable appearance, appreciatior of worth in other people, and smiling words,—these are known to be the indispensable qualifications for a sovereign.

20. Under a king unmoved by the passions and possessed of all these qualifications and perfectly acquainted with men and manners, the subjects live as happily as under the roof of their own father; such a sovereign is worthy of the name *Parthiva*.*

21. A kingdom increases in prosperity, having obtained a *Mahendra*-like† king, who is well-adorned with these royal qualities, and all whose acts are just and impartial.

22. Desire for inbibing knowledge,‡ attentive audition of the lessons taught, their assimilation, retention and the comprehension of their various meanings,§ the discussion of the *pros* and *cons* of a question,|| a close application to the study

* Lit. A ruler of earth. As we have written in the introduction, the author is indebted to the *Rajdharmánusasana Parva* of the *Mahábhárata* for his treatise; there occur many Slokas in the latter work which may aptly be cited as parallels. For instance here we give the translation of a Sloka from the *Mahabharata* :—"He is the best of kings in whose dominions men live fearlessly like sons in the house of their sire,"

† Mahendra—or the great *Indra* is the Jupiter Pluvius of the Hindu mythology. He is the god of the firmament, the regent of the atmosphere and of the east quarter, and his world is called *Svarga*. In the *Vedas*, he is placed in the first rank among the gods, but in later mythology, he falls in the second rank. He is inferior to the Trinity *Brahmá Vishnu* and *Mahesa*, but he is the chief of all the other gods. He sends the lightning, wields thunder-bolt and pours down rain.

‡ This thirst for knowledge the commentator ascribes to causes that were existent in a previous birth.

§ The word in the text may have another meaning, viz., 'knowledge of the diverse ways regarding the acquisition of wealth.'

|| *Uha*—means conjecture as 'what can this be' &c. *Apoha*—means rejection of doubtful propositions after full discussion. The two taken together gives the meaning we have embodied in our rendering.

of the real nature of things,*—these are the characteristic features of the intellect.

23. Skilfulness, activity, living animosity for an enemy, and bravery, these are the characteristic features of energy. Well-accmplished in these attributes (of the intellect and energy), a man deserves to assume the royal functions.

24. Benignity, truthfulness and valour, these are the three noblest† of all royal qualities; possessing these, a king easily attains the rest.

25. The attendants‡ of a monarch should be high-born, pure-natured, heroic, learned, loyal and experts in the practical application of the science of Polity.

26. §All the actions and omissions of a king should be examined by his loyal attendants, whose honesty has been tested by the *Upadhás*|| and who follow up their schemes until they are successful.

27. *Upadhá*¶ is so called because it brings people near the king and can make them enter into his service. *Upadhâs* are the means for testing honesty, and by these a king should try his dependents.

28—30. A person, who has got good many friends to deter him from the paths of vice, who is not a foreigner by

---

* The commentator suggests another meaning, namely, 'yearning for spiritual knowledge or knowledge of the Supreme Being.'

† 'For,' as the commentator explains 'they are most efficacious as means to an end.'

‡ The word in the text is *Sachiva*, which generally means a minister; but here the commentator takes it to mean, 'those who seek the same interest with the king.'

§ Having enumerated the necessary qualifications for a king, the author how proceeds to describe the qualities of good attendants and ministers.

|| The *Visarga* after *Upadhá* in the text is a palpable mistake.

¶ The *Upadhâs* have been explained as above by the author himself. They are four in kind, being (*a*) the test of loyalty, (*b*) the test of disinterestedness, (*c*) the test of courage, and (*d*) the test of continence.

birth,* who possesses a noble lineage and character and great physical strength, who is eloquent and audacious in speech† and is far-sighted,‡ energetic and ready-witted, who is free from obstinacy§ and fickleness and is faithful to his friends, who is painstaking and pure and truthful, who is blessed with eqanimity, cheerfulness, patience, gravity and health, who is a master of all the arts, and dexterous and is prudent and retentive, who is unswerving in his devotion and does not revenge the wrongs done to him by his sovereign,—such a person should be elected as a minister.

31. Accuracy of memory, exclusive devotion to the ways and means and the empire, grave consideration of the *pros* and *cons* of a question, unerring judgment, firmness, and observance of secrecy regarding all counsels—these are known to be the necessary qualifications of a minister.

32. ‖A person well-versed in *Trayee* and *Dandaniti*¶ should be appointed as the royal priest. He should accom-

---

* Literally translated, it would be, 'born in the self-same country with his sovereign;' the author denounces the appointment of a foreigner as a minister, on the ground that such a man can have no natural sympathy for his master. In this way no good feeling will cement their alliance.

† The commentator gives a different meaning, namely, 'unrivalled.'

‡ Lit. translated it would be 'having eyes'; but in Sanskrit literature *Shâstras* are often identified with the eyes, for they help in clearing many doubts and can enable men to divine what is in store for them. *c.f.*

'Anêka samsaya chchedi parokshârthasya darsamam
Sarvasya lochanam Shâstram yasya nâstyandha eb sa.'

Hence the word in the text may mean 'learned in the *Shâstras* or having the eye of knowledge.'

§ The word may have another signification, namely, 'rigidity of manners.'

‖ The Author now goes on to describe the qualifications of the royal priest and astrologer.

¶ Criminal Jurispend nce or the Science of chastisement.

plish *Sántica, Poustica** and other benedictory rites according to the ordinances of the *Atharva Veda.*

33. A person investigating the nature of the science of Astrology and clever in putting questions to other, and proficient in the computation of hours and minutes,† should be appointed as the king's astrologer.

34. An intelligent monarch should seek information about the honesty of his dependents from men of their stamp and position ; he should have their artistic acquirements examined by connoisseurs.‡

35. From their (deqendents') kinsmen, he (the king) should gather information regarding their natural temparament, successful career, serviceability, and their skilfulness, capacity for knowledge and power of assimilation.

36. He should assure himself of the measure of their self-confidence and ingenuity : and he should also examine their fluency and truthfulness by holding conversation with them.

---

* *Sántica* literally means, that which brings about *Sânti* or peace ; it is a special designation of the expiatory ceremonies or observances calculated to remove or avert danger. *Poustica* literally means 'promoting growth (*poosti*) ; hence it is a name for those rites that conduce to the welfare of the kingdom.

† The word in the text is '*hora,*' which may mean 'hours' as well as 'zodiacal signs.' If we accept the latter signification, then the text would mean 'proficient in interpreting zodiacal signs.' The use of this word has given rise to a controversy regarding the antiquity of this work, (Vide Introduction).

‡ The author in this and in the following four Slokas goes on to enumerate the sources and measures, from and by which, a king should gather information regarding his dependents and ministers. The syntactical and grammatical structure of this and the one following Sloka is hopelessly defective. The commentary, though needlessly elaborate at other places, is discreetly silent here. So there is no chance of making out what the exact meanings of the Slokas are ; what we embody in our rendering is the product of conjecture and common sense.

37. He should mark if they possess energy, prowess, endurance, memory, devotion. and steadiness.

38. By their behaviour, he should know their devotion, faithfuluess and purity of intention. He should enlighten himself regarding their physical strength, their evenmindedness and their healthiness, from those who live with them.

39. He should directly* ascertain their tractability and resoluteness and their power of keeping their enemies under control and their meanness or gentility.

40. The presence,of secondary qualities beyond direct perception, is inferred by their workings; and the success of their workings again is measured† by the results they achieve.

41. A king inclined to evil deeds should be prevented by his ministers; he should regard their advice in the same light as those of his spiritual guide.‡

42. The monarchy collapses with the collapse of the king, while it revives with his revival, like the lotus reviving at the rising of the sun.§

43. Thorefore ministers endued with genius, energy, and equanimity, and devoted to the interests of their master, should instil knowledge|| into him in a suitable manner.¶

---

* That is, 'not through secondary sources, but personally.'

† Fer *Bibhávayét* the commentary gives *Bibhávyaté*.

‡ The text, if translated as it is, would be 'he should pay heed to their words as well as to the words of his spiritual guides.' But there is another reading and we accept that.

§ Sanskrit poetry abounds in instances in which the lotus is regarded as the mistress of the Sun. This metaphor probably has its origin in the fact that lotuses blossom forth at the early dawn. In this natural phenomenon, the 'poet's eye in fine frenzy rolling' finds the delight the sweet-heart feels at the advent of her lord that was away.

|| We would rather prefer this to be substituted by 'should guide him'; but the tent does not allow it; and a tanslator is fast bound to the oar.

¶ That is, 'by reciting proverbs, apologues and moral tales,' these being considered to be the easiest means of imparting knowledge.

44. Those ministers only are considered to be the true friends and spiritual guides of a king, who deter him from going astray, disregarding repeated warnings not to do so.

45. Those who restrain a king inclined to evil deeds,* are to him his most worshipful preceptors and not mere friends.

46. Even persons well-grounded in knowledge are ensnared by the irristible attractions of the sensual enjoyments. What wrongful act can not then a man, whose heart is enslaved to the pleasures of the senses, commit?

47. A king perpetrating transgressions is said to be blind in spite of his eyes.†. His friends, assuming the functions of physicians, cure him of his blindness by applying the collyrium‡ of modesty.

48. When a king,blinded by passions, pride and arrogance, falls into the snare set forth by his enemies, the exertions of his ministers serve to extricate him, even as the support of the hand aids a fallen man.

49. Like the *Mâhutas*§ of infuriated elephants, the the ministers of a king are held to blame, when, intoxicated with pride, he goes astray.

50. A kingdom flourishes through the fertility of its soil, and the king prospers through the flourishing condition of the kingdom. Therefore, for his own prosperity, a king should try to make his territory as fertile as possible.

51—52. ‖A land adorned with crops, rich in mines,

---

* The commentary paraphrases 'acts which are prohibited by the *Shâstras.*'

† 'For,' goes on the commentator, 'he can not perceive the sin of his violations.'

‡ Collyrium is described in the Hindu books of medicine to be a well-tried remedy for all disorders of the eye.

§ The *Mâhuta* is the technical oriental name for the keepers of elephants; one of their duties is to guide them when the king rides on them. Buffon in his 'Natural History,' calls these leaders of elephants *Cornca.*

‖ Having explained the necessary qalifications for monarchs and ministers, the author now proceeds to describe what kind of land is best

minerals, and commodities for trade, conducive to the breed of cattle, copiously watered, (thickly) inhabited by virtuous people and pious sects, possessed of all the charms of nature, abounding in woods swarming with elephants,* having inland and navigable communications, and not depending upon showers of rain for agricultural purposes†—such a land is specially favourable to the welfare and prosperity of kings.

53. A land, overspread with gravels and fragments of stones‡ and covered with forests and thorny brush-woods, and molested by depridators, and arid and infested with beasts of prey, such a land is not worthy of the name.

54—56. A country where living is cheap, the soil of which is fertile§ and copiously irrigated,|| which is situated at the foot of a mountain,¶ which contains a large number of

---

suited to the establishment of a kingdom, and what kind of kingdom brings prosperity on the king.

* The necessity of such woods may at first seem incomprehensible; but it will be obvious when we say that the ancient Aryans, like the Greeks of yore, utilized elephants in martial purposes; and invariably these monsters of the forest constituted a good portion of their army. They were also used in pageants and royal processions.

† *Adevamâtrikâ.*—Lit. translated would mean, 'not having the god of rain or clouds as foster-mother;' hence an *Adevamâtrikâ* land is that which does not entirely depend on rain-water, but has other sources of water-supply, namely, irrigation and floods, for agricultural purposes. Egypt and the countries, through which the Nile flows, can be cited as examples. The opposite of *Adevamâtrikâ* is *Nadimâtrikâ* *i.e.*, having a river as foster-mother.

‡ The commentary here suggests another reading namely *Sakkar-osharapâshânâ* (or covered over with gravels, saline soil, and fragments of stones), for which we see no occasion.

§ Or, as the commentator remarks, 'which possesses all the above-mentioned qualifications.'

|| The word in the text is *Sârupa* for which the commentary suggests *Sânupa*.

¶ So that its inhabitants might have an abundant supply of fire-wood and fuels.

Sudras,* traders and artisans, where the farmers and husbandmen are enterprizing and energetic, which is loyal to its ruler and inhospitable to its enemies, which ungrudgingly bears heavy taxation (for replenishing the treasury), which is extensive in area and is crowded with men from various foreign countries, which is rich and pious and abounds in cattle, and where the popular leaders are not foolish and voluptuous†—such a country is the best of all others. A king should, by all means, endeavour to promote the welfare of such a land, for, with its prosperity, the other constituents of government would also prosper.

57. ‡A king should settle in such a fortress, which has an extensive area, and is environed by a wide ditch and secured with gates strengthened with high and massive walls, and which is sheltered by mighty mountains, forests and deserts.§

58. He should have a castle proof against the inclemencies of the weather, well stuffed with provisions and money, and having an abundant supply of water. A king without a castle is unsteady like patches of clouds before a strong wind.

59. A fort, containing copious water and thickly interspersed with hillocks and trees and situated in a desert and

---

* The serving class. The fact of their being numerous in a country would render labour cheap.

† According to the reading accepted in the note (which is *Murkha* &c.) the translation would be 'foolish and voluptuous.' The commentator goes on to explain his curious interpretation by asserting that such leaders do not brother their heads with politics and are not intriguing and capable of deception. They are contented with their lot and leave the king free to govern according to his own whim and caprice ; surely the explation is very ingenious.

‡ The author now gives directions which will help a king to select a suitable site for his castle. These directions, as the reader will see, do credit even to a military engineer of the highest rank.

§ These mountains and forests and deserts would stand in the way of an enemy coming to assault the fort. For *ghana* the commentary gives *Maru*.

arid soil, has been said to be impregnable, by persons well-read in the *Shâstras* and by men proficient in the art of castle-building.*

60. The *Achâryyas*† hold that fortress to be the best which is sufficiently stored with provisions, water, weapons, and other implements of war, and is garrisoned by cool-headed soldiers‡ and has numerous defences.

61. A country, having communications both by land and by water§ and furnished with castles affording shelter to the royal family at the time of a siege,—such a country is suitable for the habitation for a king who seeks prosperity.

62—63. ||A treasury, the collections of which are vast and disbursements limited, which is far-famed, where adoration is offered to the gods,¶ which is full of desirable things, a sight of which is charming, which is superintended over by trustworthy people and is enriched with gold, pearls, and jewels, which redounds to the credit of the forefathers, which

* What the author means is this :—Inside the fort there should be natural hillocks and a large number of trees, under the cover of which, the garrison at the time of a siege would be able to give battle to the assaulting army. The site of the fort should be in a desert soil, so that the besiegers would be compelled to give up their attempt out of sheer want of food and water. The garrison should have abundant supply of provision and drinking water, so that they would be able to hold out long, while the ranks of the besiegers would be thinned by famine.

† *Achâryya* lit: means a spiritual preceptor, here the preceptors of the gods and demons (Vrihaspati and Sukra) are alluded to.

‡ So that in case of a siege, they will not rashly venture a battle, for, by holding out, they are sure to conquer in the long run.

§ The word in the text is explained in the commentary as follows, 'covered equally with land and water.' We do not find any appropriateness of the interpretation and so reject it.

|| Here begins the description of the treasury, which is also very sound and statesman-like.

¶ 'Specially' goes on the commentator, 'to Sri and Dhanada.' The former is the Goddess of prosperity, and the latter the Lord of wealth, the Plutus of the Grecian mythology.

6

has been filled by lawful means, and which can defray any amount of expenditure,—such a treasury wins the approval of men of financial acumen.

64. Persons possessing treasures should preserve them for purposes of piety, for increasing their wealth, for times of danger and for maintaining their dependents.

65—67. An army* inherited from the forefathers,† throughly obedient and disciplined, firmly united, well-paid, well-known for bravery and manliness, skilful in handling all kinds of weapons, commanded by experts in the science of war, equipped with various implements of war, trained in various modes of warfare, crowded with legions of warriors, swarming with elephants and horses purified by the *Nirâjana*‡ ceremony, accustomed to stay abroad and to troubles and distresses, indefatigable in fight, having its ranks filled with never vacillating *Kshatriyas*,§ such an army has been commended by persons proficient in the science of Polity.

68. A king should form alliance with a person, illustrious, well-spoken, benevolent, learned, even-minded, having numerous partisans, and who would remain constant in faithfulness for all future periods.||

---

* The author now proceeds to describe the qualifications that make an army efficient.

† What the author means is 'which has served his forefathers' &c.

‡ A kind of military and religious ceremony performed, by kings and generals of armies, in the month of *Asvina*, (September, October) before they took the field. It was, so to say, a general purification of the king's *Purohita* (priest), the ministers and the various component parts of the army, together with the arms and implements of war, by sacred *mantras*. Some time *Nirâjana* means only lustration of arms.

§ *Advaidha*.—Lit. means 'having no sense of distinction,' *i.e.*, who do not distinguish between life and death. But *dvaidha* also means duplicity and a vacillating tendency. *Kshatriyas* are the ruling and fighting caste and stand second in the scale of castes.

|| The author here gives rules for forming alliances and for selecting allies. Here also he is very wise and far-seeing. The *Ayatikshama* in

69. A pure-hearted and high-born ally surely displays ingenuity and versatility* when great difficulties present themselves.

70. A man, who was in friendly relations with his ancestors, who is steady and unwavering, and who has a deep insight into his nature† and who is generous and unostentatious, is to be desired as an ally by a king.

71. To come out to accord a cordial welcome even from a distance, to speak agreeable words coveying distinct sense, and to offer a warm hospitality, these are the three methods of making friends.

72. The realisation of virtue, wealth and desire, is the fruit of friendship; and a prudent person does not form such a friendship which is barren of these three.

73. The friendship of the pious is like a river, shallow in the beginning, deep in the middle, widening at each step, and ever-flowing and never-ceasing.

74. Friends are of four kinds, being separately derived from birth, relationship, ancestral obligation, and protection from danger.

75. Integrity in money matters, freedom from temptation, manliness, participation in weal and woe, fidelity, ingenuity, truthfulness, these are the necessary qualifications for an ally.

76. In short, unswerving devotion to the interests of his friends is the principal characteristic of a friend. He is not a friend in whom this quality is not found; and a man should not throw himself on the mercy of such a one.

77. Thus, government and its seven constituents have been explained by us; its main stay is the treasury and the

---

the text of this Sloka means, 'the friendship of whom has not the slightest chance of melting away even in the remotest future.'

* The world in the text lit: translated would be 'squareness'.

† Another interpretation is possible, namely, 'to the liking of his heart.'

army; and administered by a skilful minister, it leads to the eternal consummation of *Trivarga*.

78. Just as the spiritual Principle combined with matter pervades this universe, so a king united with his subjects extends his dominions all over the earth.

79. Thus a king worshipped by his subjects and held in high honor by them, should protect his own kingdom. By promoting the welfare of his own kingdom, he speedily reaches the zenith of prosperity and progress.

80. A king, possessed of loyal subjects and royal qualities, is greatly to be desired.* In the field of battle he sweeps his enemies before him like chaff before the wind.†

Thus ends the fourth Section, the description of the essential constituents of government, namely, king, ministers, kingdom, castle, treasury, army and allies, in the Nitisâra of Kâmandaka.

SECTION V.

1. PERSONS depending on others for their livelihood should enter into the services of a king who is like the celestial tree *Kalpa* itself‡; who is ever devoted to his duties; and

* The commentator gives a different explanation, viz., 'is always resorted to as a refuge.'

† Literally translated the passage would be 'is as formidable an opponent to his enemies as the strong wind is to the clouds.'

‡ A tree fabled to be in Indra's paradise. It is supposed to grant all desires. There is also a creeper of the same name possessing the same qualities. The idea of comparing a generous person with this tree or creeper is a very favorite one with Sanskrit poets.

who possesses an ample treasury* and qualities that attract his subjects to him.

2. A king, even when deprived of his subjects and substance, should be resorted to, if only, he possesses good qualities.† For, (if not then, but) after a while, an honourable living could be secured from him.

3. A wise man should rather remain inactive like a branch less trunk, and wither away with oppressive hunger, than seek a means of maintenance from the worthless.

4. A worthless and unjust monarch carrying his prosperity to the very zenith,‡ meets with destruction even during his (apparently) sunny days.

5. Having been once admitted into the royal service, a skilful,§ self-possessed and never-veering|| person can secure the permanence of his office, by being decided in his judgments.¶

6. A person should choose such a living which would be relished at present and in future ; he should never select one that would be disliked by the world.$

---

* Here the commentary differs from the text and substitutes another reading, namely '*Vrittastham Vrittisampannam*' which we have accepted.

† The royal qualities enumerated in Slokas 15 to 19 in Section IV.

‡ There is another reading namely *Arisampada* which means 'the prosperity of his foes.' In this case the first line would mean, 'an unjust and worthless king indirectly helps in enhancing the prosperity of his foes.'

§ For *Nipuna* the commentary reads *Nipunam* which would be an adverb qualifying 'secure.'

|| The commentary explains 'never harbouring the remotest ill-will against his master.'

¶ Lit: translated would be, 'resolving to do everything that human understanding is capable of.'

$ In translating the Sloka we have followed the commentary. But another meaning seems possible to us which we give below. The reader is left free to compare and to judge. "A servant should only execute those behests of his royal master which would be relished by the people

7. Sesamum seeds, when kept together with *Champaca** flowers, acquire the latter's fragrance; but then the fluid that is pressed out of them cannot be taken. Thus all qualities (good or bad) are contagious.†

8. A stream of tasteful‡ water, having flown into the sea, becomes saline and thus undrinkable. For this simple reason, a wise man should never associate with one of wicked and impure soul.

9. Even when hard pressed with difficulties, a wise person should betake to none but an honourable living. Through such a living, he earns respectibility and is not cast out of this world and the next.§

10. As a man desirous of seeing a mountain should go to the deep-rooted, majestic, sacred and far-famed Vindhya hills, inhabited by numberless pious people, so a person, seeking a successful career should employ himself in the services of a master who is desirable, faithful to the usages, virtuous, illustrious, praiseworthy and served by other pious people.||

11. (By strenuous efforts) a persevering person¶ gets

---

at present and in the future; and he should never do what would be injurious to the interests of the people in general."

* A kind of yellow fragrant flower, (Michelia *Champaca*).

† In this and in the several following Slokas the author goes on to describe the influence of company. This Sloka and the next are put in by way of preamble.

‡ The text lit: translated would be 'a stream of Ganges water'. But the Ganges being the most sacred river, her water is typically used to signify all tasteful water.

§ There seems to be a pun upon the word '*loka*' which means both regions and persons. If the second signification is accepted, the last portion of the Sloka would mean 'is not forsaken by his friends.'

|| What the author wants to impress, is, that when a man has no other means of livelihood but service, he should select a master who tallies with this description. For, he thinks, such a wise selection will diminish the unpalatableness and rigours of servitude.

¶ The word in the text means 'having an accurate memory'; but this signification will be out-of-place here.

at all those objects that he may desire, even if they be hard to obtain. Therefore, assiduous endeavour should always be put forth (in accomplishing an action).

12. A dependent, willing to promote the real service of his royal master, should qualify himself with learning, humility, and knowledge of all the arts.*

13—14. That person is only fit to serve a worthy master who possesses a noble lineage, learning, proficiency in the *Srutis*,† liberality, good character, prowess and patience; who is blessed with an amiable appearance, and even-mindedness, physical might, healthiness, firmness of mind, honesty of intentions and kindness of disposition; who is beyond the reach of malevolence, treacherousness, a spirit of sowing dissensions, guilefulness, avidity and falseness, and (lastly) who has cast off obstinacy‡ and fickleness alike.

15. Ingeniousness, gentleness, constancy, forbearance, § capacity for enduring pain, cheerfulness, good character, and fortitude—these are the qualities that are said to ornament a dependent.

16. Endowed with all these attributes and observing a most scrupulous integrity about pecuniary matters, a dependent should, for his own advancement, try to win the confidence of his prosperous royal master.

17. Having obtained an access into the king's court, he

---

* Arts must be taken to include fine arts as well as mechanical arts; no less than sixty-four arts have been enumerated in Sanskrit lexicons.

† *Srutis*—*sruti* means what is heard or revealed as distinguished from *Smritis*; *Srutis* or Vedas are '*a-paurusheya*' works or 'not human compositions.' They are supposed to have been directly revealed by the Supreme Being, Brahman.

‡ The word in the text may also have this meaning namely, 'rigidity or stiffness of manners.'

§ The word in the text is *Kshanti* which is defined as *Satyapi sâmarthyé apakarin doshasahanam* or indulgence towards offenders or enemies in spite of the power of revenging.

should go there in decent garments,* and occupy the seat allotted to him (by the usher); then in proper time, and with becoming humility, he should pay his homage to his sovereign lord.

18. He should ever shun the seats and places of other courtiers and should avoid crookedness, gaudy garments, and enviousness; he should never discourse with his superiors (in age, rank and knowledge), contradicting them in a disrespectful manner.

19. A dependent should avoid prevarication, trickery, deceitfulness and thievishness. He should do obeisance to the sons and favorite attendants of his royal master.†

20. He should speak nothing unpalatable to the king's jesters;‡ for then, in the very midst of the assembly, they will pierce him to the core with their withering sarcasms.

21. Occupying a seat adjacent to (that of) his master, he should not allow his eyes to wander, but keep them

---

* For *Savesavan* the commentary reads *Suvesavan* which reading we have accepted.

† 'Then these latter,' goes on the commentator, 'will recommend him to the good graces of the king.'

‡ As we have written *Narmasachiva* means a jester or more correctly, an associate of amusements of princes and persons of high rank. But the reader must not confound him with English 'fools' aud 'buffoons' whose model-type we find in the 'Ivanhœ' of S. W. Scott. The position of western buffoons is inferior to that of the oriental *Vidusakas*. These latter are recruited from illustrious families and often from amongst the spiritual caste (Brahmanas). They are exceptionally intelligent and sound counselors. They are the humour-companions as well as confidential friends of a monarch, (some times of the hero of a play), who excite mirth by their fantastical motley dresses, their speeches, gestures, appearances, movements &c., and by allowing themselves to be the butt of redicule by almost everybody. In spite of all these, they are held in high honor by the other courtiers and exercise a considerable amount of influcnce over the king who regards them as his best and foremost counselors, and who never goes against what they advise.

riveted on the countenance of his master, to watch what he would do.

22. When the king says 'who is there,' the retainer should respond saying 'here am I at your Majesty's entire command?'* He should with promptitude give effect to his lord's behests to the best of his abilities.

23. He† should avoid (in the presence of his master) breaking out into roars of laughter, coughing, expectorating, yawning, stretching his limbs and body,‡ and making sounds with his finger tips.§

24. Divining his affectionate master's purposes, in a manner approved of by others proficient in thought-reading, he should speak distinctly, when asked to do so, upholding his master's views.

25. When a dispute or debate arises among the assembly of courtiers,|| the dependent, being directed by his royal master, should cite the opinions of the experts¶ regarding the point at issue, and should ascribe such signification to the disputed term, about which there can be doubt whatever.

---

* The text lit: translated would be 'I am here, command me fully.'

† No doubt some of our readers will wonder to find the rules of etiquette laid down here to be perfectly at one with those recognised in western society. In nicety and in minuteness of detail they are in no way inferior or wanting. In the *Mahâbhârata* also we find a denouncement of these actions (laughing&c.,) as breaches of etiquette. *C.f.* 'They become so shameless as to indulge in eructations and the like, and expectorate in the very presence of their master.' Sec. LVI., S. 53. *Râjadharmânusasana Parva*

‡ The original word in the text is *Gâtrabhanga*, which is taken to signify that peculiar kind of bodily movement which is calculated to shake off idleness.

§ The word in the text is *Parvâsfota; parva* means fingure-joints and *ásfota* means sound. In ordinary English it is termed 'filliping.'

|| The compound lit: translated would be 'the assembly of courtiers, which has been enlarged for the king's pleasure.'

¶ Specially used for any expounder of any particular system.

26. Though thoroughly informed on any point, yet, a prudent servant should never speak in such a way as to silence his master. Though eloquent, he should forego self-gratification on this score.*

27. A dependent should speak of what he knows best as though he knew very little. But with becoming modesty, he should display the superiority of his knowledge by his actions.†

28. A dependent, who is truly anxious for the welfare of his master, should proffer his wholesome advice uncalled-for, only when the latter deviates from the path of rectitude, or when any emergency is imminent,‡ or when a favorable opportunity for any particular action slips away unnoticed.

29. For the interests of justice,§ a retainer should speak sweet, salutary and truthful words, and he should avoid telling what is incredible, indecent,‖ uncouth and jarring to the ear.

30. A servant knowing the proper use of time and place, should, when they are favorable, do good to other people; he should also promote his own interests in a skilful manner.

31. He should not (prematurely) divulge those counsels

---

* In rendering this portion of the text we have followed the commentary, though another interpretation is apparent, namely, 'Even possessing vast experience, he should not be proud of it.'

† For a similar sentiment campare,

> 'Pitch thy behaviours low, thy projects high,
> So shalt thou humble and magnanimous be.
> Sink not in spirit ; who aimeth at the sky
> Shoots higher much than he that means a tree.'
>
> *George Herbert.*

‡ The nature of the emergency has been defined in the commentary to be 'warlike preparations by an inimical sovereign.'

§ The word in the text may have another import, namely 'to secure religious merit.'

‖ For *Asatya* or false, the commentary reads *Asabhya* or indecent.

and measures* of his master that ought to be kept secret. Even in his mind, he should never harbour the remotest thought of his master's dethronement and death.

32. He should shun the company and close association of women, of those sinful wretches who lustfully gaze at them, of the emissaries of a hostile monarch, of those who had been turned out by his master; he should have no interest to serve with these in common.

33. He should never try to imitate his sovereign lord in his habits and habiliments†; a wise servant should never endeavour to emulate his royal master, even if he might be gifted with royal qualities.

34. A servant, understanding signs and experssions of the face and capable of achieving acts accomplished by experts, should interpret the internal sentiments, sympathy or antipathy (towards himself), of his master, with the assistance of external gestures, appearances and signs.

35. A master, when satisfied with his servant, rejoices at his sight, accepts his advices gladly, offers him a seat near his own and enquires after his health and welfare.‡

36. Then the master does not fear to accompany his servant to sequestered places and to entrust him with secret commissions. Then he attentively listens to conversations relating to his servant or carried on by the latter.

37. The master then feels proud when his servant is praised by others, and congratulates him on his good fortune. The master remembers him (dependent) in the course of any

---

* The commentary explains the 'measures' to be *Avichára* &c, for which vide supra, Sec I. Sloka 4th note.

† The reading in the text is '*Vesabhásá*' which we have changed in to '*Vesabhusa*.' The original reading lit: rendered would mean 'the dress and manner of speaking.'

‡ In this and in the following Slokas, the author goes on to describe the behaviour, a servant is to expect, in the hands of his master, first, when he is pleased, and next when he is displeased with him.

conversation* and begins, out of delight, to expatiate on the latter's good qualities.

38. Then the master tolerates the unpalatable language† uttered by his servant and puts up with the censure passed by him.‡ The former then acts up to the latter's advices and highly prizes his counsel.

39. On the other hand, when a master is dis-satisfied with his servant, he treats him with indifference, even if the latter may have rendered many precious services to him. Acts done by his servant, he ascribes to the agency of others.§

40. Then the master incites the rivals of his servant and neglects him when he is afflicted by his enemies. When there is an act to be done by his servant, the master encourages the latter's hopes, but when it is accomplished, he never fulfils them.||

41. Whatever language, (apparently) sweet, the master might address to his servant, would be very cruel in its import; the former smells abuse even in the encomiums the latter offers to him.

42. The master shows himself to be out of temper even when in reality he is not so.¶ When he is pleased with

---

* The commentator explains 'when others speak favourably of his servant.'

† In the text the word *pathya* is evidently a misprint for *Apathya*. Accepting the latter reading the commentary gives this meaning, *viz* 'advocates his servant's views even if they be harmful.' But we do not see any reason for twisting this meaning out of the original line, specially as in the next line the author lays down a similar assertion. *Apathya* of course means 'unwholesome'; but if we are to accept this meaning, we are sure to be involved in a needless tautology, which it is the duty of every annotator to avoid.

‡ Another meaning is possible, 'overlooks the blame that he (dependent) may lay on his shoulders.'

§ Supply 'to deprive him of his due rewards.'

|| Lit: translated 'acts otherwise.'

¶ So that the dependent may not approach and solicit any favour from him.

his servant, he does not grant him any reward.* Then the master sometimes begins to speak suddenly† and moves towards his servant‡ and casts petrifying glances on him.

43. The master speaks words that cut his servant to the quick,§ and then he breaks out into a derisive laugh.|| He saddles his servant with false accusations¶ and for no reason whatever deprives the latter of his means of subsistence.

44. The master then contradicts the words which have been very rightly remarked by his servant; sometimes, suddenly wearing a disagreeable look, he unseasonably halts in the very midst of his speech.**

45. If entreated for a favor when lying on bed,†† the master simulates sleep; and even if awakened by the servants solicitations,‡‡ he still behaves like one in a dream.

46. These are the characteristics of a pleased and displeased master respectively. A servant should earn his

---

* For his satisfaction is not genuine.

† And thus cuts his servant short. The commentary substitutes *Bhavati* for *Vadati*.

‡ So that, before his servant can clear out of his path, he may have a plea for insulting him saying 'why do you obstruct my way, take your detested carcass away.'

§ The annotator here very rightly suggests *Marma* for *Mantra*, but gives a different meaning to the former, namely 'demerit;' the rendering then would be 'speaks hinting at his servant's demerits.'

|| A different reading is suggested *viz* "*Gunân na Vahumanyaté*" or 'does not appreciate his merits'. The annotator further explains himself saying 'the master does not relish the jokes cut by his servant and in lieu of laughing, he wears a morose face over them.'

¶ Supply 'to hide his own faults.'

** With a view to wound the feelings of his servant.

†† The commentator thus explains; 'even if the servant, for securing a certain favor, attends his master on his bed and there shampoos and chafes and rubs the latter's legs and arms, still the latter will not be propitiated and to baffle his man he will imitate sleep.

‡‡ *Balaina* means 'by virtue of' 'through the strength of.'

living from a master who is pleased with him, and forego the one from a displeased lord.

47. A servant should never forsake his master in times of danger, even if the latter be very worthless. There is none more praise-worthy than that dependent who stands firm by his master during an emergency.*

48. Firmness and such other qualities of servants are not brought into relief when their masters enjoy peace and tranquility. But when danger presents itself, the names of these very dutiful dependents are associated with the greatest glory.†

49. The act of doing good to the great is an act which the doer may feel proud of, and which he may very well rejoice at; even though it may be a very insignificant act, it will in proper time bear splendid blessings for him.

50. The commendable duty of a man's friends, relatives and dependents is to dissuade him from acts contrary to the *Shastràs* and to persuade him to those conforming to them.‡

51. Dependents who surround a monarch should try to open his eyes to the evils of inebriety, incontinence and gambling, by means of apologues and moral tales.§ But if

* Apart from other considerations, the advisability of this principle, even from interest's point of view, is quite evident. For surely no master can overlook all the good services rendered by his servant during an emergency; and for the sake of gratitude, which finds a place even in the sternest heart, he is sure to reward, if not adequately, to some extent, the labours of his faithful dependent.

† What the author means is this:—In times of peace, courage firmness and other similar qualities of a servant have no scope for action; but when a war breaks out or any other emergency arises, these qualities stand in good stead to their possessor as well as to his master; they also invest the former with renown and make his name a proverb among his brother-servants.

‡ The author now winds up his discourse relating to the duties of servants, after which he proposes to define the duties of masters.

§ Lit: translated would be, 'the evils of drink, of close association with women, and of dice.'

in spite of their endeavours, the king becomes addicted to any of these vices, (to reclaim him) they should have recourse to *nálikâ** and other such expedients.

52. Those foolish retainers who neglect a king falling into evil ways, run into ruin even with their royal master.†

53. Out of regard for their royal master, the retainers should address him saying 'Victory unto thee,' 'Command thy servant' 'Long live the emperor,' 'My lord,' and even 'My Divinity.' Awaiting their sovereign's commands, the dependents should dance attendance upon his pleasure.

54. (Unhesitating) compliance with the desires of their masters is the foremost duty of all dependents. Even monsters‡ become graceful§ on those servants of theirs who always gratify their humours.

55. What is difficult of being attained by high-souled person endued with intelligence, even-mindedness, and energy?‖ In this earth, what man is ever unfriendly to those people who are sweet-spoken and ever ready to perform the pleasures of others?

---

* Neither *Nâdiká* or *Náliká* (the reading of the commentary) has been explained by any lexicographer. But the commentator explains himself by saying that *Náliká* &c are same with '*Saman* &c.' The latter are means of success against an enemy. There are four of them, namely, (*a*) *Sâman* conciliation or negotiation, (*b*) *Dána* gift or bribery (*c*) *Bheda* sowing dissensions (*d*) *Danda* punishments or open attack. Some authorities add three more, namely, (*e*) *Mâyâ* or deceit (*f*) *Upeksha* trick or neglect (*g*) *Indrajála* magic and conjuring. We do not know whether the author advices the dependants to employ these remedies against their royal master going astray. It may be that there is something amiss in the reading.

† 'Share his defeat with him' would be more literal.

‡ Are here intended to tipify the cruelest and most heartless and exacting masters.

§ Lit: translated would be 'are won over by.'

‖ Lest people take exception, to what he had said in the last portion of the previous Sloka, saying 'how can a man possibly know the desire of his master,' the author puts in 'What is &c.'

56. Even the mother of one idle, unambitious, illiterate and worthless, turns her face away from him when she has to give him something by way of assistance.*

57. The flourishing prosperity of their royal master is throughly participated in, by those retainers who are brave learned and studious in serving him.

58. The injunction of the elders is that a retainer, though regarded with disfavour by his royal master, should still offer wholesome advice to him. He that carries out this injunction is sure to ingratiate himslf with his sovereign.†

59. ‡In this earth, like the rain-cloud *Parjanya*§, a king should be the source of subsistence to all creatures; when he is not so, he is forsaken by his people just as a withered tree is forsaken by the birds.||

60. High lineage, virtuous conduct and heroism, these are not taken into consideration from a servant's point of view. People become attached to a liberal and charitable person in spite of his being of vile character and low extraction.¶

---

* Turning of the face signifies contempt and displeasure; what the author means, is, 'to an idle illiterate and worthless person even his mother denies the hand of help.'

† This and the previous Sloka are not to be found in some texts.

‡ As we have said before, the author, from this Sloka, begins to describe the duties of a master.

§ *Parjanya*—is the chief of that clan of clouds that by pouring their contents promote the cultivation of this earth. As cultivation greatly depends upon showers of rain, *Parjanya* therefore has been recognised to supply food for all created beings. *C. f.* "*Annât bhavanti bhutâni, Prajanyât annasambhava.*"

|| Another reading is given for the last portion viz., '*Suskam saras ibâtndajâ*' or 'just as dried-up lakes are forsaken by water-fowls.' We see no reason for this alteration.

¶ What the author wants to insinuate is, 'bravery &c. are thrown away in a monarch who is niggardly and close-fisted.

61. Lakshmi* is the highest of connections† and there is none more illustrious than her. Men resort to the king who possesses a solvent exchequer and an efficient army.

62. Only the prosperous and the exalted receive homage from men having ends to serve.‡ Like to his enemies, what man ever pays his homage to one fallen.

63. This world of living beings, ever struggling to obtain a means for maintenance, betakes to him who is in the full blaze of his prosperity.§ Even a calf forsakes its dam, when her lactation becomes scarce and she cannot give it adequate sustenance.

64. After the lapse of short periods,‖ a monarch should endow his servants looking up to him for support¶ with remunerations proportionate to the measure of their services.

65. A monarch should never abolish any endowment with respect to any person, place or time; for, by such abolition of endowments, a king brings disgrace upon himself.

66. A monarch should never waste his riches on undeserving persons, as such an act has been denounced by the wise. For, what else comes out of such showering of wealth on the unworthy, but the exhaustion of the exchequer.

---

* Lakshmi—is the tutelary goddess of prosperity, good fortune and beauty.

† *Anvaya*—has diverse significations, besides what we have given; for instance it may mean, 'retinue' 'drift or tenor' 'grammatical order,' &c. So, the first line can have another meaning, if we take *Anvaya* to mean 'retinue.' As it is, we shall explain clearly the meaning we have accepted. When a man is blessed with prosperity, and good fortune, no one ever thinks of the family he comes from, but takes it for granted that he is high-born. Such is the magic of wealth!

‡ Another meaning is possible viz., 'seeking employment.'

§ But the commentator gives, 'who is conspicuous for his munificence,'

‖ These we take to be the periods of probation.

¶ For '*Anujivinám*' the commenator gives *Anuvartinám*, which means 'those who gratify his humour or perform his pleasures;' this makes slight difference.

67. A high-souled monarch should select* those men to be the recepients of his favour, about whose high-birth, proficiency in the three divisions of learning, knowledge of the *Shâstras*, bravery, good behaviour, anticedents, age† and circumstances, he had thoroughly enlightened himself.

68. A sovereign should never contemn high-born, wise, and right-behaved persons; because, for the sake of their honor, these men forsake or even kill him that slights them.

69. A monarch should promote those dependents of his, who are of mediocre or low origin‡ if only they are endued with sterling qualities. For, attaining greatness, these men, (out of gratitude), try hard to enhance the prosperity of their (beneficient) royal master.

70. A monarch should never promote the high-born equally with the low-born.§ A judicious monarch, though he may be weak, is resorted to as a refuge.

71. In this blind world‖ of ours, the wise do not remain there where a precious gem is regarded in the same light with a piece of crystal.

72. That king is praise-worthy and lives a long life and is attended with prosperity, under whose fostering care his pious dependents thrive as under the balmy shade of the

---

* For *Adriaita* (appreciate) of the text the commentary gives *Svadriaita*, which latter we have translated.

† The word in text is *Vayas* which may mean any age or period of life. But the annotator takes it to mean youth, which we do not accept; he would have been more consistent had he suggested *Vayas* to mean old age.

‡ Another interpretation is put forth, viz., 'those occupying middle and lower grades in the royal service.' The reader is free to judge for himself.

§ The commentator reads *Samvardhayait* for *Vardhayait* and thus explains himself—'should never bring together, by appointment.'

‖ Blind or indiscriminate regarding the recognition of merit and demerit.

Kalpa-tree* itself. Prosperity is truly fruitful when it is enjoyed by the pious.†

73. What availeth the ever-flourishing prosperity of the monarchs on whom fortune smiles, if it is not enjoyed by their friends and relatives to the full satisfaction of their hearts.

74. A monarch should appoint his kinsmen of tested fidelity to look after all the different sources of his income.‡ Through their assistance he should collect taxes from his subjects, like the lustrous orb drawing moisture up through its rays.

75. A monarch should employ those men to be the general superintendents of all his business, who have both theoretical and practical knowledge of all works, whose honesty has been put to the test, who have under them copyists,§ composers and other useful hands, and who are greatly energetic.

76. Whoever is specially proficient in anything should be entrusted to do that thing only, just as a particular sense is employed to perceive its special objects among other inumerable sense-objects.

77. A monarch should take special care for his store-house,|| for life depends solely on it. He should not extravagantly spend its contents and should personally inspect it.

---

* Vide *Supra* note to Sloka I.

† For *Satyam Vogafalá* the commentary reads *Satsamvogafalá*, making a slight difference in import.

‡ The original Sloka, if taken as it is, can give a reasonable meaning, but that does not suit the context. So here we agree with the commentator and accept his emendations. For *Apadvarésu* he reads *Ayadvarésu* and for *Tévya* he reads *Taistu*. We give below the translation of the original Sloka. 'A king should examine the fidelity of his friends at times of emergency; and he should draw money from them as imperceptibly as the sun draws water up with its rays.'

§ For *Sujnänasammatän* the commentator reads *Sujnäna samgatän* ; the translation, we have given, tallies with the emendation.

|| Store-house includes both treasury and granary.

78—79. Agriculture, communications to facilitate commercial traffic, entrenchment of strong-holds for soldiers in the capital,* construction of dams and bridges across rivers, erection of enclosures for elephants,† working of mines, and quarries, felling and selling of timber,‡ and the peopling of uninhabited tracts—these eight-fold sources of revenue a sovereign should ever enhance; his officers,§ looking up to him for livelihood, should also do so, for maintaining themselves.

80. A weak monarch|| should never hamper his subjects in the profession which they might choose, but should encourage them therein; and specially he should patronize the trading class.

81. Just as an expert farmer intent on reaping a rich harvest secures his field of crop by paling it with thorny

---

* It may at first seem curious as to how fortifications for soldiers can be a probable source of income. But we should bear in mind that when merchants and traders are aware that a country is well-protected, they bring unhesitatingly all their merchandise to sell in the markets, and thus unconsciously add an impetus to the commerce of the land, the improvement of which is no doubt the cardinal source of income.

† The same observations we have made regarding forfications for soldiers being the source of income, apply here also.

‡ The commentary reads *Vanâdânam* for *Dhanâdânam* of the text; the latter means the 'collection of money'; but it is superfluous to say that 'collection of money' is a 'source of income,' therefore we accept the emendation. The commentary further explains the reading it gives, in the way in which we have translated; but one thing suggests itself to us; it is this; the commentary paraphrases *Vana* by *Sâradâru* i.e., timber; but if the words of this latter compound be inverted, then it will be *Dârusâra* and will mean sandal-wood, in which the Indian forests abound and which is very precious. The reader may judge for himself.

§ For *Karanâdhikai* of the text the commentary supplies *Karanâdhipais* which is more sense-conveying.

|| The word in the text corresponding to our 'weak' is *Ksheena*; weak in matters of finance; this condition may induce him to levy heavier taxes and thus he may obstruct the progress of his kingdom.

plants, and protects it by freely using the cudgel against thieves and beasts that come to destroy it, so should a monarch by the infliction of meet chastisements protect his own kingdom against thieves, depredators, enemies and Foresters. Thus protected, it truly becomes an object of his enjoyment.*

82. The royal officers, the thieves, the enemies of the land, the king's favourites, and the covetuousness of the monarch himself—these are the five sources of apprehension to the subjects.†

83. Removing these five-fold source of fear, a monarch, with a view to increase his *Trivarga*, should in proper season ingather tributes (in the shape of money and crops) from his subjects.‡

84. Just as cows are at one time to be tended and nourished and at other times to be milked, so are the subjects to be helped at one time with provisions and money and at other times to levied taxes upon. A florist both tends and sprinkles water on his plants and culls flowers from them.§

85. A monarch should bleed freely his subordinates swelling with unlawful wealth, like a surgeon bleeding a swelling abscess. Thus stripped of their unlawful gains, they stand by their sovereign like men standing by fire.||

---

* For the sake of lucidity we have been a little free in our rendering of the last portion of the Sloka which is very terse in the original.

† This speaks volumes for the political insight of the author.

‡ This Sloka bristles with errors and obscurities, and but for the commentary it would have been impossible for us to render it. The commentary substitutes (1) *Ityaitad* for *apyaitad*, (2) *Apohya* for *Apohyam* (3) *Nripati* for *Nripate* and (4) *falam* for *dhanam*. We can do without the first and last of these emendatious but the rest we can not reject.

§ We are here free for lucidity's sake.

|| The last portion of the Sloka has been thus explained by the annotator. Just as people though afraid of keeping in the vicinity of fire can not help handling it for dressing their dishes, so these men though afraid of living near the king can not help doing so for fear of

86. Those foolish and wicked wretches who injure their sovereign in the least, are burnt like insects on the flame of lamps.

87. A monarch should ever endeavour to increase his treasures superintended over by trustworthy persons of financial abilities.* He should in proper time spend them for the realisation of *Trivarga.*

88. The waning condition of a monarch who drains his treasury for religious purposes is commendable, like that of the autumnal moon whose digits are drank off by the celestials.†

89. The one essential injunction laid down in *Vrihaspati's* work on Polity is "Be suspicious". ‡ The measure of this suspicion should be such as not to hinder in any way the work of administration.

---

being punished for desertion. The commentary reads *Asakta* for *Amukta*

87. For the first line of the text the commentary reads :—

Aptai samvardhayait Kosam, sada tajnairadhisttitam.

88. The last portion of the Sloka is based on the tradition which explains the decrease in the digits of the moon during the dark half of a month, by saying that the gods suck them in. We give below the trans lation of the Slokas that define which god sucks which digit.

'The first digit is drunk by the god of Fire, the second by the Sun, the third by the *Visvadevas,* the fourth by the sovereign of the waters, and the fifth by the *Vasatkara.* Indra drinks the sixth digit, the celestial sages the seventh, and the Unborn Divinity sucks the eighth digit. The ninth digit of the moon in the dark half of a month is sucked in by Yama or the god of Death, the tenth by the Wind god and the eleventh by Uma; the *Pitris* drink the twelfth in equal portions; the thirteenth is sucked by Kuvera, the celestial Treasurer, the fourteenth by Pasupati and the fifteenth by Prajapati.'

89. For *Shástrárthanischaya* (the true signification of his work) the commentary reads *Shástrasya Nirnaya* (the cheese of this teachings) which latter we accept. What *Vrihaspati* enjoins seems to be that monarchs should never implictly trust any body about them.

90. A king should create confidence in those who have no trust in him; he should not place unusual confidence on those who are already in his confidence. He on whom the monarch puts his faith becomes the favorite of fortune.*

91. Because human heart is always susceptible of change with the success achieved in any action, therefore a man should look upon such success as indifferently as a *Yogi* with a sedate understanding does regard the concerns of this earth.

92. The glory of that monarch blazes for a long time, whose dependents are fully obedient and satisfied; to whom the subjects are attached for his mellifluous speech and amiable character, and who prudently entrusts his nearest and dearest kinsmen with the task of governing his kingdom.

Thus ends the fifth Section, the duties of master and servant, in the Nitisára of Kámandaka.

—:o:—

SECTION VI.

1. PERFECTLY familiar with the popular customs and with the contents of the *Vedas*, and assisted by skilful† dependents, a monarch should, with close application, direct his thoughts to the administration of his inner and outer states.‡

* There is a supplement to this Sloka the translation of which we subjoin—'The Goddess of good luck ever attends him and follows him like his own shadow, who is never tired of striving, who is aided by the wise and who is endued with native intelligence.'

† The commentary explains the word thus, 'who are like the king himself, acquainted with the customs and the contents of the *Vedas*.'

‡ The 'inner and outer states' of a sovereign at first would respectively seem to mean, 'his dominions which have been bequeathed to him by

2. His inner state is said to be his own body, and his outer state is the territory over which he rules. In consequence of the relation of mutual support obtaining between these, they are considered to be identical with each other.

3. The growth of all the other constituents of regal power depends upon the dominions of a sovereign ; therefore with all his endeavours, he should acquire and administrate territories.

4. A monarch, who desires to win the good-will of his subjects,* should carefully cherish his body ; the highest duty† of a king is to protect‡ his subjects ; and his body becmes (directly) instrumental in fulfilling this duty.

5. Monarchs can inflict tortures for the purposes of justice, just as sages can immolate animals for the purposes of virtue ; therefore kings are not tained with sin when they put impious wretches to death.§

---

his forefathers, and territorries which he has himself acquired. But the author explains himself in a different way in the next Sloka.

* An other meaning is possible, namely 'seeking to be graceful to wards his subjects, a king should preserve his own body.'

† For *Dhâma* of the text, the commentator substitutes *Dharma* which reading we adopt.

‡ For *'Samsaranam'* of the text the commentary suggests *Samrakshanam* which tatter yields a good signification.

§ For the sake of lucidity we have been a little free here ; the strictly literal translation of the passage will be, 'the sovereigns of the earth, like the sages, can commit lawful harm.' We have rendered *hinsâ* into harm ; the sanskrit word is very comprehensive being derived from the root *hins* (to injure life) ; it has no appropriate equivalent in English, for it includes all kinds and degrees of harm, namely, injuries, torture, persecution, death, slaughter &c. What the author means is this :—*Hinsa* or doing harm is universally considered to be attended with sin ; but there are circumstances when even the doing of harm can be justified, and is not attended with sin, for instance, when a king punishes a thief or a murderer, or when a sage sacrifices an animal. These acts of *hinsa* are said to be done for the furtherance of the ends of virtue and justice. The ethics of this principle, from a worldly point of view, is unimpeachble.

6. Anxious for preserving justice, and increasing his wealth by lawful means, a ruler of earth should visit those of his subjects with chatisement, who would venture to stand in his way (of government).

7. That is said to be justice, the administration of which is upheld by venerable people proficient in the codes of law, and that injustice, the execution of which is denounced by them.

8. Thus knowing what is just and what is unjust, and abiding by the decrees of the pious, a monarch should cherish his subjects and should extirpate his adversaries.*

9. Those sinful favorites of a monarch, who separately or in a body smite against the regal power, are regarded as culpable.

10. A monarch, after having sufficiently accused† the wicked persons who have incurred public displeasure, should do away with them without the least delay, by underhand measures.‡

---

*. Lit: traslated *paripanthin* would be 'standing in the way' hence it has come to mean an antagonist. The commentator gives this meaning, viz, those who persecute the subjects. *Pânini* the great grammarian says that the use of this word is only admissible in the *Vedas*, but as a matter fact the word has been freely introduced in their compositions by sanskrit writers. May not the use of this word go to prove the antiquity of this treatise?

† The reading given in the text is vicious, for it involves a needless tautology. Thereforc we accept the reading given the commentary which is '*Pradusya cha Prakâmam hi.*'

‡ Such as assassination, poisoning &c. What the author advises seems to be this:—A king, when he finds that any one among his officers has incurred public displeasure, should try to do away with him; but he should not use open violence which may have other pernicious results. He must devise some means to saddle the offender with a serious charge; then he should have recourse to secret measures in order to remove the offender from his path. In the next two Slokas the author suggests a means by which a king may do away with the offender.

11. The king should invite the offender to meet him in a deserted and secret chamber; when the person would enter the appointed chamber, several menials who had previously been instructed and gathered together by the king,* should enter after him, with arms hidden about them.

12. Then the royal door-keepers, would seem to suspect these trusty servants who had now entered the room, and would at once begin to search their persons. There-after those armed men would openly declare that they had been employed (by the offender to slay the king).†

13. Thus imputing criminality to the offenders, a king should, for the amelioration of his subjects and for pleasing them,‡ weed out the thorns of his government.

14. As a delicate seed-shoot, nourished and cared for, in due time, yields ample harvest, so also do the subjects of a king.

15. Inflicting punishments heavier than the offences, a king terrifies his subjects, whilst dealing out lighter ones, he is held in contempt by them. Therefore a monarch should impartially mete out chastisements proportionate to the offences.

Thus ends the sixth Section, the weeding out of the thorns of government, in the Nitisâra of Kâmandaka.

---

* For *Asajnitâs* of the text the commentator gives *Asanjnâta* which latter reading we have accepted.

† As we have said in the introduction, the author was a disciple of the celebrated Chanakya whose whole life was devoted to one eternal round of stratagems; hence it is not to be wondered at, that the author should retain some tortuosity of policy which he had inherited from his preceptor.

‡ What the author means is this :—The people, when well-cared for and cherished by their sovereign, try with all their heart to bring about the prosperity of the latter.

SECTION VII.

1. FOR his own safety and for the safety of his subjects, a king should keep his sons under proper control; for, when left to themselves, these latter might kill him, yielding to an ardent longing for the enjoyment of wealth.

2. Princes, intoxicated with pride and having none to restrain them, are like elephants maddened with shedding* ichor and having none to use the goad† on them.‡ Labour-

---

* Here is what Professor Wilson says regarding the fragrant juice exuding from the temples of elephants:—"It is rather extraordinary that this juice which exudes from the temples of the elephant, especially in the season of rut, should have been unnoticed by writers on Natural History. I have not found any mention of it in the works of Buffon nor in the more recent publications of Shaw; neither do any other writer on this subject seems to have observed it. The author of the 'Wild Sports of the East' states that on each side of the elephant's temples there is an aperture about the size of a pin's head, whence an ichor exudes; but he does not appear to have been aware of its nature." In the lexicon of Amara this juice is termed *Mada* and *Dânam*, and the elephant, while it flows, is distinguished by the names '*Pravinna Garjjito Matta.*' When the animal is out of rut or after the juice has ceased to exude he is then called *Udhantta* or *Nirmada*. The exudation and fragrance of this fluid is frequently alluded to in Sanskrit poetry. The scent of the juice is commonly compared to the odor of the sweetest flowers and is supposed to deceive and attract bees. *c. f.* Sloka 45 Sec I.

† *Ankusa* as applied to elephants means the iron-hook used by elephant-drivers to keep these animals under control when they become unmanageable; these hooks are technically called goads.

‡ The adjectives, contained in the first part of the Sloka, are applicable both to princes and elephants, each of them having two meanings.

ing under a strong conceit that they are rightfully entitled to the royalty,* they can kill their royal sire or their brother.†

3. A kingdom, which, princes inflamed with arrogance aspire after, is defended with great difficulty, like prey‡ scented by a tiger.

4. When held under control, these princes, if they find any the slightest weakness in him that exercises authority over them, are sure to slay this latter, like lion-cubs slaying their keepers at any the slightest inadvertence.

5. A monarch should, through the agency of his faithful servants, coach his sons in lessons of humility.§ A dynasty, of which the princes are immodest, speedily meets with its falls.

6. A son of his loins, graced with good manners, should be crowned by the king as the heir-apparent to the throne; and a prince, transgressing the limits of decent behaviour, should, like a vicious elephant, be tethered to inferior pleasures.||

7. Princes of the blood do not deserve disownment, even when they are hopelessly corrupt; for, when in distress, resorting to a monarch hostile to their royal sire, they can assassinate the latter.

8. A king should cause difficulties to a prince inordi-

---

* The words in the text is *Avimaninas*, in rendering which we have followed the explanation embodied in the notes.

† The commentary explains 'that brother only who is the heir-apparent to the throne or the crown-prince as he is called.'

‡ Lit: translated the word in the text would be 'flesh.'

§ The commentator here very aptly points out that there are two kinds of modesty, one that is born with the man, and the other the result of culture; both these kinds are indespensable for a prince.

|| 'For then' says the commentator, 'engrossed in low, carnal enjoyments, he will have no leisure to hatch any conspiracy against his royal father.'

nately addicted to any *vyasana*,* by encouraging him in that *vyasana*;† he should so torment the prince, so that the latter might be speedily transported to the side of his forefathers.‡

9. A monarch§ should always be very careful regarding his conveyances, beds, seats, drinks, eatables, garments, and ornaments and in every thing else.|| He should shun these, even if the slightest suspicion of their being poisoned is present.

10. Having bathed in waters capable of counteracting the (baneful) effects of poison,¶ and having decorated his person with antidotary gems,$ a king should take thoroughly-

* The lexicographer Amara gives the following significations of *Vyasana* (1) calamity or disaster, (2) fall or defeat (3) and vicious habits engendered by lust and anger, *c.f.* '*Vyasanam vipadi Vranse dosé Kāmajakopaje*.' The last-mentioned meaning is applicable here. The vices of lust have been said to be ten and the vices of anger, eight in number. (For a full explanation of the term vide Introduction.)

† Another meaning seems possible, which is, 'through the agency of his boon-companions.' The commentator is silent on the point.

‡ This Sloka, of course, suggests the measure, which is to be resorted to, at the very last, when all others have failed, for the correction of an incorrigible prince. It is better, in the opinion of the author, that a vicious prince should die than live to add to the anxieties of his royal father.

§ Having finished his advices regarding the training up of princes, the author now begins his somewhat tedious discourse about the nature of poisons and their effects on various objects and things, as also about the expedients which are calculated to guard a monarch from being administered poison to.

|| The commentary explains, 'even in his intercourse with respectable ladies.'

¶ At the time when the author wrote it was believed, that water guarded and preserved with the flowers and stems of the white *Puskara* (*Nelumbium speciosum*) could nullify the effects of poison. We do not know whether mordern Botany ascribes any such virtue to the above-named plant or not.

$ This gem is said to possess antidotary virtues and is fabled to

examined food, being surrounded by physicians well-read in the science of Toxicology.*

11. *Vringa-raja*† *Suka* and *Sharikâ*,‡ these birds emit distressful notes, being greatly terrified at the sight of a venomous serpent.§

---

have been vomitted forth by Gadura, the great winged enemy of the serpent species, on whom even the virulent venom of the snakes can produce no injurious effect. Even in these days, snake-charmers are found to apply a kind of black stone on that part of their body where the deadly reptile they dangle may happen to drive its fangs. This stone is popularly known as the *visa pāthara* or the poison-stone ; it is believed that the stone has power to extract all poison that the system may absorb. We can not vouch for the identity of the *visa pāthara* with the antidotary gem of the author's days ; nor can we assert that really the stone has any property for counteracting the effects of poison. For further enlightening our readers on the point, we quote below an ancient Sloka and subjoin its translation :

'*Rachito Gadurodgāra maniryasya vibhusanam,*
'*Sthāvaram jangamam tasya visam nirvisatām vrajét.*'

For him, who has adorned his person with the gem vomitted forth by Gadura, all sorts of poisons, either mobile or immobile, are turned into no poison i.e., loose their baneful power. Probably this poison-stone has some affinity with the bezoar (vide *infra* note to Sloka 14th).

* *Jângulâ*—means poison, the word is very rarely used ; *jângulâvit* is a dealer in antidotes. The use of this compound goes far to establish the antiquity of this book.

† A sort of bird, apparently a variety of the shrike termed *malabar*—Lanius Malabaricus.

‡ Suka (Parrot) and *Sharikâ* (*gracula religisoa*) are represented in all Hindu tales as the male and the female, both gifted with human speech ; they are constantly introduced, the one exposing the defects of the fair sex and the other inveighing against the faults of the male sex. The fancy of maintaining these pets seems to have been equally prevalent in the East and the West. As to the fact of their crying out at the sight of a serpent, to which the author alludes, we are not in a position to enlighten our readers.

§ The text of this part of the Sloka is surely vicious. The one difficulty, one has to face in rendering works of this nature, is to detect

12. At the sight of poison, the eyes of the *chokara** lose their natural hue, the *chrouncha*† is visibly intoxicated, and the *kokila*,‡ becoming mad, pays his debt of nature.§

13. Always at the sight of poison, a feeling of languor takes possession of creatures. Examining, through one of these methods, his eatables, a king should put them into his mouth.

14. Snakes cannot exist where the droppings of the peacock‖ and the *Prisata*¶ are kept. Therefore a king

---

the errors that have crept into them; the last portion, if substituted by 'envenomed eatables' will convey a meaning appropriate to the text.

* *Chakora (Perdix rufa)* is a crimson-eyed bird that is fabled to live in the air and never to descend on earth. It is said that the bird sustains itself on moon-beams, and so has virtually to starve during the greater portion of the dark-half of a month. Some authorities identify it with the Greek partridge. But the *chakora* resembles the bird of paradise still more closely which latter are described to be the inhabitants of the air, only living on the dew of heaven and never resting on earth.

† *Crouncha*—This bird belongs to the genus of aquatic fowls with cloven feet. It is said to be the same with the heron or the curlew *(Ardea jaculator)*; the *Crouncha* is well known among Sanskrit writers for its connubial affections.

‡ *Kokila (Cuculus Indicus)* is the Indian cuckoo. As in the West, so also in the East, the rich melody of the note of this bird harbingers the arrival of the Spring.

§ Regarding the changes, which, the author says, all these birds undergo at the sight of poison, we can not enlighten our readers.

‖ The idea that the fæces of peacocks can drive away snakes has probably originated out of the belief so much current in the East, that the peacocks devour serpents. Naturalists, at least Buffon, do not make mention of any such phenomenon. Here is what he says regarding the food of the peacocks. 'The peacock lives on corn, but its favorite food is barley. However it does not reject insects and tender plants, and so capricious are its appetites that it is not easily restrained from the most unaccountable depredations on the dwelling, the firm, or the garden.'

¶ *Prisata*—is the porcine deer; regarding the virtues of the dung of *Prisata* we can not enlighten our readers. But an idea suggests itself to us, which is, that the author may refer to the bezoar stone produced by

should always allow peacocks and *Prisatas* to roam at liberty inside his manson.*

15. In order to examine the rice offered to him for his meal, a king should at first throw some of it on fire ; then he should throw some of the same to the birds, and watch the indications.

16. †(If the rice is contaminated with poison) then the fumes and flames of the fire will assume a blue color,‡ and it will produce crackling sounds ; the birds (that have eaten the envenomed rice) will also die from the effects of poison.

17. Rice mixed with poison is characterised by the absence of unctuousity,§ by intoxicating properties, by rapid cooling,‖ and by pallidness ; and the vapour it emits is light-blue in hue.

---

gazelles, antelopes, wild and domestic goat and sheep. Two kinds of this stone were particularly esteemed, the *Bezoar orientale* from India and the *Bezoar occidentale* from Peru. Some authorities have asserted that the true occidental bezoar is the production of monkeys. The oriental bezoar was prodigiously in vogue in Asia and in Europe and it used to be administered in all cases in which our present physicians prescribe cordials and other antidotes. This calculous concretion was formerly regarded as an unfailing antidote to poison. Probably the bezoar is the thing which in a previous Sloka the author has denominated as the gem vomitted forth by Gadura.

* Over and above the usefulness of peacocks and the *Prisatas*, they were considered as objects of luxury by oriental sovereigns.

† The author now proceeds to describe the indications, for the accuracy of which we cannot pledge ourselves.

‡ We can not say, whether or not, what the author asserts will be corroborated by the conclusions of chemistry. But so far we can say, that arsenic or any preparation of it, acted upon by fire, may emit a blue flame and fume. As there are various sorts and kinds of poison, we cannot specify all the reactions that will be produced when they are thrown on fire. The latter portion of the Sloka is self-evident.

§ The commentator explains, 'is not boiled and softened even in the highest temperature.'

‖ For *Salyam* of the text the commentary substitutes *Saityam* which yields a rational meaning'.

18. Curry contaminated with poison soon becomes juiceless and vapid ; when decocted it yields blue spume, and then its savoriness, delicacy and sapidness are all dostroyed.

19. The shine of liquid substances mixed with poison, is either hightened or lightened ; their surface looks bright* and fringed with foam.

20. The shine of envenomed fluids† becomes blue, of milk and its preparations becomes coppery, of wine and other intoxicating drinks and of water resembles the hue of the *Kokila*‡ ; their dimples become blue and broken and sometimes a little elevated.

21. All hydrous substances,§ when envenomed, soon become faded, and persons well-read in toxicology assert that though not decocted, the juice of these substances seems to be extracted ; their color turns dark.

22. All anhydrous substances‖ when mixed with poison becomes withered, and tarnished in color. All acrid things (when envenomed,) become delicate and all delicate things become acrid. Who can say that poisoning destroys a small number of animals ? ¶

23. When smeared with poison, blankets and carpets

---

* For *Räjirurdhä* of the text the commentary gives *Räjatdurdham* which reading we adopt.

† Says the commentator 'such as, the juice pressed out of sugarcane &c.'

‡ Vide supra note to Sloka 12th.

§ The word in the text is *Adra* ; the commentary explains the line saying, 'Raw fruits and paddy, when envenomed, become faded in color near their foot-stalk ; never ripening, they appear to be withered and their color turns dark ; so say those who are versed in toxicology.'

‖ The commentary hints at a different signification by asserting that *Suska* things mean Katakaş (bracelets) and other such ornaments.

¶ The last line of the text is surely vicious, as no appropriate meaning can be made out of it. It is a marring interpolation which has been foistered into the text in lieu of a line in the original M.S.

are covered over with black round spots, and stuffs made of cotton* down and fur, become totally destroyed.†

24. When envenomed, minerals and gems are tarnished with stains ; and their spendour, glossiness, weight, hue, and agreeableness to the touch, are all destroyed.

25.—26. Pallidness of countenance, faltering speech,‡ constant yawning,§ stumbling steps,|| tremor of the body¶ perspiration,** anxiety without cause, casting of watch ful glances on all sides,†† avoidance of necessary occupations‡‡ and of their abode—these signs a clever man should mark, as they betray those who administer poison to others.

27. A king should take his medicines and cordials after having made his medical attendants take a portion of them. He should take his drinks and potions and edibles after they had been tasted by those who offer them to himself.§§

28. The female attendants|||| of a monarch should place before him only those articles of toilet which have been thoroughly examined and then (packed and) sealed (by the ministers).

29. Whatever things come from unknown persons and sources should be thoroughly examined (before they reach the

---

* For *tantu* the commentary supplies *taru* or the barks of trees, which we cannot accept.

† For *Dhansa* the commentary gives *Vransa* which means 'to fall off'. We see no necessity for this change.

‡ For *tagveda* of the text the commentary gives *Vàgvanga* which reading we have accepted.

§ Like one recently awakened from sleep.

|| Supply 'even in level tracks.'

¶ Supply 'in the absence of cold.'

** Even when a breeze is blowing.

†† As if to descry whether somebody is coming to punish them.

‡‡ Such as, cooking of articles of food.

§§ For lucidity's sake we have deviated a little from the text.

|||| For *Parichārikā* the commentary gives *Parichāraka* which makes no material difference.

king). A monarch should always be carefully guarded, against his friends and foes alike, by his body-guards.

30. A king should ride on conveyances and vehicles which have either been thoroughly examined by himself or which have been recommended by his acquaintances. He should never pass unknown* and narrow roads.†

31. A monarch should keep near him, as his body-guards, those persons, all whose secret designs are known to him,‡ whose family had served his own forefathers, who are trustworthy and on whom endowments have been settled.

32. A king should shun at a distance those who are sinful, those who are crooked, those whose faults have been detected§, those who have been ostracised and those who come from the enemy.

33 ‖ A king should not go on board a vessel which is being tossed by the tempest, the crew of which have not been previously tried, which is fastened to any other vessel¶ and which is frail and rolling.

34. In very sultry days, accompanied by his friends, a monarch should immerse himself into waters, which he himself has examined, which are pure and shorn of shoals of fishes and alligators, and on the banks of which, his own soldiers stand in a circle.

---

* Unknown both to himself and to his ministers and followers.

† So that he will have no possibility of falling into an ambush laid by his foes.

‡ The commentary explains the word otherwise, viz.—'whose evil deeds have been seen and overlooked by the king.'

§ The commentary explains, 'those who act in open defiance to the ordinances of the *Shastras*.'.

‖ The author now proceeds to give directions which are calculated to insure the safety of kings during voyages and sports and hunting parties and meetings, visits &c.

¶ Or more correctly 'which is being towed by any other vessel.'

35. Avoiding dense forests,* a monarch should resort to parks, the inside and outside of which have been thoroughly cleared by the guards. There he should indulge in pleasant pastimes agreeably to his age, and should not plunge headlong into sensual enjoyments.†

36. Desirous of hunting, a light-handed‡ monarch, in order that his aim might not fail, should enter, being followed by a well-disciplined and well-accoutered§ army, a wood, the access to which is easy, the outskirts of which have been reconnoitered and are guarded by soldiers, and which abound in game and is (therefore) a suitable place (to hunt in).

37. Even when a monarch wants to see to his own mother, he should at first have the apartments thoroughly searched; he should then enter (the apartments of his mother) being followed by trustworthy and armed guards. He should never linger in narrow and perilous woods.||

38. When a tempest rages blowing dusts and gravels, when dense clouds swelling with rain overspread the firmament, when the sun-shine is exceedingly severe,¶ and when the darkness is impenetrable—at these times, a king should never, during seasons of peace, stir out.

39. At the time of going out and coming in, a king, with a view to display the elegance of his proportions, should pass by high-ways, clearing the crowd that obstruct him on all sides.

---

* The commentator explains, 'rendered impassable by copses, creepers and underwoods.'

† According to the commentator, the rendering would be, 'should not run in pursuit of objects of sensual enjoyment.'

‡ That is, 'swift in discharging missiles.'

§ For *Suvega*, the commentary reads *Suvesha* which reading we have adopted.

|| This line is misplaced or there is something vicious in the text; it would be more appropriate to place this line in the beginning of this stanza, in which case it would be taken with the previous stanza.

¶ Supply 'generating great heat and sultriness.'

40. A king should never join a fair or a festive train;* he should not go to a place where there is a great conflux of men.† He should never go anywhere, when the appointed hour for such going is past.

41. (During the night)‡ a king should roam inside his own seraglio, being attended upon by hunch-backs, dwarfs, *Kirâtas*§ and eunuchs clad in mail and graced with turbans.

42. Honest|| attendants of the harem, knowing the king's pleasure, should, with becoming humility, entertain him with pastimes which have nothing to do with weapons, fire and poison.¶

43. When the king remains inside the seraglio, the guards of the women's apartments, whose honesty has been

---

* More lit: 'Entertainments given by native theatrical parties at a fair or festive scene.'

† The text is vicious and for *Jalasambâdha* we substitute *Janasambâdha.*

‡ It was a custom with oriental monarchs to wander at night inside their own seraglios and sometimes in their town, in order to inform themselves about the real state of their dominions and whether the subjects are all in peace and satisfied with themselves,or they bear any malice towards them. The author now goes on to give directions which will protect monarchs from being surprised during such rounds.

§ They are a degraded mountain tribe, living by hunting, fowling &c. At first it would seem curious that a king should be advised to take the help of the hunch-backs and dwarfs, incapable as they are, of rendering it, at the time of a surprise. But we should remember that the king is also guarded by a most formidable band of Mountaineers and eunuchs who naturally form the most faithful and vigilant guards. The usefulness of the dwarfs and the hunch-backs lies in their very great intellectual powers. The last portion of our remark is illustrated by *Kuvjâ* of the Ramayana, the maid of Kaikeyi. The custom of employing eunuchs in protecting the harems was prevalent from time immemorial in Hindustan, whence perhaps the Mahomedans transplanted it to their country.

|| Whose honesty has been tested by the 'test of continence.'

¶ As these naturally breed danger.

commended by the virtuous and who are skilful in the act of protection* should protect him, with weapons ready for use.

44. Men of the venerable age of eighty and women of the age of fifty,† and orderlies belonging to the harem should be entrusted to look after the purity and cleanliness of the inner apartments.

45. Courtezans, having bathed and changed their garments and being decked with pure ornaments and garlands of flowers, should dance attendance upon the king.‡

46. An attendant of the inner apartments should hold no intercourse with magicians, *Jatilas*§, and *Mundas*|| and harlots. (For, being employed by hostile monarchs, these might induce the attendant to do injuries to his royal master).

47. The attendants of the seraglio should be allowed to go out and come in, only when the things they carry would be known to the guards and when, if questioned, they would be in a position to furnish sufficient reasons for their egress and ingress.¶

---

* For *Ayuktakusala*, the commentary gives *Ayudhakusala*.

† The warmth of passions having subsided, they will not indulge in any amorous caprices and intrigues.

‡ The readers may take exception to this Sloka; but admitted or not, it is a fact, that with royalty this vice (of maintaining harlots in their keeping) is more or less prevalent. Perfectly aware of this fact, the author wisely provides courtezans in the harem rather than allow kings to frequent places of evil repute where danger is possible at each step.

§ Lit: those who bear matted locks on their head; here the *Saivites* are referred to.

|| Lit: those who bear a hairless head; the mendicants and *vaishnavites* are referred to.

¶ The last line, the commentary explains thus "to say that they are going on the king's errands."

48. A king should not see any one of his dependents suffering from any disease.* But when his principal attendant is attacked with any virulent malady, the king should see him (having taken proper precautions for his own safety); for, one afflicted with disease is worthy of everybody's regard.

49. Having bathed and having smeared his person with unguents and perfumes and being decked with garlands of flowers and magnificient ornaments, a king should hold intercourse with his spouse who had also bathed and decked herself with pure garments and excellent ornaments.†

50. From his own apartments, a king should never go to see his royal spouse to the suit of chambers belonging to her. He should not place too much confidence on his wives, even if he might be greatly beloved of them.

51. His brother‡ slew king Bhadrasena, when he was staying in the apartment of his queen.§ The son of his own loins, hidding himself underneath the bed of his mother, slew the king of the Karusa.||

52. The king of the Kasis, when indulging in dalliances in secret, was assasinated by his queen who gave him some fried

---

* In order to prevent contagion as well as infection.

† The commentator remarks, 'such nice attention in matters of dress and toilet goes to enhance the affection of the couple, which is very desirable.'

‡ The pertinency of his remark contained in the last line of the previous sloka, the author now goes on to illustrate.

§ The allusions are obscure and in explaining them we entirely depend on the commentary which in some places again is silent. King Bhaddrasena, suspecting some illicit alliance between his spouse and his younger brother Virasena, prohibited all access of the latter to his queen. This exasperated the couple, and Virasena being urged and assisted by his royal mistress assassinated his brother.

|| The ruler of the Karusas incurred the displeasure of one of his wives, for having bequeathed his kingdom to a son of his, by another wife. The displeased lady, with her disappointed son, hatched a conspiracy to assasinate the king and actually carried it into action.

grain mixed with poison to eat, assuring him, at the same time, that they were mixed with honey.*

53. King Souvira's consort slew him by the poisoned jewel of her waist-band. King Vairanta was slain by the *nupura*† and king Jarusa by the mirror (which both were poisoned) of their queens.

54. King Viduratha fell by the dagger of his spouse which she kept concealed in her hair-knot.‡ A king should avoid all serpentine dealings with his friends, but have recourse to them against his foes.

55. A monarch, whose wives are properly protected (from evil influences) by his well-wishing dependents, holds in his possession this world and the next abounding in all sorts of enjoyments.

56. A king, desirous of securing virtue, should, in due order, hold sexual intercourse with his wives, night after night, having increased his potency by the ceremony of *Vâjikarana*.§

57. At the end of the day, ascertaining his routine of business (for the next day), and taking leave of his dependents, and having all necessary acts performed by maid-servants and women, a king should moderately indulge in sleep, grasping his weapons in his hands,|| and being well-guarded by his trusty relatives.

---

* The commentary is silent on the point so we can not enlighten our readers.

† A girdle of small bells, a favourite Hindu ornament, worn round the ankles and the wrists, which emits a ringing noise as the wearer moves. Professor Wilson renders it into 'tinkling zone.'

‡ The word in the text is *Veni*, which Professor Wilson explains thus: 'The *Veni* is a braid in which the long hair of the Hindustanee women is collected.'

§ The act of stimulating or exciting desire by aphrodisiacs.

|| For *âshastra* the commentary gives *ashastra* which reading we reject.

58. When a ruler of men in perfect accordance to the rules of Polity, keeps his eyes open to all affairs of the state, then do his subjects enjoy a peaceful sleep being relieved of the burden of anxiety. But when their sire-like* sovereign is demented (by the objects of plasure) their sleep is disturbed by apprehensions of the wicked† (thieves, assassins, &c). When the king keeps awake all his myriad subjects cannot sleep.

59. The sages of the past have said these to be the characteristics of a perfect monarch and monarchy. In this way, preserving justice, a ruler of men steps into the status of the foster-father of his subjects.

Thus ends the seventh Section, the guarding of his sons and his self by a king, in the Nitisâra of Kâmandaka.

SECTION VIII.

—oo—

1. SUPPORTED by a solvent treasury and an efficient army, assisted by his ministers and officers of state, and secure in his own castle, a central monarch should direct his his attention to the consolidation of his kingdom.‡

* For *Svapiti* of the text, the commentary gives *Swapitari* which yields a better meaning.

† For *Sambhaydt* the commentary gives *Asatbhayàt* which reading we have adopted.

‡ As the word *Mandala* occurs too often in this Section, we should, at the very outtset, give our readers an idea of the meaning of this word, so that they might be, hereinafter, able to comprehend clearly what the author would say. *Mandala*, ordinarily, means a circle ; derived from this meaning, a secondary signification is ascribed to the word where

2. An warlike sovereign, environed by a number of friendly dependencies and subordinate chiefs, reaches the zenith of prosperity,* while encompassed by a circle of inimical (royal) neighbours, he wears away like the wheels of a chariot.

3. Like the moon with all her digits full, a sovereign with the constituents of his government perfect,† appears agreeable to all beings. For this reason, a sovereign, desirous of victory,‡ should keep the limbs of his government in tact.

4. Minister, castle, kingdom, treasury and army,—these five have been said, by persons well-versed in Polity to be the principal constituents of a central sovereign.

5. These five and the allied sovereigns and, in the seventh place, the central monarch himself,—these together, have been said by *Vrihaspati* to compose what is known as 'government with seven constituents.'

---

it is used in political diction. According to our author, *Mandala*, in politics, signifies 'the circle of a king's near and distant royal neighbours.' The number of foes and allies included inside this circle varies according to the opinions of diverse authorities on the subject. As the reader will see, our author has furnished an exhaustive list embodying the opinions of the experts on this point. Generally twelve kings from a *Mandala*, namely, the *Vijigisu* or the central sovereign (lit: one who wants to consolidate his kingdom by obtaining victory over his royal neighbours), the five kings whose dominions are in the front, and the four kings whose dominions are in the rear of his kingdom, the *Madhyama* or the intermidiate monarch and the *Udàsina* or the indifferent king. The designations, duties and natures of the kings, in front and in the rear, have been specified by the author himself, and so we need not anticipate him. When the description of the *Mandala* will begin, we shall furnish our readers with a diagram, which we think, will help them in understanding the true signification of the word.

* The word in the text lit: translated would be, 'appears beautiful.'

† Though the word in the text is *Mandala*, yet on the authority of the commentary, we render it into 'government with its constituents.' This also is another signification of the word in politics.

‡ For the true signification of word vide *suprà* note to Sloka I. also Sloka 6th.

6. A monarch, who is equipped with these constituents (in a thriving slate), and is endued with irrepressible energy,* and is pains-taking and who, ever ardently, longs to obtain victory over others,—such a monarch is worthy of the designation of *Vijigisu*.

7. †Nobility of extraction, serving of the elders (in age and in knowledge), energeticalness, ambitiousness in aims,‡ power of penetrating into the hearts of others, keeness of intelligence, boldness,§ truthfulness,

8. Expeditiousness,|| generosity,¶ humility,$ self-reliance, conversance with the propriety of place and time (for the successful execution of an act), resoluteness,** patience for the endurance of all kinds of sufferings††,

9. Knowledge of all things‡‡ skilfulness, physical strength,§§ secrecy of counsels,|||| consistency,¶¶ courageousness, appreciation of the devotion displayed by servants, gratefulness,

---

* The reference is to the *Utsāhasakti*, for which vide note to Sloka l. Sec. I.

† The author now proceeds to enumerate the qualities that are indispensable for the *Vijigisu*.

‡ The commentary explains, 'who disdains to give away things of very small value' i.e., 'who is very liberal.'

§ The commentary explains 'absence of the fear of his councilors.'

|| Lit: translated the word would be 'absence of procrastination.'

¶ Lit: translated, 'absence of meanness (i.e., enviousness).'

$ Also 'absence of covetuousness.'

** The commentary explains 'determination of not to abondon one seeking protection.'

†† The commentary explains, 'capability for suffering the pangs of hunger and thirst.'

‡‡ The commentary says 'proficiency in all the arts.'

§§ For *Sadà* of the text the commentary gives *Urja*s which reading we have accepted.

|||| 'Owing to his countenance and designs being inscrutable' goes on the commentator.

¶¶ The commentator explains 'avoidance of sophistical reasoning.'

10. Affection for those seeking protection, forgiveness, avoidance of fickleness, knowledge of his own duty* and of the *Shàstras*,† sagacity, far-sightedness,

11. Indefatigability, righteousness, shunning of crooked councilors, and a natural swell of soul,‡ these are said to be the necessary qualifications of a *Vijigisu*§.

12. Though devoid of all these qualities, yet a king is worthy of the name *Ràjan*,|| if only he possesses Regal prowess.¶ A king, endued with Regal prowess, inspires terror into the hearts of his enemies, like a lion striking terror into the hearts of the inferior beasts.$

13. By the substantiation of his prowess,** a king attains to the highest pitch of prosperity ; for this reason, always putting forth his endeavours,†† he should establish his prowess.

14. The mark, that distinguishes the enemy of a monarch (from his friends), is the pursuance of one and the same object by the former in common with the monarch him-

---

* The commentator specifies the duty saying it to be 'the act of cherishing his subjects.'

† *Shástras* here mean Military sciences.

‡ The word may yield another meaning namely 'geneality of temperament.'

§ Instead of every time repeating a long-winded phrase we propose to use the original word, which we have explained in a previous note.

|| Lit. 'one who cherishes his subjects.' *c. f. Rájá prakriti ranjanàt.*

¶ Vide note to Sloka I. Section I.

$ The last line of the Sloka is hopelessly vicious, which, without the help of the commentary, cannot be at all understood. The commentary reads "*Pratàpayuktát trasyanti pare singhàt mrigá iba.*"

** The commentary, not accepting the ordinary meaning of the word, suggests, 'the fame that a monarch earns by subjugating all monarchs hostile to him.'

†† The commentary adds, 'by way of making war-like preparations, and waging wars.'

self.* And that enemy is to be regarded formidable who is endued with the characteristic qualities of the *Vijigisu*.

15. A covetuous,† and inexorable‡, and inactive,§ and untruthful,|| and inadvertent and cowardly and delinquent, and injudicious monarch, who dispises skilful warriors, is said to constitute an enemy who may be eradicated with ease.

16. ¶The *Ari*, the *Mitram*, the *Arimitram*, the *Mitra-*

---

* What the author means seems to be this. 'A monarch should regard those among his royal contemporaries to be his enemies, who endeavour to appropriate to themselves the dominions and wealth, on which he himself has set his eyes. The pursuance of one and the same purpose (regarding a certain territory &c.) by two rival sovereigns, goes to engender ill-feeling and enmity between them. The truth of this proposition needs no illucidation ; *c. f.* 'Two of a trade can never agree.' The reading in this part of the Sloka is vicious and *Avilakshanam* should be *Arilakshanam*.

† The commentator adds, 'hence illiberal ; and illiberality estranges his subjects from him, which again renders him materially weak.'

‡ Says the commentator, 'who by his sternness inspires his people with terror.'

§ The king being inactive, the subjects also, becoming lethargic and idle, render themselves susceptible of an easy victory.

|| The subjects also catch the same habit from their sovereign, which materially diminishes their moral courage.

¶ Now the author proceeds to describe what is called a *Mandala*, and he quotes the different opinions of the different authorities regarding the definition of the term. The diagram interleaved represents a *Mandala* containing the three hundred and twenty-four monarchies (each marked by a circle), the highest number, as the reader will see, that is included in a *Mandala*. Of these, the circles marked, 1. 2. 3. 4. 5. 6. 7. 8. 9. 10. 11. 12. are of importance,explanations whereof are subjoined.

The circle marked 1. represents the dominions of the *Vijigisu* or the central sovereign, who wants to consolidate his empire by conquering and befriending the other sovereigns whose domains are represented by circles marked 2. 3. 4. 5. 6. 7. 8. 9. 10. 11. and 12. The circles marked 2. 3. 4. 5. and 6. represent the monarchies which lie in front of the domain of the central sovereign.

mitram, and the *Arimitramitram*, these are the five sovereigns

---

The circle marked 2. represents the dominions of the *Ari* or the enemy (of the *Vijigisu*). The contiguity of these two dominions often gives rise to disputes regarding the boundaries thereof, and so ferment an implacable enmity between the sovereigns ruling over them. It is also generally observed that the adjacency of two monarchies naturally causes disputes between their sovereigns.

The circle marked 3. represents the dominions of the *Mitram* or the ally (of the *Vijigisu*). This alliance results in this way. The dominions of the sovereign of the 3rd circle are adjacent to those of the sovereign of the 2nd circle, and consequently, as before, they become hostile to each other. The sovereign of the 1st circle or the *Vijigisu*, taking advantage of this hostility, befriends the sovereign of the circle marked 3.

The circle marked 4. represents the dominions of the *Arimitram* or the enemy's ally. His kingdom being contiguous to that of the *Vijigisu's* ally, he turns hostile to the latter, and consequently becomes the opponent of the *Vijigisu*, and the ally of his (*Vijigisu's*) enemy.

The circle marked 5. represents the dominions of the *Mitramitram* or the ally of the *Vijigisu's* ally, whose attitude, as may easily be supposed, is friendly to the *Vijigisu* and his allies, and hostile to the *Vijigisu's* enemies and their allies. Here also the rule of contiguity determines the attitude.

The circle marked 6. represents the kingdom of the *Arimitramitram* or the ally of the enemy's ally. His dominions being contiguous to those of the ally of the *Vijigisu's* ally, he naturally stands in unfriendly relations with the *Vijigisu* and his allies. This hostility with the *Vijigisu* prompts him to side with the former's enemies.

The circle marked 7. represents the dominions of the *Madhyama* or the intermidiate king, whose dominions are contiguous both to the dominions of the *Vijigisu* and his enemy. So this king may become either an ally or an enemy to either of them. His power and his attitude have been described by the author himself and we need not anticipate him.

The circles marked 8. 9. 10. and 11. signify the monarchies situated in the rear of the *Vijigisu*.

The circle marked 8. represents the domain of the *Pârshnigràha* or one who is situated in the rear. The attitude of this monarch has not been defined, which may both be hostile and friendly; but more often it is hostile.

The circle marked 9. represents the dominions of the *Akranda* or the king whose kingdom lies, in the rear, next but one, to that of the

whose domains lie consecutively in front of the dominions of the *Vijigisu*.

17. The king just in the rear of the *Vijigisu* is designated *Pârshnigràha*; after him comes the *Akranda*; then comes the *Asârâs* of these two. This is the *Mandala* of ten kings in respect of the *Vijigisu*.*

18. The sovereign, whose domain lies intervening† the dominions of the *Ari* and the *Vijigisu*, is denominated

---

Vijigisu. *Akranda* has been defined to be a king who prevents an ally from aiding another. If the *Pârshnigrâha* be inimical to the *Vijigisu*, *Akranda* prevents the ally of the *Pârshnigrâha* to join him, and this he can do easily, as his kingdom lies intervening those of the *Pàrshnigrâha* and his ally. *Akranda* is therefore naturally friendly to the *Vijigisu*.

The circles marked 10. and 11. represent the domains of the two *Asàràs*, or the two monarchs who respectively support the *Pârshnigràha* and the *Akranda*; they are respectively called *Pārshnigràhàsàra* and *Akrandàsàra*. Their attitude may be easily divined.

The circle marked 12. represents the dominions of the *Udâsina* or the neutral sovereign; his dominions lie beyond those of the enemies and allies of the *Vijigisu*. The power, nature and attitude of this king have been described by the author himself hereinafter, and so we refrain from entering into details regarding him.

These twelve kings ordinarily constitute what is called a *Mandala*. Of the rest of the three hundred and twenty-four monarchies, no special explanation is necessary, as their respective relation may be considered in the same light as before. The description of a *Mandala* has also been given by *Kullukabhatta* and *Mallinàtha* in their respective commentaries on *Manu* and *Sisupàlabadha*; *Manu's* description of a *Mandala* completely tallies with what is given by our author. We need not quote *Manu* here, as the number of Sections and Slokas has been given by the commentator in course of his explanation of every Sloka. The reader may compare *Manu* at his leisure.

* The commentator in annotating this Sloka says that the *Pràshnigràha's* attitude towards the central sovereign is hostile, in spite of which, he is called a *Pràshnigràha* or a supporting sovereign.

† Strictly speaking, the dominions of the *Madhyama* do not intervene those of the *Ari* and the *Vijigisu*, but verge on them. Refer to our diagram.

the *Madhyama*. His attitude becomes friendly* when the *Ari* and the *Vijigisu* are united together, and it is hostile to them both when they are disunited from each other.†

19. Beyond the *Mandala* composed of these sovereigns,‡ lies the domain of the *Udàsina*, who is by far the most powerful of them all. He is capable of showing grace to them all, when they are united, and of crushing them when they are separated.§

20. These four, namely, the *Vijigisu*, the *Ari*, the *Madhyama* and the *Udàsina*, have been said to be the principal components of a *Mandala*.|| This is the *Mandala* of four sovereigns described by Maya conversant with the Political science.¶

21. According to Puloma$ and Indra, the *Vijigisu* the *Ari*, the *Mitram*, the *Párshnigráha*, the *Madhyama* and the *Udàsiua*, constitute what is known as a *Mandala* of six monarchs.

---

* This friendliness he shows by helping them with men and money.

† In rendering the last portion of the Sloka, we have been a little free. Lit : translated, it would be, 'this *Madhyama* is capable of showing grace to the *Ari* and the *Vijigisu* when they are united,and he is capable of slaying them when they are disunited.

‡ The reading in the text is vicious, which ought to be *Mandalàt Vahis chaiteshàm*.

§ For *Dhyastànàm* read *Vyastānàm* which will yield the proper meaning.

|| The commentary explains *Mula Prakritayas* in a different ma nner, saying that 'these four constitute the primary source of all the other constituents of government.'

¶ For *Mantrakusala* of the text the commentary reads *Trantrakusala*. *Mantra* means counsel and *Tantra* means here the science of Polity. Maya is one of the many *Acharyyas* or teachers of the people. We can not say whether this Maya built the great court-hall for the son of Pandu.

$ Is the name of a demon, the father-in-law of Indra. For Indra, Vide note to Sec, II. Sloka 35, also Sec. IV. Sloka 21.

22. The *Udàsina*, the *Madhyama*, and the *Mandala* of the *Vijigisu**, taken together, constitute the *Mandala* of twelve kings, mentioned by Usanas.†

23. The above-mentioned twelve kings, together with an ally and an enemy of each,‡ constitute the *Mandala* of thirty-six kings§ to which Maya again has referred.

24. The disciples of Manu|| (men) enumerate five *Prakritis*,¶ namely, minister, &c., for each of these twelve kings of a *Mandala*.

25. These twelve cardinal sovereigns, together with their respective five *Prakritis*, constitute the *Prakriti Mandala* consisting of seventy-two elements.$

26. A common enemy of the *Vijigisu* and the *Ári*, and a common ally of them both, these two, each of them again

---

* Vide the last portion of Sloka 17th *supra*.

† Another name for the preceptor of the Demons. Vide note, Sloka 8th Section I.

‡ Twelve kings of the Mandala and their twelve allies and their twelve enemies raise the number to thirty-six.

§ The text before us has here *sadvingsatkam* or twenty-six, which, no doubt, is a mistake of printing.

|| Vide note to Sloka 3rd Section II.

¶ Hitherto we have rendered *prakritis* into 'the constituents of a government.' Here, according to the commentator, the same meaning applies. But to enlighten our readers on the point, we must remark that *prakriti* also has another meaning in politics, which is 'the circle of various sovereigns near a king, to be taken into consideration in case of a war.' The number of the *prakritis* is, as the reader is aware, seven in all; the five, here referred to, are, according to the commentator, minister, castle, kingdom, treasury, and army. The reader should mark that the allies and the king are left out in this enumeration. Each of these seven *prakritis* is to be considered equal to a sovereign. *Prakritis* rendered into a single phrase would be 'the stamina of a state.'

$ Twelve kings of the *Mandala*, together with the five *prakritis* of each, raise the number to seventy-two. The last part of the text contains a misprint; for *saptatischádikà* read *dywadhikásaptati*. This *prakriti mandala* has also been spoken of by Manu.

12

with an ally and an enemy of his own, together with the twelve cardinal kings, constitute the *Mandala* of eighteen monarchs mentioned by Guru.*

27. The six *Prakritis*, namely, minister, kingdom, castle treasury, army and ally, of each of these eighteen monarchs, taken together, form the *Mandala* of hundred and eight elements, which has been recognised by the wise.

28. These eighteen monarchs, each with an ally and an enemy, constitute the *Mdndala* of fifty-four kings, spoken of by Vishālāksha.†

29. The six *Prakritis*, namely, minister, kingdom, castle, treasury, army and ally, of each of these fifty-four kings, taken together, again form the *Mandala*‡ of three hundred and twenty-four elements.

30. The seven constituents of the government of the *Vijigisu*, together with the seven constituents of the *Ari*, constitute what is known as the *Mandala* of fourteen components.

31. The *Vijigisu*, the *Ari*, and the *Madhyama* form the *Mandala* of three kings. These three§ monarchs, with an ally

---

* Another name for Vrihaspati, for which vide note to Sloka 8th Sec. I.

† Literally means 'of expanded eyes,' but it is an especial epithet of Siva, one of the Hindu Trinity, whose function is to annihilate the world at the end of a *Yuga*. By a reference to the Introduction, the reader will see, that Siva was one among the many who abridged the voluminous work of Brahma on Polity. In explaining this Sloka, the commentary does not follow the text, at least the one before us. It says that 'the '*Mandala* of fifty-four elements is composed of the three *prakritis*, viz., minister, kingdom and castle, of each of these eighteen sovereigns taken together.'

‡ Over and above the meaning of the *Mandala* elaborately explained by us, it seems, that it may sometimes mean 'the conglomeration of constituents.'

§ For *Atais* read *Até*.

of each of them, together constitute what others call the *Mandala* of six kings.

32. The six *Prakritis*, namely, minister &c., of each these six kings, taken together, compose what persons conversant with the formation of *Mandalas* designate as the Mandala of thirty-six parts.

33. The seven constituents of the *Vijigisu*, those of the *Ari*, and those of the *Madhyama*, taken together, constitute what other politicians call the *Mandala* of twenty-one elements.

34. The four cardinal monarchs of a *Mandala* (viz., the *Vijigisu*, the *Ari*, the *Madhyama*, and the *Udásina*), each with an ally of his own, become eight in number. These eight kings with their respective *Prakritis*, minister &c., form the *Mandala*, the number of whose components is as many as that of the syllables contained in a stanza composed in the *Jagati** metre.

35. Those monarchs who are in the front of the *Vijigisu* and those who are in his rear, together with himself, constitute the *Mandala* of ten monarchs, spoken of by those who are acquainted with the nature of *Mandalas*.

36. The six *Prakritis*, namely, minister, kingdom, castle, treasury, army and ally, of each of these ten sovereigns, taken together, compose what is designated as the *Mandala* of sixty elements by those who are conversant with the nature of *Mandalas*.

37. An ally and an enemy in front of the *Vijigisu*, also an ally and an enemy in his rear, together with himself,

---

* A kind of metre with twelve syllables in a quarter ; so that the number of the total syllables in a stanza is 12 by 4 or 48. This metre again is divided into fifteen subdivisions, namely, (1) *Indravansa* (2) *Chandravartma*, (3) *Jaladharamálá*, (4) *Jaloddhatagati*, (5) *Támarasa* (6) *Totaka* (7) *Drutavilamvitam* (8) *Pravá* (9) *Pramitákshará* (10) *Bhujangaprayáta* (11) *Manimálá* (12) *Màlati* (13) *Vangsasthavila*, (14) *Vaiswadevee* and (15) *Sragvini*.

form five in number. The six *Prakritis*, namely minister &c., of each of these five sovereigns, taken together, constitute what is recognised as the *Mandala* of thirty elements.

38. Those best conversant with the *Shastras** also recognise these *Mandalas* in respect of the *Ari*. The intelligent ascribe the *Mandala* of five kings and the *Mandala* of thirty elements also to the *Ari*.

39. Parāsara† says that two *Prakritis*‡ are only to be recognised in polity; of them, the important is he that assails, and the other is he that is assailed.

40. In consequence of the *Vijigisu* and the *Ari* assailing each other, their relation of *Vijigisu* and *Ari* becomes interchangeable. And thus there appears to be one *Prakriti* only.§

41. Thus various other kinds of *Mandalas* have been mentioned (by the Achāryyas of yore). But the *Mandala* consisting of twelve kings is universally known and accepted.

42. He is a real politician who knows a tree‖, having

---

* For this interpretation of *Dristimatàm*, we refer our readers to an earlier note; vide note to Sloka 29. Sec. IV.

† A celebrated sage, the father of Vyasa the famous compiler of of the Puranas and the author of the Mahábhárata. Parasara has a *Smriti* ascribed to his authorship.

‡ Vide *supra*, note to Sloka 24th; the second meaning is applicable here.

§ What the author means is this. According to Parasàra the number of *prakritis* is two. But others again say that, virtually these two *prakritis*, the assailant *Vijigisu* and the assailed *Ari*, are one and the same. The contention of these latter is that, as the *Vijigisu* assails the *Ari*, so also does the *Ari* attack the *Vijigisu*. In this way, the *Ari* also becomes the assailant *Vijigisu*. So, of the *Vijigisu* and the *Ari*, each may be called both the assailant and the assailed. Thus it comes to be only one *prakriti* and this is the *Mandala* of one *Prakriti*, viz., the *Vijigisu*.

‖ The author now compares a *Mandala* to a tree.

four roots,* eight branches,† sixty leaves,‡ two props,§ six flowers,|| and three fruits.¶

43. The *Pârshnigrâha* and his *Asâra* (or the *Pàrshnigrà-hâsàra*) are said to be allies of the *Vijigisu's* enemy.$ The *Akranda* and his *Asâra*** (or the *Akrandàsàra*) maintain a friendly attitude towards the *Vijigisu*.

47. Through his own agency and through that of the *Mitram*, the *Vijigisu* should exterminate his enemy (the *Ari*); and through the agency of the *Mitram* assisted by his *Mitram* (*Mitramitram*), he should crush the ally of his enemy (the *Arimitram*).

48. Through the agency of the common ally (the *Udâsina*) and of the *Mitramitram*, a ruler of earth should crush the ally of the enemy's ally (the *Arimitramitram*).

49. Thus, in gradual order, the *Vijigisu* endued with unceasing activity, should crush his ever-molesting enemy

---

* The *Vijigisu*, the *Ari*, the *Madhyama* and the *Udàsina*, these constitute the four roots, Vide *supra* Sloka 20th.

† An enemy and an ally of each of these four cardinal kings, taken together, constitute the eight branches of the tree.

‡ The five *Prakritis* of each of the twelve kings of a *Maudala*, taken together, constitute the sixty leaves of the tree. Vide *supra* Sloka 25th.

§ The two primary stays are Destiny and human endeavour.

|| The six expedients to be used by a sovereign in foreign politics constitute the six flowers. For an explanation of these expedients, Vide note to Sloka 16th, Sec. IV.

¶ The results of the application of these expedients, namely, the diminution, preservation and the aggrandisement of the territorial wealth of a kingdom, are the fruits.

$ Consequently the *Pàrshnigràha's* and his *Asàrà's* attitude towards the *Vijigisu* becomes one of hostility, whereas the attitude of the *Akranda* and his *Asâra* becomes one of friendliness.

** The commentator defines *Akranda* to be 'one who is called upon by the *Vijigisu* to make war upon his *Pàrshnigrâha*; from the root *Kranda*, to call. He defines *Asàra* to be 'one that comes to save (the *Vijigsu*) in times of danger.' From the root *Sri* to move, or come.

(the *Ari*), and also him whose dominions lie intervening the dominions of his allies in the front (*i. e.* the *Arimitram*).

44. Having at first caused his enemies in the rear (the *Pârshnigràha* and his *Asâra*) to be engaged in a war with his friends (the *Arkanda* and his *Asàra*) therein, and, like his enemies in the rear, compelling his enemies in the front (the *Ari* and the *Arimitram*) to be engaged with his friends therein (the *Mitram* and the *Mitramitram*), a king should march out for conquest.*

45. A ruler of earth should march out for conquest, after having paralysed the ally of the enemy's ally through the instrumentality of a powerful common ally (the *Udàsina*) who had been won over by various good services.†

46. The *Vijigisu* united with the *Akranda* should crush the *Pàrshnigràha*.‡ Through the instrumentality of the *Akranda* assisted by his *Asàra*, the *Vijigisu* should crush the *Asàra* of the *Pàrshnigràha*.

50. Thus hemmed in and opposed on both sides by ever-active and intelligent monarchs,§ the enemy either soon becomes exterminated or resigns himself to the rule of the *Vijigisu*.||

51. By all means, the *Vijigisu* should try to win over to his side an ally common to him and to his enemy. Enemies, alienated from their allies, become easily extirpable.

52. It is causes that create enemies and allies¶; there-

---

* Thus the enemies in the front and in the rear of the *Vijigisu*, being engaged, they will not be able to watch his movements. So that at any time he will be able to crush them by surprise.

† The explanation, given in the commentary, being a little awkward, we have rejected it.

‡ Which act would be very easy, as the dominions of the *Párshnigráha* intervene those of the *Vijigisu* and the *Akranda*.

§ The *Vijigisu* and his ally.

|| For *Cha* read *Vá*.

¶ What the author means seems to be, that men are not born either mutual friends or mutual enemies. There must be some cause or causes

fore, always, should the *Vijigisu* shun such causes that might create enemies.

53. In every part of his dominions, by far, a king should cherish every one of his subjects.* By cherishing his people, a king enjoys a prosperity developing into the flourishing condition of all the constituents of his government.†

54. The *Vijigisu* should cultivate the alliance of monarchs stationed far off, of those who constitute his *Mandala*, of local governors‡ and also of the Foresters.§ It is those monarchs well-supported by their allies that can consolidate their empire.

55. When out of a desire for conquest, the *Madhyama*, swelling with the *Saktis*,|| marches forth, the *Vijigisu* united to his enemy, should withstand the former; if he is unable to do so, he should submit to make peace with the *Madhyama*.¶

---

to establish a relation either of friendship or enmity. By causes the commentator understands *Upakära* or good service and *Apåkåra* or injury. It is superfluous to say that the former creates allies, and the latter enemies.

* What the author means is, that a king should not only cherish his influential subjects, but also those who are poor and helpless. The means of cherishing are *Sáma* &c., for which *vide* an earlier note.

† The commentator explains the passage differently saying 'enjoys all-round prosperity.

‡ *Sthåna* has a diversity of meaning in politics. Kallukabhata takes it to signify the essential requisites for a monarchy, namely, army, treasure, town and territory; but this meaning does not apply here.

§ *Durga* ordinarily means a castle, but its derivative meaning is 'that to which the access is very difficult.' The commentator takes it to mean 'forest.' So we have rendered *Durganivåsina* into Foresters. But it may also mean, 'those who hold forts and castles to themselves.'

|| Vide note to Sloka 1st Section I.

¶ The text in the last part of the Sloka is vicious; for *Sandhimånnamet* read *Sandhinånamet*.

56. Enemies are of two kinds, namely, the natural and those created by acts. A natural enemy is he who is born in the self-same dynasty with the king,* and an enemy other than the natural, falls under the second head.

57. Ceding of his own territory*, weaning away of the officers of his enemy†, and *Karsana* and *Pidana*‡ of the enemy in opportune moments,—these four have been asserted, by men proficient in the science of chastisement, to be the duties of the *Vijigisu* in respect to his enemy.

58. Disablement of the treasury and of the machinery for awarding punishments, and the assassination of the prime-minister,these have been defined by *Acharyyas* to be *Karsana*. Acts, still more oppressive than these, have been called *Pidana*.

59. Destitute of all shelter,§ or seeking shelter with

There are two Slokas supplementary to this one, which have been omitted in the text. We subjoin their translations :—

(*a*). When the *Udásina* marches forth for conquest, all the other monarchs of the *Mandala*, firmly united together and with a sense of common duty, should await the assault of the former. If they are unable to withstand the former, they should bow down before him.

(*b*). When a calamity threatens, what ought to be done to avert it, by monarchs united together, for the fulfilment of their objects, is said to be the common duty of them all.

* Under the category of 'natural enemies' come the cognates and agnates, who have any claim on the inheritance. The second class is the ordinary class of enemies men have, and who are made such, by dealings and behaviours.

* The word in the text is *Uchcheda* which means extirpation. This meaning we should like to accept.

† Another meaning is possible, which is, 'undermining the strength of the enemy.'

‡ These words have been explained by the author himself in the next Sloka. The nearest approach in English to these words would be 'tormenting and crushing.'

§ The 'shelters' are specified by the commentator to be, castle, treasury, and army.

the weak, the *Ari* of the adjacent domain, inspite of his prosperity, can be easily extirpated.*

60. Of a monarch confident of his shelter, *Karsana* and *Pidana* should be done in opportune season. Either a castle, or an ally of honesty commended by the pious, has been defined to be a shelter.

61. An intestine enemy deserves extirpation, in consequence of his having the power to rob the monarch of all his authority.† Witness, the case of Vibhisana‡ and the son of Suryya,§ whose natural enemies were their uterine brothers (Rāvana and Vāli respectively).

62. An intestine enemy knows very well the laches, actions, and resources|| of a monarch. Thus knowing the

---

* As a supplement to this Sloka, Sloka 15th of this Section has been repeated here.

† The word in the text is *Tantra*, which the commentator explains to be 'ministers and kingdom &c.' But *Tantra* also means 'authority,' or more properly, 'the royal prerogative.'

‡ The brother of Ravana the well-known ten-headed demon of the great epic Ramayana. He was extremely sorry for the abduction of Sita by Ravana, and several times advised the latter to restore her to her husband Rama. But the proud Ravana turned deaf ears to all his remonstrances and entreaties. At last Vibhisana, forsaking his brother, repaired to Rama, and became instrumental in destroying his brother Ravana. After the death of Ravana, he was installed on the throne of *Lanka* (Ravana's kingdom) by Rama.

§ The son of Suryya (Sun) is Sugriva the brother of Vali the great monkey chief of *Kiskindhā*. During Vali's absence from the kingdom, Sugriva usurped the throne, considering the former to be dead. But when Vali returned, he had to run away to the *Rishyamukha* hills. His wife was seized by Vali. When latterly, he met Rama, he told the latter how he had been treated by his brother and besought his assistance for recovering his wife, promising at the same time that he would assist Rama in recovering his wife Sita. Rama killed Vali and installed Sugriva on the throne of *Kishkindhà*.

|| For *Karma* and *vittam* the commentary reads *Marma* and *Viryyam*, which respectively mean, 'vitals of the state, or intention' and 'prowess.'

secrets,* he consumes the latter, like fire consuming a withered tree.

63. †The *Vijigisu* should, with all speed, eradicate a common ally who behaves with open partiality towards the *Ari*, like the wielder of the thunder-bolt‡ slaying Trisiras.§

64. Apprehending his own extirpation, the *Vijigisu* should render assistance to his enemy, when the latter is in danger, being afflicted by a very powerful assailant.||

65. The *Vijigisu* should not seek to extirpate that enemy, by whose extirpation there is the slightest chance of making an enemy of another; but he should turn the latter's domain into a dependency.

66. If a family-born¶ enemy of great implacability is

---

* *Antargatas* literally means 'remaining inside or penetrating.' This Sloka, with the alterations in reading noted above, has been quoted in the Section on war of the Hitopadesha, Sloka No. 62. We subjoin Sir W. Jone's translation of it. "Our natural enemy knows our former crimes, our heart, and our strength; so that he penetrates and destroys, as fire burns a dry tree."

† The commentator goes on to say that, not only enemies but sometimes allies also deserve eradication.

‡ Or Indra, for which vide note to Sloka. 21 Sec. IV.

§ Trisiras was one of the gods; he was inimical to the interests of Indra; seeing him delight in the supremacy of the Asuras, Indra killed him. There was another Trisiras, a demon by birth, who was killed by Rama.

|| What the author means is that, there are occasions when help ought to be given even to an enemy. When the enemy is in danger of being extirpated, the *Vijigisu* has also reason to fear. For if the enemy's powerful assailant succeeds in driving out the former, he will occupy the domain adjacent to that of the *Vijigisu*. Then the *Vijigisu* will have the sword of Democlese hanging over his head. There are several vicious readings in the text of this Sloka. For *Dwisata* and *Apachaya* read *Dwisatá* and *Upachaya*.

¶ Instead of tiring our readers every time with a long-winded phrase, we take the liberty of coining this compound, which is equivalent to 'natural enemy' defined in Sloka 56th.

seen to deviate from his natural course of conduct,* then for his subjugation, the *Vijigisu* should incite an enemy born in the self-same dynasty with him (family-born enemy).

67. Poison is counteracted by poison, a piece of adamant is penetrated into by another piece of the same, and a wild elephant is crushed by a rival of known prowess.†

68. A fish devours another fish,‡ so also does a blood-relation, without doubt, destroy another blood-relation. Rāma honoured Vibhisana for the extirpation of Rāvana.§

69. The intelligent *Vijigisu* should never do such an act, the performance of which would agitate|| the whole *Mandala*. He should ever cherish the *Prakritis*¶ and their ministers &c.

70. A king should please his own *Prakritis* by conciliation, gift (or bribery) and bestowal of honour; and he should crush the *Prakritis* of his enemies by sowing dissensions among them and by openly attacking them.

71. The whole extent of the dominions comprised in a *Mandala* is overspread with hostile and friendly sovereigns. Every one of these sovereigns is exceedingly selfish.$ How then is neutrality of attitude possible in any one of them?

72. The *Vijigisu* should afflict even an ally having the

---

* Which would be 'to persecute constantly the *Vijigisu*.'

† Hence 'domestic,' so says the commentator. What the author seems to suggest in this Sloka appears to be that, 'to slay a family-born enemy, a monarch should skilfully employ another of the same nature.'

‡ The reference seems to be to the maxim of *Nyàya* philosophy known as *Mátsya nyáya*, vide note to Sloka 40 Sec. II.

§ It was Vibhisana who apprised Rama of the mortal dart being lodged with *Mandodari*, the wife of Ravana.

|| The commentator explains, 'give reason, to the other sovereigns of the *Mandala*, for the persecution of himself.'

¶ The second meaning, given in an earlier note to this word, applies here.

$ I.e. every one is anxious to aggrandise his own interests at the expense of others. So there can be no true alliance among them.

means for enjoyment,* if the latter goes astray. But when the latter is hopelessly corrupt, then the *Vijigisu* should crush him, for, then he is to be regarded as a very sinful enemy.†

73. The *Vijigisu* should make friends even with his foes, if they become instrumental in his own aggrandisement. He should forsake even his allies, if they are intent on doing evil to him.

74. Either he that seeks to promote real service, or he that is anxious for the welfare of a monarch, is to be regarded as a friend.‡ He is an ally who renders effectual service, no matter whether he is satisfied or not.

75. After grave considerations, a monarch should abjure allegiance to an ally whose offences have been repeatedly brought to notice. But by abandoning an unoffending ally, a monarch destroys his religious merit as well as his worldly prosperity.§

76. A monarch should, at every time and in every instance, enquire into the guilt and innocence of others personally. When he has thus personally found out the guilty, the infliction of punishment becomes praiseworthy.‖

---

* The commentator says, 'the means is treasure.'

† The commentary paraphrases the word in text by 'still worse.'

‡ The commentary gives a different reading, for which we see no occasion ; still we subjoin it. '*Bandhurapyahité yuktas Satrustam Parivarjayet.*' 'A friend intent on doing evil is to be regarded as a foe, and he should be shunned.'

§ For *hi* the commentary reads *Sa*. The last portion is explained by the commentator thus :—' By forsaking an ally, a monarch loses the chance of reaping that worldly profit which otherwise he may have realised.'

‖ Compare Sloka 142, in *Suhridveda* (Breach of friendship) in the Hitopadesha. We subjoin Sir W. Jone's translation of it.

'Without distinguishing virtues or vices, let neither favor be granted nor severity used ; as a hand placed with pride in the nest of a serpent occasions destruction.'

77. The *Vijigisu* should never work himself up with ire, without having obtained sufficient information regarding the real state of affairs. Men regard him as a snake who becomes angry on the innocent.

78. A monarch should be cognisant of the degrees of difference among excellent, mediocre, and ordinary allies. The services, done by these three classes of allies, are accordingly excellent, mediocre, and ordinary.*

79. A monarch should never accuse others falsely, nor should he listen to false accusations.† He should ever shun them who try to cause disunion among allies.

80. A monarch should be able to comprehend utterances known as *Prâyogika*,‡ *Mâtsarika*,§

---

* Compare Sloka 69 Hitopadesha, Section *Suhridveda.* 'Three sorts of men, O king, the highest, the middle and the lowest; let their master exercise them alike in three sorts of employment.'

† For the first portion of the Sloka, compare Hitopadesha Sloka 141 Sec. Suhridveda. We subjoin Sir W. Jone's translation.

'Let not a prince punish men from the words of others; let him examine the facts, himself, and then imprison, or dismiss with respect.'

‡ *Prâyogika*—Lit: relating to *Pràyoga* or the expedients of foreign policy (Vide note to Sloka 51. Sec., V.); hence *pràyogika* utterances are those that are calculated to promote the interests of foreign policy. For instance, we quote below, from the Drama *Mudràràkshasa*, the words, the *Vaitàlika* (ministrel) deputed by Rakshasa uttered, with a view to estrange the alliance between Chanakya and Chandragupta, when these latter merely feigned a quarrel.

Bhusânadyupabhogèna prabhurbhavati na prabhus,
Parairaparibhutojnairmanyatè twamiba prabhus.

'Lord are not lords for their enjoyment of ornaments &c., but they are regarded to be so by the wise, for, their authority can not be thwarted by others.' The *Vaitàlika* knew perfectly well that Chandragupta virtually had no authority independent of the power of Chanakya, and to bring home into the former's mind the subserviency of his position, he uttered the above words, expecting thereby to sow dissensions between them.

§ *Màtsarika*—These are utterances indicative of *Matsara* or indignation or spite; by such expressions, the speaker wants to thwart the measures of policy adopted by an enemy or his emissary, by apprising

*Mâdhyastham,** *Pâkshapâtikam,*† *Sopanyàsa,*‡ and *Sanusaya.*§

---

the latter that he is perfectly cognisant of his machinations and intrigues. For instance, we quote from the above-named Drama, the words of Chanakya in reply to the words of the *Nata* (actor).

A ! Ka ésa mayisthité Chandraguptam Abhivabitumichchati.

(Chanakya in the tiring room)—What, who is he that wants to crush Chandragupta, so long as I am here.

* *Mùdhyastam*—These are utterances expressive of outward indifference towards a certain matter while there may be real concern about it in the mind ; or as the commentator adds, words that do not betray any malice, but on the other hand express friendliness and a conciliatory spirit. For instance, we quote and translate from the same Drama, the words Chanakya uttered, when he was apprised of the movements of Rakshasa's family.

Nanu Suhrittomas na hyanàtmasadrisesu Ràkshasa Kalatram nyàsee Karisyati.

'Surely our best friend Rakshasa will not entrust the protection of his family to one unworthy of his friendship.'

† *Pàkshapàtika*—These are utterances signifying an excessive partiality for one's own party. For instance, we quote from the said Drama, the words Chanakya uttered (aside), when he put in his finger the signet ring of Rakshasa presented to him by his spy.

Nanu Rákshasa eba Ashmàkam Angulipranayee Samvrittas' 'surely even Rakshasa himself will now like our finger.'

‡ *Sopanyàsam*—These are words uttered, with an under-current of irony, to invite one to take his seat near his superior, with a view to throw the former off his guard. (From *upa* near and *nyàsa* to sit). For instance, we translate, from the same Drama, the dialogue between the Banker Chandanadasa, and Chanakya.

Chanakya—All hail, O Banker, sit thyself on this seat.

Chandanadasa (doing obeisance)—Dost thou not know, O sire, that undeserved welcome causes greater pain to the sincere than even the most biting sarcasm ? So permit me to sit on this bare earth which is fit for me.

Chanakya—Not so, not so, O Banker ; you deserve to sit with us, so occupy this seat.

Chandanadasa (aside)—I know not what is he driving at.

§ *Sànusaya*—These are utterances that indicate repentance for

81. He should not openly take the side of any one of his allies, but should encourage a feeling of rivalry among them in securing his grace.*

82. As the responsibilities of royalty are very onerous, a monarch therefore, adapting himself to circumstances, should, overlooking the prominent failings of even his mean allies, attribute to them qualities which they do not possess.†

---

an act or omission resulting in an irreparable loss. We quote and translate from the same Drama.

Rákshasa—Mayi sthité kas Kusumapuram abarotsasi. Praviraka Praviraka, kshipramidáning,

Prákáràn paritas saráasanadharais kshipram parikshipyatám,
Dwàresu dwiradais paradwipaghatávedakshamais stheeyatám
Muktá mritubhayam prahartu manasas satrorvalé durvalé
Tés niryántu mayà sahaika manasas yesámabhistam yasas.

Viràdha—Amâtya, Alamâvégéna, Vrittamidam varnyaté.

Rákshasa—Katham vrittamidam, mayá punarjnâtam sa eba kâla varttate.

Rakshasa (drawing his sword)—Who dares invade the city of Kusumapura whilst I am here. Ho, Pravirarka, Praviraka, 'Let men with bows and arrows speedily mount guard on the ramparts; station, in the city-gates, elephants capable of rending the temples of those of the enemy. Let those, who want to crush the weak host of the enemy and who desire to acquire fame, follow me with a singleness of purpose, disregardful of the fear of death.

Viradhas—Minister, this excitement avails nothing. I was only recounting what had already happened.

Rakshasa (shyly)—What, mere description! I thought that, that hour has come back again.

For *Samsaya* in the text, the commentary gives *Sánusaya*.

* What the author means is this. 'If a king shows any marked partiality for any individual ally, then the others are estranged from him.'

† What the author means seems to be this :—'To aggrandise his own interests, a monarch may even have recourse to sycophancy; and he should neither hesitate to attribute good qualities to persons who do not really possess them, nor should he take notice of any vice in any one of his allies.

83. A ruler of earth should secure to himself a large number of allies of various descriptions. For, a monarch, supported by a large number of allies, is capable of keeping his enemies under his sway.

84. The danger, which the true ally of a sovereign runs to remedy the evil that has befallen the latter, that danger is such, that even his brother, father, or other people cannot face it (for his sake).*

85. A king should not assail an enemy, who is being supported by his allies of firm vows. This is the one duty to be observed in a *Mandala*, and this has been mentioned to be so, by those who know how to consolidate an empire.

86. A *Mandala* virtually consists of allies and enemies and the *Udâsina*; and the purification of the *Mandala* means the purification of these three.†

87. Thus a monarch, treading the path of justice, and bringing about the purification of the *Mandala* with all endeavours, shines resplendent like the autumnal moon of pure beams, affording delight to the hearts of the people.

Thus ends the eighth Section, the construction and characteristics of a Mandala, in the Nitisâra of Kâmandaka.

—oo—

* The author wants to insinuate the superiority of an ally to one's father, brother &c.

† Consolidation means the subjugation of, and the alliance with, these kings.

SECTION IX.

1. WHEN assaulted by a monarch,* more powerful than himself, and (thus) involved in a great jeopardy, a ruler of men, having no other remedy,† should seek peace, delaying as much as possible.‡

2. §*Kapâla, Upahâras, Santânas,* and *Sangatas; Upanyâsas, Pratikàras, Samyogas, Purushântaras,*

---

* In lieu of *Valiyasâbhiyuktastu*, the commentator suggests a different reading *viz. Valavatvigrihitastu*; this does not materially change the signification. 'Power' must be taken here, as before, to be synonymous with *Prabhàva* or the *Saktis*, for which vide note to sloka I Sec I.

† The commentary explains, 'deprived of the support of his allies, and the security of his castles, wherewith to withstand the invador; thus highly distrsssed.'

‡ The meaning of the author is more clearly explained by the comtator thus:—" The assailed king should not, with unceremonious haste, ratify a treaty or peace; he should occupy as much time as possible in settling the preliminary negotiations, thus leaving room for himself to fall upon the assailant, if through chance, some calamity in the meanwhile, overtake the latter; but this would be impossible if the treaty be ratified before the advent of the calamity."

In his translation of the Hitopadesha in which these *Slokas* have been embodied, S. W. Jones curiously renders this sloka thus:—" When a prince is engaged in war with a stronger prince, there is no other remedy. When he is in danger, let him seek peace, and reserve his exertions for another occasion."

§ The author now proceeds to enumerate the different kinds of peace, the number of which, as the reader will presently see, is so many as sixteen. These Slokas have been incorporated *verbatim* in the *Hitopodesha* (Salutary counsel) of Vishnu Sarman, which undoubtedly is a later work (see Introduction). In the several following Slokas, the author himself explains these kinds of peace, and the provisions for each of them.

3. *Adrishtanaras*, *Adishtas*, *Atmàmisha*,* *Upagrahas*, *Parikrayas* and *Uchchinnas* and *Paribushanas*,†

4. And *Skandhopaneyas*; these sixteen kinds of peace are celebrated. Thus have they, who are learned in peace-making, named sixteen sorts of peace.‡

5. Only that kind of peace is said to be *Kapàla-sandhi*,§ that is concluded between two parties of equal resources. The peace that is concluded through the offer of presents is called *Upahára*.||

---

* In the enumeration contained in the Hitopadesha, referred to above, we find *Atmàdishtà* for *Atmámisha*.

† In the Hitopadesha we have *Parabhusana* for this designation.

‡ The slokas marked 2. 3. 4. should be read all together.

§ As to the interpretation of the first line, opinions vary considerably. The word in dispute seems to be *Samasandhitas*, which is a compound formed of the two words "*Sama*" or equal and *Sandhitas* or peace. Some explain this to mean (1) " Peace in which the considerations for the parties are equal; no one deriving advantage over the other; or "peace on equal terms." (2) Others explain it to mean, ' Peace between two contending parties whose resources (*Saktis*) are equal, and where no surrender of troops or treasure is made by any of the parties. (3) Others again, who number S. W. Jones among them, explain it thus, their explanation being more etymological. "*Kapála*" means a potsherd or a piece of broken jar. Just as an earthen jar broken in some portion when repaired by the placing of another sherd on the broken part, appears to be intact, but as in reality it is not so, so the peace that is concluded by mere words of mouth and where there is no pledge or promise indicating a permanent alliance, is said to be *Kapála-sandhi*. This kind of peace can be violated at any time, as the parties to it are not bound by any formal pledge or promise. Hence it comes to what S. W. Jones has termed it, *viz*., a simple cessation of hostilities. The commentator accepts this last interpration.

|| *Upahára* means presents or gifts in general. Sometimes the use of the word is limited to 'complimentary gifts or gifts to a superior alone.' The latter meaning seems to be more appropriate here, inasmuch as the commentator explains *Upahára-sandhi* thus:—'Peace that a vanquished monarch concludes with his conqueror by surrendering to the latter his army and treasury, is called *Upahára*.' The nearest approach

6. *Santána-sandhi** is that which is concluded by a king by giving a daughter in marriage to his royal adversary. That peace is named *Sangatas*† which is founded on friendship between good men.

7. This kind of peace lasts as long as the parties to it live; under it, the parties identify their acts and their resources; ‡ it is not broken by any cause whatever, either in seasons of properity or adversity.

8. This kind of peace namely *Sangata-sandhi* is excellent,§ like gold among other metals. People versed in peace making also call this *Sandhi*, *Kánchana* or golden.

---

in English to *Upahára* in this connection would be, "indemnity, or presents given as the price of peace."

* *Santána* means a child ; therefore *Santána-sandhi* has been taken to mean 'peace made through the giving up of one the female children of the family.' The compound *Darikádána* means, 'to give a daughter (*Dáriká*) in marriage.' S. W. Jones is not very clear in his translation of this passage ; he renders it thus :—"*Santána* is known by having first given up one of the family."

† In the body we have given the rendering of S. W. Jones. A strictly literal translation of the passage would however be this; 'That is called *Sangata-sandhi* by the pious, of which the foundation is laid in friendship. *Sangatas* means 'union,' hence *Sangata-sandhi* has come to denote 'association and intimacy resulting from friendship.' In the next two Slokas, the author puts forth the other distinguishing marks of this kind of peace, and tries to prove its superiority over the rest.

‡ The word in the text is *Samànàrthaprayojanas* which is a compound formed of three words, *viz.*, *Samànà* (identical), *Artha* (treasure) *Prayojana* or (necessities). The commentator takes *Prayojana* to mean, 'acts done for the furtherance of righteousness, worldly profit, or the attainment of desires. What the author means seems to be this :—"Those that are bound by the ties of this particular kind of peace do not observe any difference with regard to their respective treasures and acts. They consider one another's wealth and interest as good as their own, and act accordingly."

§ For *Prahrista* of the text, the commentary reads *Prakrista*, which undoubtedly is an emendation.

9. Peace that is concluded with a view to bring into a remarkably successful termination all the controversies of the occasion, has been named *Upanyâsa** by those acquainted with its nature.

10. 'I did him good, he will also do so to me'—when peace is concluded under such considerations, it is called *Pratikâra-sandhi*.†

11. 'I shall do him good, he will also do so to me,'—when peace is concluded under such considerations, it is called *Pratikâra-sandhi*; ‡ and it was such an alliance that was formed between Rāma and Sugriva.§

12. When two parties join one another for accomplishing an act that is equally interesting to both of them, and if they

---

* Opinions also vary regarding the definition of this kind of peace. For *Ekârtha* of the text we have substituted *Sarvârtha*. The commentator however does not change the reading, but explains the word *Ekârthasamsidhi* thus, *viz.*, the fulfilment of one of the objects of desire. According to the commentator then the definition is something like this ;—*Upanyâsa-sandhi* is that in which the parties come to conclude it with a previously-formed resoultion that, by such conclusion of peace some of their objects will be fulfilled, such as, the acquirement of a certain territory, &c. The translation given by S. W. Jones of this passage is incomprehensible to ourselves. We therefore quote it below for our readers to judge. 'Upanyasa—prosperity through wealth being given, and thence peace concluded by those empowered to make it."

† To make our meaning explicit, we subjoin S. W. Jone's definition of this kind of peace.

"*Pratikâra* is peace concluded through benefits conferred and received." The reader should mark the past tense in 'I did &c.,' for in the next Sloka, the author gives another definition of *Pratikàra* in which a slight and insignificant change in tense only occurs.

‡ The definitions of *Pratikâra* embodied in Slokas 10 and 11 are both covered by the one given by S. W. Jones. The distinction between these two definitions, is immaterial.

§ For the allusion contained in this part of the Sloka, refer to an earlier note (vide note to Sloka 61, Section VIII). Though it is not explained in full there, it will be enough to serve our present purpose.

enjoy one another's confidence, the peace that is then concluded between them, is called *Samyoga.**

13. 'The best of your troops should join those of mine to aggrandise my interests'—when under such a condition dictated by the conqueror upon the conquered, peace is concluded, it is called *Purushântara.*†

14. 'You shall have to accomplish this act for me, without getting any help whatever from me'—when under some such condition specified by the (conquering) enemy, peace is concluded, it is designated *Adristapurusha-sandhi.*‡

15. When peace is made with a powerful adversary through the cession of a portion of the territories, it is called *Adista-sandhi* by those who are versed in the principles of peace-making.§

---

* *Samyoga* literally means a 'firm union,' and what can bring about a firm alliance but a common by interest? Here also the definition given by S. W. Jones is very curious. We give it below.

'*Samyoga*—Where the advantages are equal.' If this definition is accepted, *Samyoga* virtually becomes identical with *Kapàla.*

† For *Madartha*, the commentary gives *Sadartha*, and explains it to mean 'acquirement of territory,' &c. The definition of this kind of peace would be something like this—"*Purushántara sandhi* is that, to secure which the weaker party surrenders his troops to the use of the stronger." S. W. Jone's definition is entirely different, and we know not what the cause of it may be; it is this:—

Purushàntara—When two monarchs meet face to face in battle, the wealth of one procures peace.

‡ *Adrista-purusha* is a compound formed of *Adrista* (not seen) and *Purusha* man. Hence *Adrista-purusha Sandhi* is that, in which some of the conqueror's men are bound to help those of the conquered, when the latter called upon by the former, goes to perform some act for the former's benefit. The definition given by S. W. Jones is incomprehensible. It is this:—"Adrista-purusha—when after peace, thus bought, the foe joins in a treaty."

§ The commentary gives a different reading for *Ripuvarjita viz. Ripururjita.* This makes the meaning of the Sloka more explicit and therefore we have accepted it. The original if translated literally will stand thus, though the difference between the two translations (one in

16. The compact that is formed between a sovereign and his own troops, is called *Atmàmisha-sandhi.* Peace that is concluded for the preservation of self by the surrender of everything else, is called *Upagraha-sandhi.**

17. Where, for the preservation of the rest of the *Prakritis,*† peace is concluded through the surrender of a part or the whole of the treasure,‡ or by giving metals other than gold and silver,§ it is called *Parikraya.*||

18. *Uchchinna Sandhi* (destructive peace) is so called inasmuch as it is concluded by the cession of the most excellent lands to the foe. *Paribhusana-sandhi*¶ is that which is concluded by giving up the products of the whole territory.

19. That kind of peace, in which the indemnity (in money or territorial produces) agreed upon by the parties

---

the body and the subjoined one) will be very immaterial. "When an enemy is shunned by the stipulation that a portion of the territory should be ceded to him, and when peace is concluded accordingly, it is called *Adista* by those versed in the principles of peace-making." S. W. Jone's definition is as follows. "*Adista*—Where land is given in one part."

* The definitions, given by S. W. Jones, of these two kinds of peace are as follows :—

Atmàmisha,—that concluded with a king's own forces.

Upagraha,—that concluded for the preservation of life.

† For *Prakritis* vide note to Sloka 24 Section VIII.

‡ This is also a *Prakriti* (vide note referred to above).

§ The original word is *Kupyam* which means a base metal, hence, any metal, except gold and silver.

|| The following is the definition given by S. W. Jones, in which he has omitted one element. '*Parikraya*—that concluded by a part or the whole of the treasure.'

¶ In different texts this word *Paribhusana* is substituted by one of the two words *Parabhusana* and *Paradusana,* the latter being the reading of the commentary. S. W. Jones, definitions are :—" (1) *Uchchana,* —concluded by giving the most excellent lands, (2) *Parabhusana*—concluded by giving up the fruits arising from the whole territory."

is given by instalments, is called *Skandhopancya-sandhi*,* by those who are conversant with the natures of peace.

20. Of these sixteen sorts of peace, the following four—viz—(1) that concluded through benefits conferred and received (*Pratikâra*), (2) that through friendship (*Sangata*) (3) that through (marital) relation-ship (*Santâna*) and (4) that through the presentation of gifts (*Upahàra*)—are mostly recognised.

21. In our opinion, the *Upahâra* is the only sort of peace that deserves the name. Except that concluded through friendship, all the other kinds of peace are only varieties of the *Upahara*†.

22. Inasmuch as a powerful assailant never returns without obtaining (considerable) presents, therefore is it said that there is no other kind of peace more excellent than the *Upahàra*.‡

---

* Different interpretations of this sloka have been suggested. We however have followed the commentary, which has introduced one emendation into the text viz., *Skandhaskandhena* for *Skandhas Skandhena.* Another explanation is this :—*Skandhopaneya-sandhi* is that in which the vanguished party is required to carry what the conquer may demand of money &c., on his shoulder to the place of the latter. The framer of this definition has evidently erred by trying to be too much true to the etymology of word which is *Skandha* (or shoulder) and *Upaneya* (to be carried). What S. W. Jones gives is this :—" Where only a part of the produce of the land is given."

† If the reader examines the definitions of these fifteen kinds of peace, save that of the Sangata (which is formed through friendship), he will find that every one of them contains the elements that are essential to the *Upahára-sandhi*,

‡ What the author means seems to be this :—A powerful monarch invading another's territory does so with a view to obtain handsome booty and unless he is offered valuable presents he will not give up his attempt. And it is the *Upahāra-sandhi* that enjoins the weaker party to offer those presents. Thus the *Upahāra* is the kind of peace that is ordinarily concluded ; hence its superiority.

23. *A young prince†, an old one, one long sick,‡ one discarded by his cognates,§ a cowardly sovereign,|| one having cowards for his followers,¶ one covetous,** one whose officers and followers are greedy and covetous,††

24. One whose *Prakritis* are disaffected,‡‡ one excessively addicted to sensual pleasures, one who is fickle-hearted about his counsels,§§ one who desecrates the gods|||| and the Brahmanas,

---

* The author now proceeds to specify the parties with whom peace should not be concluded. These parties, as the reader will see, are twenty in number. Immediately after, the author, furnishes reasons why peace should not be made with them.

† The Sanskrit word is *Vála* and S. W. Jones renders it into "A boy"; of course what the author means is not an ordinary boy, but a boy-king.

‡ This is S. W. Jones's translation, the original word is a compound, meaning literally "one suffering long from an illness."

§ S. W. Jones's rendering is 'an outcast.' Ours is strictly literal.

|| Who flinches from a fight.

¶ S. W. Jones's translation of the original word is curious; it is, 'a cause of terror.' It is incomprehensible, inasmuch as 'a cause of terror' is rather the party with whom a hasty conclusion of peace would be politic. Our rendering is appropriate and strictly literal.

** A covetous prince naturally appropriates all booties to himself, and deprives his soldiers of their rightful dues. Thus he cultivates their ill-will, which goes to weaken him materially.

†† If the followers of a king be covetous, they do not hesitate to sacrifice their sovereign's interests for a paltry consideration. Such a prince therefore, is always in danger.

‡‡ For *Prakriti* refer to an earlier note. The *Prakriti's* when dissatisfied undermine the king's power and bring about his speedy fall. S. W. Jones renders the original word into 'ill-natured.'

§§ The prince who divulges prematurely his counsels, renders himself susceptible of an easy victory. S. W. Jones's translation is wide of the mark here also. This is it :—"He who has many schemes and different counsels."

|||| S. W. Jones's rendering is this, a contemner of the gods and priests. It is believed that when the gods and the Brahmanas are

25. One who is under the influence of adverse fate,* one who relies too much on chance (or fate),† one who is famine-stricken,‡ one whose armies are in disorder,§.

26—27. One in an unfamiliar land,|| one whose foes number many, one who takes not time by the fore lock,¶ one devoid of truth and justice,**—let not a wise king conclude peace with these twenty sorts of persons, but let him ever harass them in war; for, these, when assaulted, speedily fall under the sway of their enemy.

---

offended they can bring about the ruin of a king. For 'gods' some substitute 'his family-deities,' these latter are special images that receive homage from the family as long as it continues.

* S. W. Jones's translation is "one who denies Providence." Probably the translator has been misled by the word *Upahatas*, which when compounded with *Daiva* has a different meaning altogether.

† A king depending too much on Providence, is consigned to a singular inactivity which goes to ruin him.

‡ What the author means is this:—" When the king's territory is visited with a famine, his subjects being starved, he naturally becomes incapable of fighting.

S. W. Jone's translation is this:—'One who gains a little by beggary,'

§ Supply 'through the prevalence of maladies, discontent and disobedience, &c.'

|| The original word is *Adesastha* which means 'dislodged from his natural site,' and hence, deprived of the security of his castles and advantages of the soil and treanches and ditches and fortifications in it. S. W. Jones;gives:—"One who is in any fereign country.'

¶ S. W. Jones's O translation is this:—'He who takes not the right time for action.' Some interpret the word in a different way thus:—"When the king comes upon evil times and hard days," this latter meaning is strained. So we do not accept it. Another which is prosible and meaning seems to be a little is more correct, is 'one who fights not in season.'

** A prince void of truth and justice, is alienated from his subjects by his mal-treatment of them.

With these parties a king should not make peace, inasmuch as if war is waged against them, the chances of defeat will be very little. So it would be impolitic to allow these kings their liberties through peace.

15

28. *People wish not to fight for the cause of a boy-king on account of his want of *Prabhâva*.† For, what man would fight for the interests of him who himself is unable to defend them, and who again is not in any way bound to him (by the ties of kinship).

29. An old king and one long sick, should not be concluded peace with, inasmuch as they are devoid of that element of regal prowess known as *Utsâha Sakti*,‡

* Having specified above the parties with whom it would be impolitic to conclude peace, the author now proceeds to show where the weakness of those parties lie, by a knowledge of which an assaulting monarch is sure to obtain advantage over them. The gist of what the author has said above and what he is going to say, seems to be this that, "Fight with those who would fall an easy prey to you, and do not conclude peace with them." The strength of the twenty different sorts of persons enumerated above, is undermined some way or other, and they therefore, are very susceptible of being defeated and dethroned. A wise king therefore, should not give these parties the benefit of the peace with him, but should add to his own territorial wealth by incurring the least trouble and danger.

† A young prince is naturally weak and is unacquainted with the tortuous courses and consequence of political measures, such as war and peace. His ministers, army, followers, &c., do not entertain that amount of regard for him which would deter them from violating his authority. He himself again is physically incompetent to face the hardhips of a war and to lead legions to fight. For these and many other such reasons, his subjects hesitate to risk a battle for his sake and under his leadership. In this way, he is materially weakened, and is left to the mercy of the assailant, who if prudent, should not conclude peace with him, but would crush him. (For *Prabhâva vide* note to Sloka 1, Section I.)

In rendering the first portion of the sloka, S. W. Jones commits what seems to be a mistake. His translation is this :—" Men seek not to war with a boy on account of his weakness, nor with an old man or an invalid, through want of power in them to transact business." But the author has been specifying the parties against whom war is to be waged and who should not be concluded peace with.

‡ For *Utsâhasakti*, vide note to Sloka 1, Section I.

and are sure to be crushed by their own kinsmen (or subjects).*

30. A king forsaken by his kinsmen, becomes easily extirpable,† moreover they of his own family would destroy him, if they could be won over by some personal good service.‡

31. A coward, by abandoning battle, flies to his own end.§ And even a brave monarch is deserted on the field of battle by his men, if these latter be cowards.||

---

* In rendering this Sloka we have been a little free in the use of words, with a view to make the sense all the more clear.

† So peace should not be made with him; but his dominions should be confiscated, as he would not be able to offer the least resistance, being deprived of the assistance of those who alone would have fought hard for him.

‡ The last word in the text is a compound formed of *Swartha* (self-interest) and *Satkrita* (gratified). Hence it means,—"Gratified (with the assailant) for his having helped in the furtherance of his selfish interests." What the author wants to impress seems to be this, that the assailant, when he proceeds against an out-cast-king, should win over the latter's alienated relations by helping them in advancing their personal interests; then through their agency, he should pull down the out-cast.

S. W. Jones's translation is as follows:—"An out-cast is deprived of happiness; even they of his own family seek to destroy him for their own credit."

Swartha Satkrita may mean also, "for subserving their own selfish interests", but it can never have the meaning ascribed to it by S. W. Jones, neither can *Sukhocheddya* have the meaning given to it by the same scholar.

§ A cowardly king, through a natural aversion for war, ever shuns it; and that being the case, when attacked, he is sure to surrender himself unconditionally to the assailant, which means his destruction. So, it would be impolitic to make peace with him whose kingdom could be appropriated by a mere contraction of the brow. S. W. Jones's translation is given below. "A coward, through aversion for wars, naturally flies away."

|| A king whose men and ministers are so many cowards, cannot

32. The troops of a covetous monarch,* will not fight, inasmnch as he pays them poorly,† And the king, whose officers are greedy and covetous, is destroyed by them when they are bribed by the enemy.‡

33. The king, whose *Prakritis* are disaffected, is deserted by them at the prospect of a war,§ and he who is excessively addicted to sensual pleasures, becomes so weak as to be easily crushed.||

---

stand before an assailant, inspite of all his bravery ; for they would surely abandon him to his fate, at the slightest prospect of a war breaking out. Not even the valorous achievements and feats of heroism of that king, would be enough to inspire noble sentiments in their hearts. For the last line of the text the commentary gives this line, *viz.*

"*Beeropi Bhirupurushais Sangràme, hi Pramuchyaté.*"

S. W. Jones gives—" In battle, even a hero is mixed in flight with cowards."

* The word in the text is *Auujivinas,* which literally means 'dependents.'

† The meaning given by us in the body, is based on the commentary. But another meaning is possible and that is this ; " A covetous monarch shares not the booties obtained, with his troops, who therefore naturally grudge to fight for him." The word in the text etymologically means, 'one who does not equitably distribute ;' hence the latter meaning seems to be more correct.

‡ A monarch who is imprudent enough to entertain covetous followers, is sure to be destroyed through their agency ; for these unprincipled fellows would not hesitate the least to betray their king to the enemy for a paltry bribe. Hence, if the assailant is wise enough, he makes use of these potent tools, and does not want to conclude peace with such a sovereign.

Dànabhinnais, literally means " Weaned over by means of bribery and gifts, &c." S. W. Jones's translation is as follows.

" The subjects of a miser will not fight, because they share not his riches ; and those of him who is not covetous, fight only through gift." We offer no comments.

§ Thus forsaken, he becomes virtually powerless, and is easily worsted by his enemy.

|| Such a king occupied with the task of gratifying his senses, neglects his royal functions and thus cultivates the ill-will of his people,

34. The king who is undecided in his judgments (counsels),* becomes odious to his counsellors; and owing to his infirmity of purpose, they neglect him when the time for (joint) action comes.

35. A contemner of the gods and the Brahmanas, and an ill-fated monarch, these two are reduced of their own accord, through the consequences of their arrant impiety.†

36. "Providence is certainly the cause of prosperity and adversity.' The fatalist arguing in the above manner, gives up all personal exertions.‡

---

who, at the first opportunity join with, any other king that may come with a hostile intention ; thus virtually the king becomes helpless, and is easily disposed of by his foe. The following is the rendering of S. W. Jones.

"An ill-natured man is deserted in the battle by better natures, and the sensualist who abounds in pleasure is overcome by it."

* The original word is *Anekachitta-mantras* which is a compound meaning "many-minded regarding his counsels." We translate it a little freely in order to be consistent. The following is S. W. Jones's rendering. "He who has many projects of his own is a foe to good counsellors."

† The first few words of the Sloka may have another meaning. In that case the rendering would undergo this change in the last part *viz.*, for "through the consequences, &c., we shall read "for virtue is ever powerful." The double meaning seems to hinge on the euphonic combination that may or may not be supposed to exist in *Sadàdharma*, &c. What the author means is this that, such kings are subjugated by their enemies without the least difficulty, for, by their impious deeds they alienate both God and man from themselves. Thus they form an easy prey for the conqueror. S. W. Jones's translation is this :— "A contemner of the Gods and priests, as well as the opposer of Providence, is continually tormented with grief by force of his own impiety."

‡ What the author means is this :—A monarch depending too much on Providences ascribes all that many come to pass, to its agency. And he consoles himself, in the case of an unfortunate occurrence, saying, 'what could my exertions have done when Fate was so much against me? Surely Destiny is superior to human endeavours." This

37. The monarch whose territory is visited by a famine, gives his liberty up of his own acord.* He also whose troops are discontented has not the power to risk a battle.†

38. A king in an unfamiliar‡ land is crushed even by a puny adversary; witness, the case of the king of elephants who when in water, is overpowered even by the smallest shark.

---

servile reliance on Providence prompts him not to put forth his exertions for the defence of his kingdom. Thus he remains unprepared when assaulted by an inimical sovereign, and so falls an easy prey to him. S. W. Jones's rendering of this sloka is :—Providence is certainly the giver of wealth and poverty ; let a man therefore meditate first of all on Providence ; but not so as to prevent his own exertions.

* We have been a little free here, for the sake of lucidity. The meaning of the author is this :—When famine rages in his country and when there is no food to live upon, its king surrenders himself of his own accord without offering the least resistance, merely for this two-fold consideration, (1) That none of his subjeets would then fight for him ; that even if they do so, they will be reduced through their want of food ; (2) And that by surrendering himself he would at least then be able to maintain himself and his people on the food that the conqueror would naturally import for preserving his newly acquired domain. S. W. Jones's translation of this part is this :—"A miserable beggar is self-tormented." It is needless to say that it is wide of the mark.

† The king, in whose army discontent and disorder, prevail cannot confidently encounter a foe, for it is almost certain that his troops will desert him on the field of battle. The commentary parapharases the word *Valavyasanaksaktasya* thus :—"The army whose ranks number many warriors who have not been duly honored for their services, and who, in consequence thereof, are very much disaffected." S. W. Jones's rendering is as follows :—"He who has a bad army has no power to fight."

‡ For *Adeshastha* refer to an earlier note. The commentary paraphrases it thus. "In a country which is other than the one suited for his site." For *Hanyate* the commentary substitutes *Avijiyate* which virtually conveys the same idea. S. W. Jones's translation is this. "A foreign invader is soon overpowered even by a weak foe. As the shark monster of the lake, though small, seizes the king of elephants.' *Apakarsati* in the text literally means "draggs in" from *krisa* to draw.

39. The king whose enemies number many, always trembles in fear of them, like a pigeon, surrounded by hawks; and in whatsoever path he treads, he is speedily destroyed by them.*

40. One who unseasonably launches† upon war, is speedily crushed by one who fights in season. Witness the example of the crow overpowered by the owl, when at night the former is deprived of its vision.‡

41. Under no circumstance whatever should peace be concluded with one devoid of truth and justice, in as much as owing to his vicious propensities, he will soon act in direct contravention of the treaty, howsoever sacred it may be.§

---

* A king having many foes is sure to be crushed, for it is impossible that one would stand against many. S. W. Jones's rendering is as follows :—"He who trembles among a multitude of foes (like a pegion among eagles), in whatsoever path he treads, is assuredly destroyed even by him with whom he travels on the road." The last portion is superfluous.

† For *Akâlyuktasainyastu* the commentary gives *Akâlyuktastwachirât*, which latter reading we have accepted.

‡ The enmity between the owl and the crow is well known in India, so much so, that it has past into a proverb. In the day-light the crow attacks the owl, that can not bear the sun's rays, while by night when the crows are deprived of their vision the owls attack them. Here is S. W. Jones's translation of the Sloka :—'He who engages unseasonably, is overcome by him who fights at a proper time; as the crow was reduced to weakness by the owl who attacked him by night."

§ S. W. Jones's translation of the Sloka is as follows :—"Never make peace with a man void of truth and justice who, let his treaty be ever so sacred, will soon be led by his improbity to a violation of it."

42. * A king true to his promises,† an *Aryya*,‡ a virtuous prince, an *Anâryyâ*,§ one having many|| brothers, a very powerful sovereign, and one who has come off victorious in many wars,¶ these seven are said to be the parties with whom peace should be concluded.

43. He** that keeps his troth inviolate never acts in contravention of the treaty he concludes. And it is

---

* The author now proceeds to enumerate the parties with whom it would be politic and wise to conclude peace. The principle that under lies his advice seems to be this that, it is better to be in peace with those who are difficult of being overcome and with whom, if war is waged, the chances of success will be limited. The one consideration that should always be like a sacred duty to a sovereign; is the prosperity of the territory over which he rules; and for its sake the monarch should prudently launch upon war or conclude peace. Where there is the least chance of securing any advantage by peace, it should not be discarded. But it would not be politic to risk a war merely in the hope of getting some advantage in case of victory, which in war is very doubtful. The keynote of the author's political creed seems to be :—" Move in the line of least resistance; so crush them who are weaker than yourself, and pay homage to them and cultivate their good-will who are stronger."

† The word in the text is *Satya* which means " true." Hence he who keeps his promises or troth inviolate even at the loss of his very life.

‡ *Aryya* lit means the Hindu and Aryan people as distinguished from the *Anâryyas* or the aboriginies. Hence it has come to signify one faithful to the religion and laws of his country and of noble birth and character.

§ The *Anâryyas* are the people that inhabit a land before it is conquered by an advanced race; and as such, they generally are far below in the scale of civilization than their conquerors. Hence the word has come to signify base fellows of low moral standard whose mode of life is considerably vile.

|| His power lying in the wisdom of his counsels and in the efficiency of his men and munitions.

¶ He that has obtained victory in many wars is sure to conquer ; so it is unwise to proceed hostilely against him .

** The author now proceeds to furnish reasons why peace should be concluded with these parties; he also emphasises the fact that if war be waged against these, defeat will be the inevitable result.

certain that an *Aryya* will never become an *Anáryya* even if he loses his life.*

44. All his subjects take up arms for a virtuous prince when he is assailed.† A virtuous sovereign is invincible owing to his love of his subjects, and to his piety of nature.‡

45. Peace should be made with an *Anáryya*,§ for, even he, meeting an enemy,|| eradicates him like the son of *Renuká*,¶

---

* That is, even if an honorable and high-born, person has to lose his life he will not change his nature and be vile like an *Anàryya* or dishonest fellow. S. W. Jones's translation is this :—

" He who keeps troth inviolate will not alter his nature after a peace, even if he loses his life. A good man most assuredly will not become bad."

† And when he is thus supported by his subjects, the assailant has no chance of vanquishing him ; on the other hand, it is not unlikely that the latter's troops will rebel against him for his trying to annoy a virtuous and beloved monarch.

‡ A virtuous prince naturally cherishes his subjects like his own children. So, they become very loyal to him and look upon him as their father, and do not hesitate to sacrifice their life and property for his sake ; such a prince, so dearly loved by his people, is incapable of suffering defeat. *Dukhochchedyas* lit means 'he who is extirpated with difficulty.' *Prajánurágát* may have another meaning, *viz.*, through the loyalty of his subjects. S. W. Jones's translation is as follows. " For a just man, all the world fight. A just prince prevents calamity by love of his subjects, and of virtue."

§ Vide *Supra*, note to Sloka 43. It may mean here a bad man.

|| The commentary introduces a change in reading by substituting *Sa dwisa pràpya* for *Sampràpya*. The change we have accepted.

¶ *Renukà* is the wife of the sage Jamadagni the mother of Parasuráma,a celebrated Bráhmana-warrior regarded to be the sixth incarnation of Vishnu. The allusion referred to here, is this. King *Kàrtaviryya* went to the hermitage of his father and carried off his cow. But Parasuráma when he returned home, fought with the king and killed the latter. When the king's sons heard of the fate that had overtaken their sire, they became very angry and repairing to the hermitage and finding Jamadagni alone, they shot him dead. When Parasuráma, who was not then at home, returned, he became very much exasperated and

destroying the **Kshatriyas.***

46. Just as a thick cluster of bamboos† surrounded on all sides by thorny plants, cannot be easily eradicated, so a king, supported by his many brothers, cannot be easily subdued.‡

47. When a king, ever so vigilant and assiduous,§ is assaulted by a sovereign stronger than himself, there is no

---

made the dreadful vow of exterminating the Kshatriya race. He succeeded in fulfilling his vow, and is said to have 'rid the earth thrice seven times of the royal race.'

* We can not help remarking here that this Sloka is not very definite about the idea it professes to convey. The example given seems to be out-of-place ; the reasons furnished are not cogent. However we must take it as it is. The meaning seems to be this :—A king should not hate the aborigines of a land but should be in friendly terms with them ; for there may come times when he will profit by such alliance. To cite an example from the Rámáyana, Rámachandra was saved from many dangers through his friendship with the Chandála *Guhaka,* who belonged to the vilest and most abominable caste existing in India. S. W. Jones's translation of the passage is as follows : "Peace should be made even with a bad man, when ruin is impending ; not for the sake of his protection, but from consideration of time."

† *Venu* may also mean 'reeds.'

‡ The last portion of the Sloka has been rendered a little freely. It is superflous to comment that when the several royal brothers live in amity and when there are love and respect binding them to one another, there is scarcely any chance for a foreign invader to subdue such a king. It is intestine discord that has been the ruin of many a kingdom. S. W. Jones's translation is given below .—"As dust when intermixed with thorns cannot be trampled on, so a king, who has many brethren cannot be subdued." The difference in the first portion of the translation might probably have arisen out of a misprint in the scholar's text which probably substitutes *Renu* for *Venu,* the Sanskrit letters (*Ra*) and (*Ba*) resembling one another very closely. *Renu* means 'dust.'

§ All his efforts and perseverance avail him nothing when he is to combat with superior might, and in spite of them, he is sure to be defeated.

safety for him, as there is none for a deer under the claws of a lion, (save in the conclusion of peace).

48. When a powerful sovereign wants to seize a little only (of his enemy's territory or treasure), even then will he kill the latter, like a lion killing an infuriate elephant. Therefore, one desiring his own good, should conclude peace with such an adversary.*

49. There are precedents to prove that it is better not to fight with a stronger foe.† For, never can clouds roll in a direction opposite to that of the wind.‡

50. Prosperity leaves not that king who bows low before a powerful adversary and puts forth his prowess in proper season, even as rivers (that naturally flow downwards) cannot flow upwards.§

---

* The meaning of the author is certainly this, but his expression is not clear. 'When a powerful adversary invades another's kingdom only to get a little of the latter's territory or treasure, it is advisable for the latter to conclude peace. For, like a lion that cannot possibly feed on the entire carcass of the elephant, but kills it all the same, the stronger enemy would kill the weaker one, though he does not want to appropriate the whole of the latter's dominions.' But when the powerful king wants to confiscate the whole kingdom, it is better to die fighting for liberty than to surrender one's self.

† The first part of the Sloka admits of another construction, which is as follows ;—"There is no evidence to justify the statement that a powerful antagonist should always be fought against." This though it does not change the meaning of the passage materially, is still worthy of notice. The construction becomes different as we take *Na* with *Yodhvabyam* or *Asti*. The construction we have given, points out the appropriateness of the example embodied in the next line, which in the other case seems out-of-place.

‡ S. W. Jones's translation is as follows :—"It is not advisable to fight with a hero ; even a cloud cannot go in opposition to the wind." The author enjoins the conclusion of peace with the powerful, for, trying to go against them, a king is blown away like clouds trying to go against the wind.

§ The principle inculcated in the first part of the Sloka is quite apparent. None can deny that it is safe to be in peace with one more

51. Like the son of Jamadagni,* every king who, in all places, at all times and over every enemy, obtains victory in battle, enjoys the earth merely through the prestige of prowess.†

52. He, with whom a king victorious in many battles concludes peace, is sure to bring his foes under his sway in no time, even through the prowess of his new ally.‡

53. Never should an intelligent prince trust his adversary even if he be bound by the ties of a treaty,§ inasmuch

---

powerful than one's self. But at the same time, the weaker of the two must not miss any opportunity in which, by the help of his prowess and energy, he has any chance of crushing his powerful rival. The author means this : 'The comparatively weaker sovereign should remain in apparent peace with others more powerful than himself, watching opportunities to establish his superiority. This is the high road to royal prosperity. *Pratipa* means, contrary, adverse.

* Vide *Supra* note to Sloka 45.

† What the author means is this, that a king who has had the fortune of obtaining a large number of victories, becomes so well-known and feared that, he can enjoy his kingdom even through his mere prestige although at the same time there may be serious diminution of his strength. S. W. Jones gives :—"Like the son of Jamadagni, every king who in all places and at all times, obtains victory in battle, enjoys glory."

‡ What the author means is this. A monarch concluding peace with another victorious in many battles, enjoys much profit, inasmuch as his adversaries knowing his alliance with the ever-victorious king, yield themselves up without any resistance whatever, as they know that that will be unavailing. S. W. Jones's translation of the Sloka is as follows: "He who makes peace with a prince who has been victorious in many wars, assuredly overcomes his own enemies. This king therefore who has been often a conqueror is he with whom peace ought to be made."

§ The anxiety of the author for the safety of the royal personages is so keen that after embodying such an elaborate instruction regarding how to chose parties to a peace, he would not be content; but warns the kings not to place confidence on allies, and not to be lulled in a sense of safety generated ordinarily by a thought of the conclusion of peace. Such thoughts of safety often bring disaster on a king.

as, in the days of yore, Indra while openly declaring a cessation of hostility, slew Vritra (when the latter was thrown out of his guard.)*

54. The enjoyment of royalty† either by a son or by a father, changes his nature considerably,‡ and therefore is it said that the ways of princes are different from those of ordinary people.§

55. When assaulted by a powerful adversary, a sovereign should seek shelter inside his castles, whence he should make vigorous efforts, and for his own liberation, invoke the assistance of another king still more powerful than his assailant.||

---

* The allusion in the last part of the Sloka is obscure. Vritra was a powerful demon who was killed by Indra. But we know nothing of the perfidy of Indra referred to here by the author. The reader is referred to our translation of Srimadvhagavatam, Book VI, where an elaborte description of the battle could be found.

The commentator suggests certain minor changes in readings *viz.*, *Samhita* for *Samdhita* and *Adrohé* for *Adroka*.

† For *Rajyàtnnicha* the commentary substitutes *Rajyàlida*, which latter reading we have accepted.

‡ The first line, lit. translated, would stand thus :—"A low-minded father or a son becomes susceptible of perversion when royalty devolves on them."

§ What the author means seems to be this :—"The filial or paternal affection that is ordinarily found to subsist between a father and a son, could not always be looked for in the royal father or son. Their exalted ranks swing their heads, and their conduct become unnatural. It has been wisely said "Uneasy lies the head that wears the crown" for, it cannot even find solace in the lap of the father or the son. What made the author put in this Sloka here is this that, he has already warned sovereigns not to trust allies ; he also advises them not to trust their own father or their sons, for royalty is like an intoxicating liquor having the power to corrupt the whole inner man.

|| The author now proceeds to describe what should be done by the king who is unfortunate enough to be assailed by an adversary who would not consent to conclude peace. The advice given, as the reader can see, is perfectly politic and none the less diplomatic.

56. Like* a lion attacking an elephant, a monarch forming a right estimate of his own *Utsàhasakti*,† can fall upon another superior to him. This is what the son of Bharadwaja‡ says.

57. A single lion crushes a thousand herds of huge tusked elephants; therefore, working himself up into fury equal to that of a lion, a (weaker) sovereign should fall upon his (powerful) adversary.§

58. ‖Of a sovereign, who exerting himself to the best

---

* The author now points out what is to be done in the absence of a sovereign competent to help the one assailed by a powerful adversary. In this case, the weaker monarch should at first carefully judge his *Utsàhasakti* (Vide below) and then he should fall upon the assailant. That there is chance of success, the author exemplifies by citing the case of the lion slaying the elephant, which latter is much stronger and larger in proportion than the former.

† *Utsàhasakti* we have explained in an earlier note (Vide note to Sloka I, Sec. I). But the meaning the author here wants it to convey is a little wider. It means not only the power of energy, but also agility, quickness and activity which are the qualities incident to an energetic nature. *Utsàhasakti* here refers also to the other *Saktis* of the sovereign, and it includes, the efficiency of the army and the abundance of the sinews of war.

‡ The son of Bharadwaja is the celebrated Drona, the military preceptor of the Kurus and the Pandavas. He was born out of a *Drona* or bucket in which his father preserved the seed which fell at the sight of a celestial nymph called *Ghritàchi*.

§ The author further illustrates what he has said in the previous Sloka. It is not so much the physical strength of his soldiers that gives success to a sovereign, but it is their fierceness engendered by some sense of wrong, that ensures it. Strength is as necessary for success as are agility and quickness and firmness of intention.

‖ The author now proceeds to state that as there is risk in hazarding a battle with a powerful adversary, there is also immense advantage to be derived if in any way victory may be gained. When a king can put down his assailant, his other enemies are naturally inspired with a higher estimation of his strength than they had ere now formed. Thus they are frightened and venture not to oppose him when he attacks

of his powers, can crush his superior with his army,* the other enemies become conquered by his (this display of) prowess only.†

59. Where in war victory is doubtful, (in that case) peace should be concluded even with one equal in every respect;‡ for, as Vrihaspati§ says, "Embark not in any project where success is uncertain."||.

60. For these reasons, the sovereign that desires his prosperity to reach the acme,¶ should conclude peace even with one equal to him in all respects. The clash between two unblaked jars surely becomes destructive of both.**

61. Sometimes†† by resorting to (uncertain) war both the parties reap destruction. Were not Sunda and Upasunda, both‡‡ equally powerful, destroyed by fighting with each other?

---

them; and they fall an easy prey to him. In this way, without the evils of war, he succeeds in extending his empire, which is the highest ambition a sovereign may cherish.

* For *Sasainasya* the commentator gives *Alpasainasya.*

† For *Pratápasidhena* the commentator substitutes *Pratápasidha.*

‡ The sum and substance of the author's advice is embodied in the text of this Sloka, which is very sound and statesman-like.

§ Vide an earlier note.

|| S. W. Jones's translation of the Sloka is as follows:—"Let a king seek peace for the love of religion; in war success is doubtful; but in making peace let no man doubt. So said Vrihaspati."

¶ The commentary suggests some minor changes in the readings which are as follows:—For *Tatsampraviddhé* it reads, *Asampraviddhé* and *Abhibriddhikàma* for *Ativriddhikàma.*

** The last part of the Sloka hints at the result that may be expected when two princes equal in prowess happen to fight with each other. *Apakkayo* means 'not maturely burnt.'

†† The author further illustrates the instruction given in the last part of the preceding sloka, by saying that war between two equally powerful princes is destructive of both.

‡‡ Sunda and Upasunda were two brother demons, the sons of Nikumbha. They got a boon from the Creator that they would not die

62. *Even the most degraded and powerless enemy† should be made peace‡ with, when calamity threatens,§ inasmuch as, attacking at that time, he may cause troubles (to the mind)|| like a drop of water causing pain when it falls on a lacerated limb.¶

---

until they would kill themselves. On the strength of this boon, they grew very oppressive, and Indra had at last to send down a lovely nymph named *Tilottamá*, and while quarrelling for her, they killed each other.

* The text of the Sloka has been considerabty changed by the commentator in order to wring out a plausible meaning. The Sloka specifies the occasion when peace is to be made even with a low-born person. We notice the changes of reading in the following notes.

† The word in the text is *Viheena* for which the commentary gives *Atiheena*. The commentator suggests *Atiheena* to mean 'in very bad circumstances.' This meaning is good. The author has said before that peace should not be made with those who are liable to be easily conquered; but there are occasions when even such an adversary should be made peace with.

‡ For *Susandhopi* the commentary gives *Sandheya.*

§ For *Agatas* the commentator reads *Agaté.*

|| For *Himavat* the commentary suggests *Hi manas.*

¶ For *Kshatam* the commentator gives *Kshaté*. The whole Sloka with the changes of reading noted above would read thus :—

"*Atiheenopi Sandheyas Vyasané ripurágaté,*
Patandunoti hi manas toyavinduriba kshaté."

What the autor means is this:—"Ordinarily peace should not be made with a weak and low-born adversary, as he can be defeated with ease. But when you are threatened by any grave calamity you might conclude peace with him, so that your anxiety on his score will be lessened. Monarchs weaker than yourself though ordinarily can do no harm to you, yet they may afflict you when you will be overwhelmed with a serious catastrophe; just as water though it does not give pain under ordinary circumstances will do so, when you are wounded.

63. If* on such occasions,† the comparatively weak monarch refuses to make peace, the reason is to be found in his mistrust‡ (of the other party). In that case, gaining the former's confidence, the other party should ruthlessly crush him.§

64. Having|| concluded peace with a monarch more powerful than himself, a king exerting carefully to please the former,¶ should so serve him as to gain his confidence.**

---

* As in the previous, so in this Sloka also, various changes in reading have been introduced; and in lieu of noticing the changes separately, we give below the Sloka as it would be when the readings are all amended :—

"Heena chet Sandhi na gachchet tatra heturhisamsayas
Tasya Visramvamâlakshya praharéttatinisthuram."

The author here suggests the measure that should be resorted to, in the case of the weaker king's refusal to make peace. The Sloka as given in the text, may give some meaning, but that would not be suited to the context. Literally rendered it would be this :—'Never desire to make peace with the low, the reason being, there is much uncertainty in such a treaty (and hence it will not last long). Therefore securing their confidence, a king should smite them down, actuated by desire for gain.' Even here, we have to change a little of the text.

† When calamity threatens.

‡ This part of the text seems to be vicious. The commentator has not suggested any emendation. The emendation embodied in the changed reading of the Sloka is our own. *Samsaya* means 'doubt' or 'mistrust'; therefore *Asamsaya* means 'certainty' 'belief' &c. Thus we can make out some sense if we read *Asamsayas.*

§ The last portion contains advice as to how such refractory kings should be dealt with.

|| The author now proceeds to determine the duty of a weaker monarch when he concludes peace with one stronger than himself.

¶ For *Tam pravisya pratâpavan*, the commentary gives *Tamanu pratiyâtnavân*. We have translated the reading given in the commentary. There is another minor change in the next line of the Sloka, which needs no explanation.

** The strain in which the author sings is this :—"When peace is made with a more powerful king, try to gain his confidence by hook or

65. Unsuspected* and ever watchful and always inscrutable in his expressions and designs, he (the weaker king) should speak only those words that would be agreeable.† But he should do what it is his duty to do.‡

66. Through confidence intimacy may be secured; through confidence an act (of selfish interest) may be successfully achieved.§ It was through her confidence on him that the lord of the celestials was able to destroy the fœtus of Diti.||

---

by crook; and then taking advantage of the intimate knowledge that you would gain of his affairs, crush him completely. Whether you make peace with the weaker or the stronger king, always try to crush him, so that you will be relieved of the fetter that peace necessarily puts on you." It seems that the author would not hesitate to inculcate the sacrifice of honesty and good faith at the altar of empire's advancement. We do not know what ultimate good such a policy would bring. What we have written above, would be evident from a perusal of the next Sloka.

* Lit. rendered would be, 'confided upon.'

† If he behaves in this way, not the slightest suspicion would ever fall upon him. Thus he would have every opportunity for serving his own end *viz.*, to slay the stronger king. "*Priya*" words are as "*Jaya*" "*Jiva*," "Victory" "Long live the Emperor" &c.

‡ This, according to our author, is, as the reader is aware, to slay the other superior king. The weak prince should show every possible deference to his superior in words and deeds, but he should never forget his ultimate aim of doing away with him.

§ The author now enumerates the advantages that are gained when confidence of the stronger king is obtained by the weaker. Being a confidante, the latter gradually becomes a favorite; when in that position, it becomes considerably easy to achieve the task (or the duty as the author calls it) he has in his heart *viz.*, the destruction of the former.

|| The last part contains an allusion which has not been explained in the commentary. The reference seems to be to the birth of the *Marutas* or Wind-gods. When *Diti* the mother of the demons was quick with the *Marutas*, Indra, knowing by his *yoga*-prowess that she was going to give birth to a child that would be a formidable opponent of his, entered her womb and there severed the fœtus in seven times seven parts.

67. Having* formed a firm alliance with the principal officers† or the royal son‡ of even a cool-headed§ assailant, the (assailed) king should endeavour to sow dissension|| among the former's party.

68. The¶ assailed sovereign should try to saddle the principal officers of the assailant with accusations, by spending money** lavishly (in bribes) and by (treasonable) letters and documents, in which his identity would be hidden.††

69. Thus‡‡ when an intelligent sovereign succeeds in

---

* The author now suggests other measures by which a powerful assailant may be overthrown. These measurss naturally fall under the expedients of foreign policy enumerated in an earlier note (Vide note to Sloka 51, Sec. IV). The first of these measures is to sow discord (*Veda*) among the enemy, which will considerably reduce their strength and activity. This end, according to the author, is best served, when a conspiracy or league may be formed with one of the principal officers of the assailant's state.

† Such as, the minister, the royal priest, the physician, or the commander-in-chief.

‡ The word is *Yuvaràjâk* or the heir apparent or the crown prince.

§ What the author means seems to be this :—'Even a cool-headed adversary may be overthrown in this way, not speak of him who is rash.'

|| The commentary has introduced an emendation here; it reads *Antaprakopam* for *Tatas prakopam*. The reading given in the text scarcely yields any rational meaning.

¶ The author now suggests the means by which dissension can be effectually sown. The means is this :—'The assailed sovereign after gaining the confidence of the assailant, should try to alienate him from his ministers &c. He should try to bring down the wrath of the sovereign over the officers of state by imputing false charges to them; these charges, he should uphold by producing witnesses secured through bribe, and by forged letters and documents which should be so carefully drawn up as not to cast the slightest suspicion on him.'

** The reading in the text is vicious, and we have adopted that given in the commentary, which is *Arthotsargena.*

†† The commentary suggests another reading *viz.*, *Arthasanghitais*, which means 'the meanings of which are very deep.'

‡‡ The result of sowing distrust among the adversary's party is described in this Sloka. We have, in our translation, been a little free

accusing the principal officers of the assailing monarch, the latter in spite of his being formidable, relegates all activity, inasmuch as he loses confidence over his own people.*

70. Intriguing† with the ministers of the enemy, the assailed king should tone down their efforts to crush him.‡ He should kill his enemy by weaning over his physician,§ or by administering poisonous liquids.||

71. The assailed king should, with all his efforts, try to enkindle the wrath of the monarch whose dominions lie just behind the assailant's.¶ Then, through his agency, he

---

regarding the construction of the original, but this make the translation all the more lucid.

* The last portion of this Sloka would have been unintelligible but for the reading suggested in the commentary, which reads *Yàtyaviswâsam* for *Yasya viswasa*. When a sovereign cannot trust his own people, he can scarcely risk a battle with his enemy.

† What the author says in this Sloka is this :—"The assailed king should form secret alliances with the minister &c. of the assailant, so that they would not fight to the best of their abilities. It was this principle which Lord Clive followed in making Mirzafar apathetic towards the interest of Siraj during the battle of Plassey. As is well-known, Mirzafar during the course of the battle remained with his soldiers as inert as a wall. This conduct was of course due to the league he had formed with Clive previously."

‡ For *Tadavastham Samunnayet* the commentator gives *Taddvamvam Samam nayet*, which indeed is an emendation. The former hardly gives any sense.

§ Who, of course, is able to treacherously kill him without the least difficulty.

|| The last mentioned alternative seems naturally to be connected with the other. But we have faithfully followed the construction of the original.

¶ The text of the Sloka is obscure inspite of the emendations given in the commentary. The translation given above is suited to the text and to the teachings already inculcated by the author. The Sloka would admit of another meaning, which will nearly tally with what is given above, differing in minor details only. That rendering would be something like this :—"The assailed king should fan a quarrel between

should heedfully bring about the assailant's destruction.*

72. The† assailed king should, through spies disguised as astrologers‡ inhabiting the assailant's country§ and possessing all the auspicious marks of inspired Seers, cause predictions to be made before the latter to the effect that dreadful calamities would soon overtake him.

73. Taking‖ into consideration the loss,¶ the expenditure,** the difficulty†† and the destruction‡‡ &c.,

---

the assailant and him who is looked upon with disfavor by this latter. Then, through the agency of the person out of favor, he should crush the enemy." What the author refers to is that expedient of foreign policy which is known as *Veda*. What he means is this that, when a weak monarch is assailed, he cannot but seek external help, and this he should find in the *Parshnigrâha* of the assailant, whose anger against the latter he should try to rouse. Then united with the *Parshnigrâha* he should crush the foe.

* The commentary gives *Pradharsayet* for *Prasàdhayet*; we have accepted the emendation.

† This Sloka suggests a means that would act as a deterrent to the assailant and induce him to adjourn active operations against the assailed, and thus giving the latter time to secure others' help &c. The meaning is this :—"As soon as he is assailed, the king should, by bribing, win over some of the subjects of the assailant's dominions; he should then put them in disguise as venerable astrologers with all the exterior marks of holiness. They should then repair to the assailant's camp who would naturally seek their help in determining the *finale* of the war he is going to wage. Now the disguised astrologers would tell him that the stars are impropitious and forebode great danger. In this way the assailant's spirit will be damped and he will not launch immediately on war.

§ *Naimittikai*—means those who can read the signification of *Nimittas* or omens. Hence an astrologer.

‡ For *Uddesa kritasamvàsai* the commentary reads *Taddesakrita-samvàsai*; and for *Sadhulakshanai* it reads *Siddhalakshanai*.

‖ The author now proceeds to delineate the evil effects of war, which he thinks will dissuade kings from risking wars rashly.

¶ Such as the death of the principal and trustworthy officers.

** The draining of the treasury and the devastation of the crops &c.

†† Such as the inclemency of the weather, &c.

‡‡ Of men and munition.

involved in a war, and weighing seriously its good as well as evil effects, the assailed king would rather do well to willingly * submit to certain hardships, than launch upon war; for war is ever prolific of evil consequences.

74. The body, the wife,† the friends and the wealth of a sovereign may cease to be of any avail to him, within a wink's time, when he launches on war, (in which there is every possible danger of his life).‡ These again are constantly jeopardised in war. Therefore an intelligent§ sovereign should never engage in a war.

75. What king, who is not a fool, would put his friends, his wealth, his kingdom, his fame and even his own life in the craddle of uncertainty by embarking on war? ||

76. When assailed, a sovereign desiring peace, should conclude¶ a firm treaty, by means of conciliation, gifts or or bribery or by sowing dissension** among the enemy, at a time when the latter's array of troops would cross the boundaries of his territory; before this should not betray his peaceful intentions.††

77. Protecting himself and his army effectually and concentrating all his forces, a brave king (when assailed) should

---

* When there is no other alternative except war, it is better to make peace even with certain inconveniences to one's self.

† What the author means is this:—When a king engages in war there is every danger of his being slain, in which case his body, wife, &c. will be of no use to him.

‡ For *Valam* (army) the commentary gives *Kalatram* or wife.

§ The reading in the text is *Vidyàt* which certainly is vicious. The commentator gives nothing. We substitute *Vidwan*.

|| As soon as a king engages in a war, these things become uncertain, and he may lose them any moment, being slain or defeated.

** For *Santapayet* the commentator gives *Samsthapayet* which reading we have accepted.

¶ For these Vide an earlier note (Sloka Sec.

†† In the last part of the translation, we have been a little free for the sake of lucidity.

perform many manœvours to afflict his assailant; then when the latter shall be involved in great dangers, let him make proposals of peace. For it is with hot iron that hot iron becomes fused.*

78. These are the different kinds of peace (and the modes of forming them), which have been enumerated by ancient† and mighty sages. By putting forth his prowess, a ruler of men should subdue his refractory‡ enemy. He should act after having discerned (through his prudence) what is good§ and what is bad.||

Thus ends the ninth Section, the dissertation on peace, in the Nitisara of Kamandakiya.

---

* But if the assailant refuses to make peace, the author says, the assailed should not surrender unconditionally, but to the best of his might and intelligence, fight and annoy his adversary. If at the time of his defeat he wants to make peace, the victor would be exacting in his terms. So, by equal fierceness only, can he conclude a firm treaty. S. W. Jones's translation of the Sloka is as follows.

"Preserving his secret unrevealed and his forces well-united, let a hero march and annoy his enemy, for hot iron may form an union with hot iron; so he by equal fierceness, at a time when his foe is fierce, may conclude a firm peace."

For *Samtápam* in the last line the commentator gives *Sandhànam*, which evidently is the true reading. The commentator quotes Chanakya in support of the author.

"*Nàtaptam Loham, Tapteno, Sandhatte.*"

'Cold iron cannot become fused with hot iron.'

† For *Purvatana* the commentator reads *Purvatama*.

‡ That is, unwilling to make peace.

§ The last portion of the Sloka has been considerably changed in the commentary. For the last two lines, it reads :—

Valát, Tadenam Vinayet Nareswaras
Samikshya Kàryyam Guru Chetaratdwidhà.

We have adopted the reading of the commentary; still the context seems to be vicious.

|| The word is *Guru* which lit: means, 'that which redounds to the credit of the performer.'

SECTION X.

1. POSSESSED by thoughts of revenge, and with hearts burning with anger engendered by the infliction of mutual wrongs, people proceed to fight with one another.*

2. One may also launch upon a war, for the amelioration of his own condition, or when oppressed by his foe,† if the advantages of the soil and the season be in his favor.‡

3. §Usurpation of the kingdom, abduction of females,‖ seizure of provinces and portions of territory,¶ carrying away

---

* The author's meaning, explained by the commentator, seems to be this :—" Wrath and resentment caused by the infliction of injuries, are the chief causes of war."

† What the author means to say is this :—Wrath and resentment are not the only causes that breed war, but a desire for elevating one's position, or excessive oppression by the foe, may also lead one to hazard a war. But there is a provisio in the latter case, which is this that before declaring war, one must see that the advantages of the land and time are in his favor ; if they are not so, he must not go to war, for, in that case defeat will be inevitable.

‡ *Désakàlavalopétas.*—Another meaning of this compound different from what we have embodied above, is suggested by the commentator ; it is this :—Supported by the advantages of the land and the season, and by an army well-equipped with men and munition.

§ This and the following two Slokas should be read together. The author now enumerates all the causes and occasions when war is launched upon by kings and sovereigns.

‖ For example the commentator cites the case of the abduction of Sita by Ravana, (refer to Ramayana).

¶ *Sthana* and *Desa* mean almost the same thing ; in our rendering we follow the commentary strictly.

of vehicles and treasures,* arrogance,† morbid sense of honor,‡ molestation of dominions,§

4. Extinction of erudition,|| destruction of property, violation of laws,¶ prostration of the regal powers, influence of evil destiny, the necessity of helping friends and allies,** disrespectful demeanour, the destruction of friends,††

5. The want of compassion on creatures,‡‡ disaffection of the *Prakriti Mandala*,§§ and common eagerness for possessing the same object, these and many others have been said to be the (prolific) sources of war.

6. The|||| means for extinguishing the wars caused by

---

* *Yána* lit means 'that which carries,' hence conveyance of any kind, including horses, elephants &c., *Dhana* the commentary explains as gems and jewels.

† The word in the text is *Mada*, explained by the commentator to mean, arrogance engendered by the sense of personal courage and heroism !

‡ Like that of Ravana, who thought, "What, shall I, Ravana the king of the three worlds, make over Sita to her husband, out of sheer fear ?"

§ The original word is *Vaisayikipida*—which lit : means 'some disorder in the kingdom.' When caused internally, it breeds civil war. *Visaya* here means 'kingdom.'

|| The original word is *Jnána-vighâta* which the commentary explains to mean the destruction of the literary class, who are instrumental in the cultivation and spread of knowledge.

¶ The commentator explains,—the infringement of the social laws, and customs.

** The word in the text is *Mitrârtham* which the commentary takes to mean, 'for the sake of friends.'

†† The word in the text is *Bandhuvinâsam* ; the author means this, that when an ally is destroyed by his enemy, a king takes up the cause of his ally and avenges his destruction or ruin.

‡‡ The commentary explains :—'To abandon creatures to the mercy of their enemy, having at first given them full assurances of safety.'

§§ *Prakriti Mandala*—refer to an earlier note.

|||| Having enumerated the sources of war, the author now goes an to describe the measures by which such wars may be put an end to. We have rendered this Sloka freely for making the sense clear.

the usurpation of kingdoms, abduction of females and seizure of provinces and portions of territory, have been specified by those skilled in the expedients of policy, to be the relinquishment of the kingdoms, the restoration of the females and the evacuation of the provinces, respectively.*

7. The means for pacifying the wars caused by the violation of laws and the spoliation of porperty† are the restoration of the laws and the restitution of the property, respectively. The means for putting an end to a war caused by the molestation of the kingdom‡ by the foe, is to molest the kingdom of the latter in return.

8. Of wars caused by the carrying away of treasures§ and by the destruction of knowledge and the prostration of the regal powers, the end is reached by the restitution of the things taken, by forgiveness and indifference.||

9. Wars brought about by allies through their oppression and persecution, should be looked upon with indifference¶;

---

* For *Madena* of the text, the commentary gives *Damena*.

† The word in the text would mean lit: "The war arising out of some cause detrimental to the interests and government (of one of the parties concerned)." We have translated this Sloka also freely.

‡ *Visaya* here, as before, means 'kingdom or the dominions of a monarch.'

§ For *Yána* of the text the commentary gives *Dhana*, which we have accepted.

|| The second line in the original bristles with bad readings. The commentary has suggested certain emendations but for which it would have been difficult to make any sense out of the line. For *Shama* it gives *Sama* and for *Tadarthaschangena* gives *Tadarthatyàgena*. Both these emendations we have accepted.

¶ The sense of the author is this :—When the allies of a king bring about a war through their wanton behaviour and policy, he should not join them, but remain indifferent; so that, none of the evils of the war may overtake him. It is always the duty of a sovereign to make common cause with his allies; but not so in this case.

but, for a generous ally* even the very life may be risked.†

10. War caused by the offer of insult should be extinguished by the offer of honor. Conciliation and propitiation are the means for pacifying a war caused by pride and arrogance of one party.

11. A brave king should reach the end of a war caused by the destruction of a friend or an ally,‡ by the application of underhand measures, or by having recourse to incantations and magical spells.§

12. For pacifying a war having for its cause the eagerness for possessing the same object (by two kings), a prudent king should give up that object, provided that his royal prestige does not suffer thereby ||

13. The war caused by the spoliation of a portion of the treasures¶ should not be prosecuted in,** inasmuch as

---

* The commentary gives *Atmavatmitravargârtham* for *Atamvatmitravargétu*.

† But when a generous and faithful ally is involved in a war, a sovereign should offer him aid, even if such conduct may cost him his very life.

‡ When the ally of a king is destroyed, it is prudent for him not to declare open war against his ally's foe, but to apply secretly the expedients of policy and thereby undermine his (the other's) strength.

§ One line of this Sloka is omitted in the text. The line as given by the commentator is this :—

Rahasyena prayogèna Rahasya karanènà va.

Rahasya-prayoga is the use of covert measures. *Rahasyakaran* is the employment of incantations and charms for some malevolent purpose; it includes *Márana*, *Vaseekarana* &c.

|| What the author means is this :—When two kings set their heart upon possessing one and the same object, war becomes inevitable. To avoid such a war, one of the contending sovereigns must withdraw himself; but the withdrawing monarch must be careful that his royal prestige is not prejudiced by his falling back; in that case, he should fight to the last rather than lose his prestige and honor.

¶ For *Dhanàpachàrajàtè* the commentator gives, *Kosàpahárajanitè*. The meaning is not materially changed by this change in reading.

** For *Tannirodham*, the commentary substitutes *Virodham*, which makes the Sloka intelligible.

by carrying on a war, a man may lose all his treasures.*

14. When the party against whom war is waged is numerous,† its end should be reached by sowing dissensions in the enemy's camp, by gift, bribery,‡ reconciliation, tempting offers, and other such expedients of policy.§

15. War caused by the want of showing compassion to creatures, should be extinguished by speaking agreeable and pleasing words to them.|| The means approved of by the pious for pacifying a war brought about by the evil influence of Fate, is to propitiate Fate.¶

16—18. War incident to the rebellion of the dis-

---

* What the author wants to emphasise is this :—When the cause of the war is the seizure of a portion of the treasure, it should not be carried on ; for, if prosecuted in, there is every chance of the rest of the treasure being drained out to meet the expenses of the war ; moreover there is no certainty about success.

† The word in the text is *Màhájana,* which the commentator takes to be equivalent to *Vahujana.*

‡ The first half of this Sloka again has been omitted in the text. The commentary supplies it. It is this :—

Trishnopanyásayuktèna Sàmadànadikènagha.

§ The author's meaning is this :—When war is inevitable with a aumerically strong party, then one should not hazard pitched battles, but try to produce intestine discord among the enemy's troops and generals, and wean over some of them to his side by gift, bribery &c. Thus weakening the odds against him, he will compel them to conclude peace.

|| The commentary quotes another reading for the first part of the Sloka, to be found in the Benares Edition. It is this :—

Bhutànugrahavíchchedajàtsyántam Vrajet vasee.

It means—'One who can control his passions, can reach the end of a war engendered by the failure of showing compassion to creatures.'

¶ When through the influence of Destiny war beeomes inevitable, the means for pacifying it, is the performance of ceremonies calculated to propitiate adverse Fate and redound to the peace and tranquility of the kingdom. These ceremonies are technically called *Sànti*, *Sastyayana* &c.

affected *Mandala*,* is to be pacified by the application of one or the other measures of policy.†

Hostilities‡ have been said, by those who know how to remove them, to be of five kinds:—(1) That produced by a spirit of rivalry,§ (2) that caused by some dispute about lands,‖ (3) that having women at the root,¶ (4) that produced by irresponsible spies,** (5) and that consequent on some fault or transgression on one side.†† The son of *Valgudanti*‡‡ speaks of four kinds of hostilities only, *viz.*, (1) that caused by the invasion of one's territory, (2) that caused

* The word in the text is *Mandalakshova; Mandala* of course here refers to the *Prakriti-mandala,* and *Kshova* means agitation or disturbance; the commentator explains *Mandalakshova* to mean, *Prakritinám Vidroha,* or the rebellion of the subjects.

† The word in original is *Upàya* (Vide note to Sloka 53 Sec V).

‡ Having enumerated the general causes of war and the means for pacifying them, the author now proceeds to define and describe the several kinds of hostilities.

§ The original word in the text is *Sàpatnyam; Sápatnya* is *Satru* or a foe; the commentary explains it to mean—'hostility ordinarily to be found existing among foes.'

‖ *Vástujam*—etymologically means 'originating from some *Vastu* or object; the commentator specifies the objeects to be, land, treasure, territory &c.

¶ The meaning of the author, as explained by the cemmentator is this:—"Hostility having for its cause the intrigue and illicit love of women." This meaning although appropriate is not comprehensive; *Strijam* would mean that kind of hostility that has anything to do with females.

** Here the commentator has introduced a change in the reading; he reads *Chárajams* for *Vájnátam. Chára* means spies scouts or emissaries; hence *cháraja* would mean, hostility, which spies cause to spring up between two parties. The *Charas* bring into notice some or other of the treacheries of one party and thereby sow in the heart of the other, the seeds of enmity.

†† This is the ordinary kind of hostility, which originates from some guilt or transgression.

‡‡ The son of *Valgudanti* is Indra; the reading in the text is *Vahudanti* for which the commentary gives *Valgudanti.*

by something (done by others) prejudicial to the exercise of the regal powers,* (3) that resulting from some dispute about the boundaries† of dominions, (4) and that produced by some disturbance of the *Mandala*.‡

19. Men take cognizance of two kinds of hostilities only *viz.*, (1) that which is hereditary,§ (2) and that bred by some fault or transgression.||

War¶ from which the benefit derived will be a little, that from which it will be nothing, that in which success is dobtful,**

20. That injurious at present,†† that without any future benefit,‡‡ that with one whose strength is unknown, that with a wicked person,§§

---

* The original word is *Sakti Vighàtajam*, which means, originating from the deadening of the *Saktis*; our rendering is a little free.

† The original word is *Bhumyanantarajàtam* which the commentator explains thus. 'Resulting in consequence of the territories bordering on one another.' Hence the meaning we have given above.

‡ *Mandala* referred to here is the *Mandala* of twelve kings (Vide an earlier note). The disturbance of this *Mandala* is equivalent to the disturbances of the balance of power that is ordinarily found to exist in it.

§ That is, handed down by the father to the son; ever constant in the family.

|| This is the common sort of hostility, bred by the offer of insult and offences.

¶ The author now goes on to describe what kinds of wars are to be avoided.

** The text-word lit translated would be, 'the result of which is uncertain.'

†† That is, 'war that alienates friends and disturbs the balance of power existing among the kings of the *Mandala*.' *Tadàtwa* means, for the time being.

‡‡ For the first line of this Sloka, the Benares Edition substitutes,

Ayatyàm cha tadàtwe cha dosa Samyamanam Tathà.

§§ The commentary paraphrases *Dusta* by deceitful; for the sake of a good construction, here we omit to translate one word, and have rendered it in the first half of the 23rd Sloka.

21. That for the sake of others,* that for the sake of a female,† that extending over a considerable length of time,‡ that against illustrious Brahmanas,§ that which is unseasonable,‖ that against one aided by the gods,¶ that with one having allies and friends proud of their prowess,**

22. That beneficial for the present but without any future good, and that from which advantages may be derived in future but not so at present,

23. These are the sixteen kinds of war that should not be launched upon and tenaciously adhered to†† by a prudent

---

* It is rather difficult to ascertain what the author means by *Parârtham* ; ordinarily it would have the meaning we have already embodied in our translation. The sense the writer wants to convey, is that a king should not without much deliberation, take up the cause of others, and even if he does so, he should not prosecute the war for a long time. Another meaning hinted at by the commentator is, 'for the sake of snatching away (or guarding and preserving) the properties of others.' A war for the only object of depriving others of their properties and rights, should not be waged and adhered to.

† Lit translated the text-word would stand thus :—' Having for the cause.' The commentator explains 'war brought about by the eagerness of two monarchs to possess one and the same women.'

‡ A lengthy war should be avoided for at the end it leaves both the parties ruined.

§ It was believed in ancient India that Brahmanas had the power to destroy their enemies by mere words of their mouth. So it is no use waging war against them.

‖ The original word is *Akāla*, which the commentator explains thus :—In seasons of the year that are not fit for declaring war, such as the rainy season &c. Autumn is the best time for declaring war in India.

¶ The word is *Daivayuktena* which according to the commentator is equivalent to *Daivasakti sampannena*. It was believed that the gods fight for men ; or the word may mean 'possessing divine or God-like power, obtained through boons &c'.

** For *Valodhritasakhnena* the commentary gives *Valodhwatasakhena*.

†† The word omitted in the last part of the 20th Sloka, is here rendered. For *Stovita* the commentator gives *Stamvita*.

king. A wise king should wage only such a war, from which advantages may be derived both at present, and in the future.

24. He should ever set his heart upon performing acts beneficial both for the time being and in future. By accomplishing such acts productive of present and future good, a king never brings shame on himself.*

25. A learned man should perform acts conducive to his good both in this and the next world. Tempted by trifling wealth and objects of enjoyment in this world, he should never do any thing detrimental to his welfare in the next.†

26. A man acting in a way prejudicial to his welfare in the next world, should be shunned at a distance.‡ The *Shastras*, bear testimony to the truth of the above proposition. Therefore, one should perform pious and beneficient acts.

27. When an intelligent§ monarch finds his own army happy and efficient|| and that of his foe in the reverse state, then may he launch upon war.

---

* In the original Sloka the verb is omitted. The commentory therefore supplies *Yâti* after *Vâchyatâm*.

† The translation given above is advisedly made free in order to bring out the meaning of the sloka clearly.

‡ The meaning of the another is explained by the commentator thus :—A person acting in a manner detrimental to his spiritual welfare is thought to be bold enough to perpetrate any sin whatever. So every body suspects and is afraid of him.

§ In this and the next two Slokas, the time and the circumstances under which war may be declared, are specified. The original text-word *Matiman* is explained by the commentator thus :—one who can judge what would conduce to his good and what not.

|| The word in the text is *Hrista-pusta*, a compound of *Hrista* (or cheerful, contented &c) and *Pusta* (well supplied with men and munetion, hence, in the most perfect condition).

28. When he finds his own *Prakriti Mandala** swelling in prosperity and very loyal to him,† and that of his enemy in the reverse condition, then may he embark upon war.

29. Territory, allies and wealth, these are the fruits of war‡; when by war the gain of these three is certain, then only may it be hazarded.

30. Wealth§ is desirable,|| allies are more desirable and lastly, acquisition of territory is most desirable. All-round prosperity is the out-come of territorial possessions, and friends and allies come in the train of prosperity.

31. Against an adversary equally prosperous, a prudent king should employ the expedients of policy. Even war against him when carried on agreeably with these sure and infallible measures of policy, is commendable.¶

32. When war has already come** a politic†† king

---

* *Prakritimandala* refers to his numerous subjects.

† That is, enjoying health and plenty and cherishing the greatest respect for their sovereign.

‡ 'By fruits of war' the author probably means this, that a king risking a war, has the chance of acquiring territory, allies, or treasures.

§ The author now institutes a comparison between the three fruits of war and thereby ascertains their relative importance. The acquisition of territory, as the reader sees, is the highest good resulting from war.

|| The word in the text is *Guru* which has numerous meanings; here probably it means—'importance,' but we have for the sake of lucidity rendered it a little freely.

¶ Previously the author has advised that war with one equal in every respeet should be avoided. When it is inevitable, pitched battle should not be fought, nor should war be declared openly. But even if war is to be declared openly and battles fought, then the measures of policy should be adhered to, in order to undermine the streugth of the enemy.

** That is, when inspite of all previous efforts to avoid it, war is declared, then the measures of policy should be had recourse to, for the pacification of the war.

†† The text-word is *Vidwan* explained by the commentator to mean, *Rájanitivisárada* or a sound and a veteran statesman.

should pacify it by means of the expedients of policy. Victory is a thing uncertain; therefore one should not suddenly* fall upon another.†

33. A king‡ desirous of enjoying never-leaving prosperity when assailed by a stronger adversary, should have recourse to the conduct of canes§ and not to that of snakes‖.

34. Having¶ recourse to the conduct of canes, one gradually reaps immeasurable prosperity, whereas one who behaves like a snake brings down destruction on him.

35. A wise king waiting like one mad or intoxicated** for the opportune moment, should when such moments come, suddenly fall upon and devour up†† even an enemy whose strength has not suffered any diminution.‡‡

---

* That is, without mature deliberation.

† The gist of the Sloka, given in the commentary is this:—Victory in war is uncertain, therefore even though there are ample resources for a king to carry on a war, he should pacify it with his best endeavours.

‡ The author here advises what is to be done when the weak monarch is assailed by the strong.

§ The original text-word is *Vaitasee* which means—"cane-like." *Vaitasee Vriti* therefore means this:—Just as a cane when forcibly bend yields easily and offers no resistance, so when assailed by a stronger foe a king should be yielding and pliant.

‖ *Voujangi Vriti*, is the serpentine conduct which is explained thus by Chanakya himself.

Amarsawa Sonitakânkhayà kim padâ Sprisantam dasati Dvijihva.

Serpents would never suffer any injury inflicted on them; on the other hand they bite men without any provocation and without any gain to themselves.

¶ The author now describes the effects of cane-like and serpentine conduct.

** That is, as if quite indifferent and careless of what is going about him. This is merely a feint.

†† That is, crush completely.

‡‡ The primary duty of the weaker of the two, kings when assailed

36. A weak king, should patiently bear the thrashing by the enemy, like a tortoise contracting within its shell when beaten ;* but when the right time comes, the inlelligent king should behave like a crooked serpent.†

37. Judging of the times, a king should be forbearing like the mountain, or furious like fire.‡ Sometimes it is advisable to bear the foe on one's shoulder and speak sweet and flattering words to him.‡

38. A king ingratiating himself into the favor of his foe§ and by conducting himself like one solicitous of his welfare, should know the purposes of the latter, which are ordinarily difficult of being known ; then exerting himself in the right hour, he should catch hold of the locks of the goddesses

---

is to keep his eyes wide open for any opportunity that may occur. Acting in season, he may even crush his powerful enemy. He should seem to be indifferent to the state of affairs around him, only to create a belief in his adversary's mind that he is quite innocent.

* The advise given here is only a continuation of what is embodied in Sloka (33). *Kurma Samkocham* means, the way in which tortoises, contract themselves within their shells when beaten or injured by men or any other animal. So, a king, if he finds himself weaker than this assailant, should behave like a *Kurma* or tortoise, that is, he should take shelter in his castles or seek it with is allies, &c.

† The serpent attacks others with fury and shows no liniency for its victim ; so should the intelligent king, acting in the right moment' should be unrelenting and stern towards his foe, and would not stop until the latter's destruction has been completely achieved.

‡ The forbearance or the fury of the king should depend on the season and his own strength. When hard pressed, it is politic to so humiliate himself as to flatter, and bear on his shoulder his strong adversary ; of course he is not to bear his foe literally on his shoulders, but the phrase is used to signify the depth of humiliation.

§ The commentary differs from the meaning we have given ; it explains *Prasadvritya* to mean, by showing that he is contented with his subjugator.

of prosperity (and drag her over to him) by means of his right hand of deplomacy.*

39. A high-born, truthful, highly powerful, resolute, grateful, forbearing, energetic, greatly munificient and affectionate (towards his subjects) king is said to constitute a foe difficult of being subdued or defeated.

43. Untruthfulness, cruelty, ungratefulness, fearfulness, carelessness, idleness, cheerlessness, useless pride or pique, and extreme procrastination, and addiction to gambling and the company of women—these are the causes that ruin prosperity.†

41. When a prudent king finds these evil habits and faults in his foe, he shall, equipped well with his three *Saktis*, march against the latter for conquering him. Disregarding this a king brings about his own destruction; this is what the sages say.‡

42. Inspired with a (laudable) desire for the amelioration of the condition of his kingdom, and the exaltation of his own position, ever seeing the affairs and movements of the (kings of his) *Mandala* by means of his eyes constituted by the spies,§ a monarch, with all his efforts concentrated, and

---

* Knowing the enemy's plans and mode of working &c. it would be easy for the subdued sovereign to overthrow him. The first part contains a metaphor, divested of which it would mean that he would gain victory and be prosperous.

† The last portion of the Sloka has been rendered a little freely for the sake of lucidity. These habits in a foe render him susceptible of easy victory.

‡ In this Sloka the author specifies the right moment for marching against a foe.

§ *Charas* or spies are said to be the eyes of the king, *i.e.*, through their agency he can know what is going on in every part of his kingdom, or anywhere else. *C.f.* Ramayana. "Inasmuch as kings though remaining far away, come to know of every object and affair through their spies, they are said to have eyes constituted by the spies."

resolute should, betaking to the path of war, exert his utmost in order to win success.

Thus ends the tenth section, the dissertation on war, in the Nitisara of Kamandaka.

——;o:——

SECTION XI.

1. THE expedition which an eminently powerful and energetic* sovereign† whose subjects are loyally attached to him through his many excellent qualities, sets out upon, in order to obtain victory,‡ is called *Yâna* §

2. *Vigrikya, Sandhàya Sambhuya Prasanga* and

* The original word is *Utkristavala viryyasya* which may have also a meaning other than what is given in our translation—*vis*—'He whose army is in an excellent condition and whose prowess is great.'

† The word is '*Vijigisu*,' for an elaborate explanation of which *vide* note to sloka 16th Sec VIII.

‡ The text word is *Jayaisina*, which means—'one ardently desirous of gaining victories.' But to avoid a clumsy construction, we have been a little tree in our translation.

§ *Yâna*—This is one of the six expedients to be had recourse to by a king in foreign politics, the root is *Yâ* 'to go out,' literally meaning setting out.' Hence 'march against an enemy or more strictly any movement of a soveregin with martial intentions. 'The other five expedients are, (1) *Sandha* peace or alliance,'(2) *Vigraha* or war (3) *Sthana* or *Asinaa* halt; (4) *Samsraya* or seeking shelter with olhers; and (5) *Dwaidhibhava* or dnplicity. C. F. *Amorakosa*; "*Sandhirna Bigraho Yanâmashanam dwaidhava 'samsrayas*"; tho two previous chapters contain the disquisitions on peace and war; in this have been described the nature and character of the other expedients.

Upeksha,* these have been said by eminent politicians,† to be the five different kinds of *Yána*.

3. When a sovereign marches forward for crushing his host of enemies by the sheer dint of his prowers, it is called *Vigrihya-yàna*,‡ by the *Acharyyas*§ conversant with the nature of *Yànas*.||

4. When¶ a monarch supported by his own allies,** marches forth for completely crushing the allies of his enemies†† by force, it is said to be *Vigrihya-gamana*.‡‡

---

* As the author subjoins elaborate explanations of these several kinds of *Yàna*, we need not anticipate him.

† The text word is *Neepuna* which lit: means clever, skilful. But here it means, proficient in politics. The reference here is perhaps to *Vrihaspati*, *Sukra* and others.

‡ *Vigrihya* comes from the root *graha* to take, with the prefix *vi*'; it means—to quarrel, fight; *vigraha* or war also comes from it. There are two different kinds of *Vigrihyayána* ; the first of these (as defined in the sloka to which this is a note) has been defined by the commentator thus :—"The expedition for the conquest of bellicose and assaulting foes.' The other has been specified in the next Sloka.

§ *Acharyya*—generally means a teacher or preceptor, hence one who expounds a particular science and teaches it to others. Here it means the preceptors of the military science, such as Drona was.

|| The original word is *Yànajna* which means 'one who knows *yanas* the translation given above is free inorder to bring out the meaning clearly.

¶ This is the second sort of *Vigrihya-yàna* referred to above. In the first kind, the march is against the foe himself, and in the second it is against his allies.

**. For the first half of this Sloka the following line is sometimes substituted :—

"*Atimitrani Sarvani Sumitrai Sarvatas Valàt*" the translation would then stand thus :—"The march for crushing the treacherous allies with the help of the faithful ones &c. "Atimitra" means—those who have trangressed the bonds of alliance and have wandered astray.

†† The word In the original is *Ari-mitra* for an elaborate explanation of which, vide note to sloka 16, Sec VIII.

‡‡ Synonymous with *Vigrihya-Yana-Gamana* being equivalent to *Yána*

5. When after concluding a treaty* with the foe in the rear†, the *Vijigisu*‡ out of a desire for victory,§ advances upon another foe,‖ it is said to be *Sanahàyagâmana*¶.

6. When a monarch, in collusion with** *Sâmantas*†† faithful,‡‡ warlike§§ and powerful, marches against a (com-

---

* The text word is *Parshingrâhena-Satrunà* for an explanation of which vide not to Sloka16, Section VIII.

† The original word is *Sandhâva* which is derived from *Sam* (completely) and *Dhà* to join or unite. *Sandhàya* lit : means in collusion with.

‡ For *Vijigisà* Vide note to Sloka 16 Section VIII.

§ The commentafor explains, " Expecting victory over his foe that is ready for the fight."

‖ For *Yatrâyamam* the commentator substitutes, *Yatyànam*.

¶ *Sandhàya-gamana* lit : means, *Gamana* (Yâna) or march, after a *Sandhi* or treaty or alliance ; hence expedition against a powerful adversary, in collusion with the *Parshuigrahas*. Although the *Parshuigraha's* attitude is hostile, yet for the sake of encountering a stronger foe, alliance must be formed with him.

** *Akeebhuya* lit means, 'being one,' *i.e.* being of the same opinion (commentary). But we take it to mean—' united together.'

†† *Sâmanta* may mean, both a neighbouring or a feudatory prince ; the commentary accepts the former, explaining it as " King's ruling over territories bordering upon those of his own." But *Sàmanta* has another meaning which may be equally appropriate here and that is,—a general entrusted with the command of the army.

‡‡ The original word is *Soucha-yuktai* which lit means—Possessed of *Soucha* or purity." Purity here of course is equivalent to political integrity. Hence, it comes to " faithful."

§§ *Sâmparàyikai* lit means,relating to *Sampàrâya* or war ; hence 'warlike' or strategic. The commentary substitutes *Sâmabayikai* here, which means—Counsellors or ministers. If this emendation be accepted then it would be more appropriate to take *Sâmanta* to mean generals ; the first part of the translation would then stand thus—' When a monarch united with his faithful and powerful generals and counsellors," &c.

mon) foe,* it is called *Sambhuya-gamana.*†

7. When, like Suryya and Hanumat‡ two kings,§ jointly undertake an expedition against a foe that threatens the safety of the *Prakritis* of both, it is called *Sambhuya-yâna.*

8. When after winning over *Sâmantas*‖ of little prowess by the promise of reward in case of success,¶ a king marches against his foes, it is called *Sambhuya gamana.*

---

* The word is *Akatra* or one against whom all should march.

† *Sambhuya-Gamanam* lit means a united advance, there are three kinds of *Sambhuya-Gaman* one is defined here and the others in the next two Slokas.

‡ *Suryya* or the sun is represented in the Hindu Mythology as the son of Kasyapa and Aditi. He runs his daily course through the heavens on a chariort and four with Aruna for his charioteer. Rahu, a demon, is his inveterate enemy who wreaks vengence on him at the time of the solar conjunction and opposition. Hanumant is the great monkey chief who played a prominent part in the Ramayana of Valmiki. He once got the sun under his armpit, for the latter trying rise in the heavens when Hahumant wanted him to remain below the horizon. Thus they were not the best of friends.

The allusion referred to here is obscure; but the commentary explains it. It says that in one occasion *Suryya* and Hanumant, jointly went to war against Rahu who wanted to swallow the sun as also the face of Hanumant which latter he probably mistook for the moon. Then though *Suryya* and Hanumant were not the best of friends, they joined together against their common foe.

§ The commentary, says that the two kings are the *Vijigisu* and the *Ari.* Although their attitude is ordinarily hostile to one another yet when both of them are threatened by a powerful adversary they join together and make a common cause.

‖ *Sámanta* here means 'neighbouring kings.'

¶ For *Falodayam* the commentary gives *Falodaye.* If the former be accepted then the translation would be 'promising them sure success.'

9. When a king, originally marching against a particular foe, afterwards through some contingency, proceeds against another, it is called *Prasanga-Yána.** Hereof king Salya is the example.†

10. When a powerful king marching against a foe has every chance of success,‡ but disregarding them, he proceeds against the latter's friends, it is called *Upekshá-Yána.*§

11. Having‖ had recourse to this *Upekshá-yána*, Dhananjaya slew the dwellers of the Golden city,¶ sparing

---

* *Prasanga* means here, 'some event, or cause.' What the author means is this:—A king sets out on a march against a particular foe, but owing to some incident on his way, he changes his original intention and proceeds against another, although at the time of setting out he had no such intention.

† King Salya, the ruler of the Madras, was the maternal uncle of the Pandavas, being the brother of Madri the second wife of Pandu. As is natural, on the declaration of the great war between the Kurus and the Pandavas, he set out to join Yudhisthira, intending to fight against Duryodhana. But on his way there, he was artfully won over by Duryodhana and subsequently fought on his behalf. He maintained the field for one day during the latter end of the war, but was at last slain by Yudhisthira himself.

‡ The original word is *Abiskritam falam* which lit: means 'sure victory.'

§ *Upekshá* means 'indifference' or 'disregard'. Hence *Upekshá-Yána* is the march undertaken by a king in utter disregard of another decided advantage which he may have turned to profit at his will. What the author means is probably this:—A king at first marches against a certain enemy of his and obtains victory over him, but without making the best of the occasion and completely crushing the foe, he assaults the latter's allies, who all the time thinking him to be satisfied with the victory obtained, were off their guard.

‖ The author now explains *Upekshá-Yána* by an example.

¶ The allusion though obscure, is explained by the commentator thus:—The Nivatakavachas, a clan of powerful demons, were attacked by Dhananjaya the third of the Pandavas. They were defeated and compelled to fly to the nether regions. But Dhananjaya, though then he

the *Nivàtkavachas* who had already been vanquished by him.*

12. Women,† (intoxicating) drinks, hunting, gambling‡ and diverse kinds of scourges of Fate,§ these are called the *Vyasanas*.‖ He who is under the influence of these, is called a *Vyasanin*, and is the right person against whom march with hostile intentions, should be directed.¶

---

was quite competent to slay them, did not do so but left them alone; he at the same time, attacked the dwellers of the Golden city (a celebrated residence of the Danavas,) and completely crushed them having taken them quite unawares.

* After the eleventh sloka, thirteen new slokas are to be found in the commentary, which do not occur in the text before us. These slokas, with some slight differences here and there, correspond to the thirteen slokas of Section X, beginning with the twenty-second. To avoid unnecessary repetition, we do not translate those slokas here again but refer our readers to their translations in Section X.

† Having defined and described the different kinds of *Yàna*, the author here specifies the party against whom *Yána* should be directed.

‡ By the enumeration of the simple names, the author really means to express that, excessive love for women, indulgence in intoxicating liquor, and addiction to gambling, hunting, &c., are culpable, and it is not they (*i.e.* women &c) that are the *Vyasana*, but over-fondness for them that constitutes the *Vyasanas*. According to the commentator, there are four kinds of *Vyasanam*, viz., *Stri-vyasanam* or excessive love for women, *Pànavyasanam*, or over indulgence in intoxicating drinks, *Aksha-vyasanams* or addiction to gambling and *Daibopaghàta vyasanam* or calamities inflicted by Fate.

§ The original word in the text is, *Daibopaghàta* which the commentary explains saying—*Daivi Apat*, or calamities inflicted by Fate, such as Famine, Pestilence &c.

‖ For an elaborate explanation of this word vide note to sloka 8 section VII., and also the Introduction.

¶ For *Sà gamyas* of the text, the commentary reads *Sugamyas*; but there is no necessity for this change; of course a *vyasanin* would be more liable to be defeated by his foes.

13. When* in consequence of the diminution their strengths suffer,† both the *Ari* and the *Vijigisu*‡ stop for a while (either in the beginning or during the progress of a war), it is called *Asana*.§ There are five kinds of *Asanas*.‖

14. When each (of the Ari and the *Vijigisu*) endeavours to thwart the plan of operation of the other, it is called *Vigrihyásana*.¶ When again a king beseiges a foe it is called *Vigrihyásana*.**

15. When†† it becomes impossible to capture a foe secure within the stronghold of his castle‡‡, then a king

---

* The author now goes on to define and describe what is known as *Asana* among the measures of policy.

† The text reads *Sámarthyàvighdtàt* for which the commentary gives *Sámarthyabighàtát*. The former reading means 'when the strength of either has not suffered any diminution.' We have accepted the reading of the commentary.

‡ Vide note to Sloka 16th Section VIII.

§ *Asana*—From *Asa* to halt or stop.—It is one of the modes of policy against an enemy. A lexicographer defines it, 'maintaining a post against an enemy.' It means the halt or stop in active operations against an enemy owing to some cause or other ; or a halt in course of a march against an enemy.

‖ The five kinds of *Asana* are (1) *Vigrihyásanam*, (2) *Sandháyásanam*, (3) *Sambhuyàsanam*, (4) *Prasangásanam* and (5) *Upekshàsanam*.

¶ The original definition of *Vigrihyásana* admits of another rendering *viz*, 'the act of attacking each other is called *Vigrihyásanam*.' The commentary explains this in another way, taking it to be identical with the definition of *Asana* as embodied in the previous sloka.

** The last part of the sloka also admits of a different rendering *viz*. "When a king capturing or crushing a foe, halts for a while, it is called *Vigrihyásanam*." Thus two kinds of *Vigrihyàsanam* have been specified here.

†† The author now mentions the time when *Vigrihyásanam* should be had recourse to.

‡‡ For *Durgasthitas* the commentary gives *Durgagatas* which makes no difference in meaning.

should lay seige to it, cutting off the *Asára** and blockading the road† (by which supporting forces from the country are likely to advance.)

16. Cutting‡ off the *Aṣára* and the communication with the country, reducing the strength of the enemy§ and disuniting his *Prakritis*,‖ a monarch should gradually bring him (his foe) under subjugation.

---

* *Asàra* is the combined force of the allies of the beseiged. Vide note to Sloka 16th Section VIII; the author says that the forces sent by the allies of the beseiged foe, should be smitten down and crushed.

† The original word is *Veevadha*. For *Asàraveevadhán* of the text the commentary reads *Asàraveevadhou* which seems to be gramatically correct.

‡ The another now points out the results of the interception of the helping troops and the prohibition of all egress from and ingress to the beseiged fort. *Cutting off the Asara* is intended to mean the complete discomfiture of the troops that come to help the beseiged king.

§ The original word is *Pràkshina-yava-saindhavam*—a compound of *Prakshinas* (utterly weakened) *Yava* and *Saindhava*. Now there is some difficulty about the meaning of the last two Sanskrit words. The commentary takes *Yava* to denote *Vega* or fleetness and *Saindhava* to mean 'horses of the Sindhu breed.' It therefore gives the compound the meaning we have embodied in the translation, taking horses to signify the whole army. But *Yava* (as spelled in the text) cannot mean *Vega*; it means, 'barley-corn.' *Saindhava* can also have a meaning other than horses of the Sindhu breed, viz., a kind of rock salt. In the age of the author there was no imported salt. It was this rock-salt which the people of India used in their meals. These considerations lead us to ascribe a totally different meaning to the word, which is—'When *Yava* or barely-corn, the staple good of the garrison, and the stock of salt are greatly reduced.' This meaning is all the more appropriate, because when food runs short in a garrison, there is no other course open to it but unconditional surrender. In accepting this meaning it must not also be forgotten that all egress and ingress have been cut off.

‖ For *Vigrihyamāna Prakritim*, the commentary substitutes, *Vibhajyamāna Prakritim* which means 'dividing the main stays of the kingdom by dissensions &c.'

17. When the *Ari* and the *Vijigisu* both suffering loss in a war, stop it by the conclusion of an armistice,* it is called *Sandháyâsanam.*†

18. Even Rāvana‡ the crusher of his foes, had recourse to the *Sandháyâsanam*, offering Brahmā§ as his hostage, when he had to fight with the Nivātakavachas.‖

19. When a monarch, thinking the *Udásina* and the *Madhyama*¶ to be equal to himself in respect of power, awaits, mustering all his forces,** ready for an attack from either of them, it is called *Sambhuyâsanam.*

20. If the *Uvayâri*†† desires the destruction of the *Ari* and the *Vijigisu*, being himself more powerful than they

---

* For *Sandhàya Yadavasthánam* the commentator gives, *Sandhàya Samavasthànam.*

† *Sandhàyásanam* etymologically means 'to stay a while, by concluding a peace.'

‡ Vide an earlier note and our translation of the Ramayana.

§ Brahman, in the Hindu mythologies, (and not in the Philosophies) is described as the creator, the first deity of the sacred Trinity. He is described to be very merciful and the only god who awards boons giving their receiver the least trouble. It was from Brahma (who is also called the grandfather of the gods) that Rávana obtained the boon of conditional immortality.

‖ The Nivatakavachas were a very poweful clan of demons always delighting in harassing the gods. They were at last extirpated by Kunti's son Arjuna one of the central figures of the great epic Mahabharata.

The allussion here is not so clear and well-known. What the commentary gives is put in English for the information of the readers. There was once a war between Rávana and the Nivatakavachas, in which the former was badly attacked and defeated by the latter. Rávana then concluded an armistice by offering Brahma, his family-preceptor, as a hostage.

¶ Vide note to Sloka 16th Section VIII.

** For *Sammuthánam* the commentary reads *Vyavasthánam* which is more intelligible and appropriate.

†† This is another name for the *Madhyama* who is so-called in consequence of his hostile attitude to both the *Ari* and *Vijigisu.*

both, he should be withstood by what is known as *Sangha-dharman.**

21. When a monarch desirous of going to a certain place (or person), halts through some contingency or other, at a place different from where he intended to go at first, it is called *Prasangâsana* by those versed in the science of Polity.†

22. The (apparent) indifferent attitude of a king before an enemy more powerful than himself, is called *Upekshàsana.*‡ Indra§ treated with indifference the carrying off of the *Pârijâta*|| from him.

---

* *Sanghadharman*—means 'to do an act in conjunction with others.' *Sangha* means 'together.' The commentary defines it—*Vahubhir Milítwa ekakâryyakaranam* or 'the performance of an act by many united together.' The reading given above is suggested by the commentary in lieu of *Tatwadharman* which can have no possible meaning in this connection. There is another emendation introduced by the commentary in this part of the sloka which is *Sambhuyainam* for *Sambhuyena.*

† What the author means appears to be this :—A king marches out with a view to join one of his allies, or to crush one of his foes. But through some contingency or other, he is compelled to stop at a place quite different from where he intended to go. As this halt or stoppage *(Asana)* is the result of some contingency, it is called *Prasaugâsana.*

‡ *Upekshâsana* means halt (or more properly here, want of active movements) seemingly the result of indifference, *i. e.* when a king finds that his foe is stronger than himself, he assumes an indifferent attitude, which in some measure goes to deter the latter whose confidence in his own efficiency receives a shaking.

§ Vide an earlier note. Indra and Upendra (Krishna) were said to be the two sons of the Rishi Kasyapa begotten upon Aditi. Upendra was more powerful than Indra.

|| *Pârijâta* is the name of one of the five trees obtained by the churning of the ocean. It was appropriated by Indra. The *Pârijâta* flower is the most fragant and charming and is always described to be the favorite of the celestial damsels who love to put them on their hair-knots, and to wear garlands made of them.

The allusion here is as follows :—On one occasion Nárada the celestial sage, when wandering through the heavens was honored by Indra with

23. When again a king, through some other cause* being led to treat with indifference certain acts, remains inactive like Rukmin† (or does not have recourse to vigorous measures) it is called *Upekshâsana.*‡

24. Hemmed§ in between two powerful enemies, a king

---

a garland of the *Pàrijâta* flowers. This garland he gave to Krishna who in his turn handed it over to Rukmini his beloved wife who was then near him. Then Narada who was very fond of brewing quarrels, went to Satyabhama another wife of Krishna, and related the incident to her, leaving her to conclude that she had been shamefully neglected by her husband who instead of giving the garland of *Pârijàta* to her, had given it to her rival. When Krishna came to her, she repremanded and chided him and lamented piteously; whereupon Krishna promised to fetch for her the *Párijâta* tree itself from heaven. He accordingly asked for it from Indra the lord of heaven who refused to part with it. A battle was thereupon fought and afterwards through the mediation of other gods, the *Pârijâta* tree was allowed to be transplanted into the garden of Satyabhama, and Indra was advised to treat that act of Krishna with indifference.

* Such as, affection, love, &c. Here the emendation given in the commentary must be accepted, which is *Anyena* for *Anyaistu.*

† Rukmin was the son of Bhishmaka and brother of Rukmini one of the favorite wives of Krishna. Rukmini was at first betrothed by her father to Sisupala, but she secretly loved Krishna, and on the day of her marriage, according to a preconcerted plan, was snatched away by Krishna. Her brother Rukmin who was engaged to protect her, did offer no resistance (the account here varies) but suffered her to be taken away, thus assuming an indifferent attitude for the love of her sister, although he might have successfully opposed Krishna.

‡ The translation given above has been advisedly made free for lucidity's sake.

§ Having described what is known as *Asana*, the author proceeds to define *Dvaidhibháva*. It is also a mode of foreign policy defined in two different manners (a) double dealing or duplicity, keeping apparently friendly relations simultaneously with two adversaries; (b) dividing one's army and encountering a superior enemy in detachments; harassing the enemy by attacking them in small bands, something like the present guerrilla mode of fighting.

surrendering himself (to both) only in words* should like the crow's eye-ball,† carry on a double dealing without being detected by either of them.‡

25. (Of the two powerful foes) the one who is (dangerously) at hand,§ should be put off assiduously with empty promises.‖ But if both of them assail him simultaneously, a king should surrender himself to the stronger of the two.¶

26. When** again both of them, seeing through his

---

* What the author means is this: The assailed king should by all sorts of flattering speech make the assailant believe that he is entirely under his command. But really he should entertain no feelings of friendship for the latter. Long-sounding and empty words should be used to beguile the assailant only for the time being.

† The allusion referred to here is founded on a very curious belief current in this part of the world. But how far this beleif is correct, we can not say. It is supposed that the crow has only one eye ball (*c. f.* such words as *Ekadristi*, *Ekakshi*) which it moves as occasion requires from one socket to another. From this supposition a maxim of Nyáya-philosophy has obtained currency, which is applied to a word or phrase which though used only once in a sentence may if occasion requires serve two purposes. Naturalists should do well to ascertain whether or not there is any truth in the above belief.

‡ The author means to say that when a king is simultaneously assailed by two powerful adversaries, he should not surrender himself to either or exasperate either, but carry on a double dealing keeping apparently friendly relations with both; of course he should be careful as not be detected in his duplicity prematurely.

§ For *Sannikristaram* some read *Sanmikristamarim*.

‖ The meaning of the author, as explained by the commentator is this: 'When a foe threatens immediate attack, he should be put off with promises of whatever he wishes the assailed to do. But those promises should never be fulfilled, as they are mere dodges to gain time.

¶ The last portion lit: translated would be 'should serve the stronger of the two.'

** This Sloka embodies the advice as to what should he done when the duplicity of a king is seen through by his foes. The first thing he should do then is to befriend a sovereign or sovereigns inimical to his foes. But in the absence of such parties, he should surrender himself to the stronger of the two.

double-dealing and becoming convinced of his duplicity, reject all overtures of peace, then he (the assailed king) should go over to (befriend) the enemies of them both; or if that is not possible, should seek shelter with the stronger of the two (as before).*

27. *Daidhibhàva*† is of two kinds, *Swatantra* and *Paratantra*.‡ What has been described above is *Swatantra Daidhibháva*; *Paratantra Daidhibháva* is of him who receives remuneration from two kings inimical to each other.§

28. When|| a king is assailed¶ by a very powerful**

* The translation is free. The last portion of the Sloka is differently put in some texts, which does not materially affect the sense.

† For an explanation of this word refer to an earlier note. '*Daidha*' means 'double' and *bhàva* the state or condition.

‡ The meaning of the author is not so clear. The kinds of *Daidhibháva* mentioned by him do not tally with the two classes explained by us in a previous note; the commentator offers some explanation which also is not comprehensive. We suggest below what seems best to us. *Swatantra* means independent. Hence *Swatantra daidhibhàva* would mean the duplicity of a king who for effecting his own safety has recourse to it, not under anybody's instructions but out of his free and independent will. He has not been deputed by others to play a double game and to ascertain the purposes of both the assailing monarchs. *Paratantra* means 'dependent.' Hence this kind of *Daidhibháva* is the double dealing that spies practice being commissioned by their employer. The double game which servants in obedience to the orders of their masters play, is *Paratantra daidhibhâva*, which does not bring any direct personal benefit to them. The commentary explains:—'the *Daidhibháva* of an independent person is *Swatantra* and that of a dependant person is *Paratantra*.

§ For *Uvayachetana* of the text which is quite unintelligeible in this context, the commentary gives *Uvayavetana* which we cannot but accept.

|| The author now proceeds to describe another mode of policy which is known as *Samsraya* or seeking protection at others' hand.

¶ The text word rendered literally would be, 'in the course of being exterminated or destroyed.'

** The commentary explains, '*Upachita Saktimata*' *i. e.* one possessing *Saktis* swelled to the highest degree.

enemy and has no other means or measure open to him to avert the calamity, then and then only,* should he seek protection from one who comes from a noble family and is truthful, generous and highly powerful.†

29. To assume worshipful attitude‡ at the sight of his protector, to be always at one with his protector in his thoughts and purposes§, to do alll his works for him and to be obedient to him|| these are said to be the duties of one who seeks shelter with another.

A. ¶Being attached to his protector as if to his own preceptor,** the protected should pass some time†† with the

---

* The stress put on this part of the sentence is advised; for, as the commentator points out, when there is any other means whatsoever for self-preservation available to a king he should not throw himself at the mercy of other kings, inasmuch as *"Mahâdosahi visistavalasamàgma Râjnâm" i. e.* for kings to implore highly powerful rivals (for protection) is the source of great evils.

† This king must be more powerful than the assailant.

‡ Such as bows, obeisance, salamas, &c.

§ *Tatbhàvabhávita* lit: means to be inspired with his thoughts and sentiments. Whatever the protector would think or intend to do, must also occupy for the time being the attention and thought of the protected. In this way the latter would be able to ingratiate himself into the favor of his protector, who if satisfied with him might give him his independence back.

|| *Prasarayita* lit: means, "courteous and polite in behaviour," or "bearing affection or love for the protector." The obedience must be one of love and not of fear.

¶ Some twenty-two Slokas have been omitted here in the printed book; of these fifteen come within the 11th Section of the Manuscript copy and seven fall in the next. The Slokas marked A. B. &c. are the wanting Slokas.

** That is, for the time being he should behave towards his protector as if he were his spiritual preceptor, who is the person deserving the highest esteem and respect at the hand of the *Mantra Sisyas* or "pupils of sacred initiation."

†† That is, live for some time with the protector, just as a Brahmana

former like one very meek and gentle.* Then gaining strength† by such association, he should once more become independent.

B. Not‡ to remain without a refuge,§ a king should seek it with the peace-breaking|| assailant by surrendering to him his army or his treasury or his lands or the products of the lands.¶

---

lives with his preceptor for a time after his investiture with the sacred thread.

* The commentator says that the meekness and humility should only be outward and not the outcome of any real affection or feeling. We do not agree with the commentator here, in as much as affection and love have been said to be the feeling that the protected should entertain towards the protector.

† The text word is "*Paripurna*" which lit: means "filled to the highest degree." Here as the commentator states, it means "swelling with strength and powers." What the author means is that while living under the protection of a stronger sovereign, the army and resources of the protected would gain strength and become numerous everyday; for meanwhile no strain would be put on them. Some substitute *Purnasakti* for *Paripurna*; this reading makes the text clear as day-light.

‡ The author now lays down the course of action to be adopted in case of the absence of a protector possessed of the qualifications enumerated by him hereinbefore.

§ The word is *Anapàsraya*; *Apàsraya* means 'without a refuge.' Hence *Anapàsraya* means 'not without a refuge.' The author wants to say that a monarch threatened by a powerful adversary should not remain without a protector and in the absence of a good one he should choose the very assailant. The advisability of the principle is apparent for, a king whose weakness is once betrayed, becomes like a piece of meat which all hawks pounce upon.

|| The original word is *Visandhim i. e.* one who violates the provisions of a peace or treaty, and acts in contravention of it. Some read *Visandhis* here.

¶ According to the commentator the "products of the land" are the rents and revenues flowing into the imperial exchequer. But *Bhumisambhava* certainly has a wider significance.

C. Involved in difficulties,* all these things (army treasury, lands, products of lands, &c.,) should be given up simultaneously for the preservation of the self.† For, living, there is every chance of regaining the kingdom‡ at the end, like king Yudhisthira.§

D. 'To a living man joy shall come, even if it be after the lapse of a century,' is a blessed verse said to be very commonly known.||

E. For the sake of one's family some particular person

---

* The Sanskrit word is *Arta* which means "distressed." The commentator takes it to mean, 'oppressed and assailed'; the difficulties must be such as to threaten the safety of life and limb.

† It will be pertinent to note here that the principle of self-preservation was not only the key note of Hindu polity but also of Philosophy Numerous saws and sayings can be quoted in support. Even the author's preceptor the celebrated Chanakya has said so in one of his slokas. *c. f.* 'Always preserve yourself in preference to your wives and wealth.' The principle is not the outcome of abject selfishness but of the belief (which is right) that self is the source all happiness, spiritual and earthly, and is instrumental in achieving religious merit.

‡ The word in the original is *Vasundharâ* which means lit: that which contains treasures. It is a special epithet of the earth; it was given to her as treasures were supposed to remain within her bowels. Here of course it means "a kingdom swelling with prosperity."

§ King Yudhisthira, the eldest son of Pandu, after having suffered numerous wrongs and injuries at the hands of his cousins, the Kouravas who for a time deprived him of his lawful inheritance to the throne, obtained it back after a severe battle extending over eighteen days. The reader is referred to our translation of the Mahabharata. For the last line of the sloka the following is substituted by the commentator "*Yudhisthira Jigàyàdou Punarjiban Vasundharàm.*"

|| What the author says is this that there is a verse full of significance known to very body that if a man lives he is sure to have joy even after the lapse of a hundred years. The author wants to impress the fact that the lot of man cannot be uniformly miserable or happy. This existence has aptly been called checquered. Weal and woe come to man as if revoling on a wheel. A man surviving the misries and sufferings of life is sure to reap joy at last. Hence the necessity of self-preservation.

should be forsaken, for the sake of his village the family should be forsaken, for the sake of the country his village should be forsaken and lastly (if need be) the earth should be forsaken after due deliberatian (for self-preservation).*

F. †When his own strength increases or when some calamity‡ threatens his foe (the assailant with whom he has sought shelter), the (protected) king should fall npon hte former, or acquiring power, he should smite his foe down by means of *saiuhee vritti*.§

G. Never rush into an union either with a stronger or a weaker rival king without sufficient cause or reason; for in such union there is danger of losing men, money and munitions and of being treacherously treated.||

---

* The author now institutes a comparison among the several interests that is likely to clash against one another. If the king finds that his family will suffer in consequence of his friendship to a certain individual, he should forsake him. And in this way he should even give up his territory in the interests of his self-preservation. This last measure of course must be had recourse to after cool and mature deliberation. Here also, as before, the refrain is that, self-preservation is the best of all virtues.

† The author now describes how the shelter-seeking king is to effect his liberation. After a period of servility during which he should try to strengthen his position and watch opportunities, he should fall suddenly upon his protector and crush him.

‡ The commentator takes *Vyasana* to mean here 'excessive fondness for wine and women and gambling &c. but we take it to mean '*Vipat* or calamity.'

§ *Sainhee* means etymologically 'pertaining to the lion' (*Sinha*) or lion-like and *vritti* means conduct. The lion before taking the leap upon his prey musters all strength and strains all his nerves. So a king before falling upon his foe should gather all his strength and leave no stone unturned to crown his effort with success. Earnest endeavour ever meets with the desired result. The last part admits of another construction which is as follows, "Acquiring strength by *Sinhavritti* a king should assail his enemy."

|| The rendering is free. The author advises against hasty unions, pointing out the dangers thereof.

H. Even going to a father for union, a king should not believe him ! The wicked when the good confide on them, almost always play these latter false.*

I. These are the six *gunas* or the modes of foreign policy.† But some say that there are only two *Gunas*, *Yâna* and *Asana* falling within the category of *Vigraha*, and the rest *(Daidhibhâva* and *Asraya)* being other forms of *Sandhi* only.

J. In as much as the assailant king marches *(Yâna)* and halts (*Asana*) in course of a war *(Vigraha)*, accordingly *Yâna* and *Asana* have been described by the wise as forms of *Vigraha*.‡

K. And in as much as, without the conclusion of some sort of a peace, double-dealing *(Daidhibhâva)* and shelter-seeking *(Samsraya)* are not possible, therefore these two also are said by the wise to be merely other forms of peace.§

L. Whatever is done after the conclusion of some sort of a peace is surely to be reckoned as a form of peace *(Sandhi)*; and whatever is done after the declaration of a war is certainly to be considered as a part of the war *(Vigraha)*.

M. Those who hold that there are only two *Gunas* or modes of foreign policy, specify them to be only *Sandhi* (peace) and *Vigraha* (war). But others again hold that there

---

* The last part lit: would be, 'when the good come to confide on the wicked they generally injure the former.

† The author concludes. The six modes are, *Sandhi, Vigraha, Yâna, Asana, Daidhibhâva* and *Asraya*.

‡ *Yàna* and *Asana* are strickly speaking operations included in wars. It is in a war that a king marches, halts or lays seige to his enemy's territories.

§ Unless there is some kind of a union between two parties, one cannot play the other false, nor can one seek refuge from the other. It is only when mutual agreement exists that they can have any dealing between them.

are three *Gunas* namely the above two (*Sandhi* and *Vigraha*) and *Samsraya*.*

N. When oppressed by a powerful assailant, a king is obliged to seek protection from another more powerful than the former, it is called *Samsraya*; the other forms of union are said to be *Sandhi* (Peace).† Thus said Vrihaspati.

O. Strictly speaking there is only one *guna, viz.*, *Vigraha* (war). *Sandhi* (Peace) and the others come out of it; and therefore these latter are only the results of the former (*Vigraha*). Modified according to circumstances (and stage) the one *guna Vigraha* multiplies itself into the six *gunas*. This is the opinion of our own preceptor.‡

P. A king,§ conversant with the nature of the six *gunas*,|| possessing spies¶ and versed in consulta-

---

* This latter class of politicians do not include *Samsraya* or shelter-seeking in *Sandhi*, hence the difference.

† Vrihaspati the preceptor of the celestials (Vide note to Sloka 8 Section I.) draws a distinction between *Sandhi* and *Samsraya*. That form of union, if it may be called an union at all, that a weak king is compelled to effect with a stronger one, inorder to save himself from the persecution of a strong foe, is called *Samsraya*; whereas *Sandhi* is concluded between *two* contending parties, the assailed and the assailant.

‡ As the reader is aware, the author's, preceptor is Chanakya. The fifteen Slokas that have been said to be included within the 11th Section of the Manuscript copy end here. In the Manuscript the 12th Section begins with the next Sloka.

§ Having finished his disquisition on the six modes of foreign policy, the author now proceeds to impress the necessity of holding consultation and counsel. As in these days, so in the past, counsels used to be held before any king proceeded to do anything. It was after mature deliberation that any project was taken in hand.

|| The original word lit. rendered would be, one whose understanding has comprehended aright the nature of the six *gunas*, and who has no doubt left about their working, employment &c.

¶ The text-word is *Guraprachárabân*, *Gurahpracharas* are they whose movements (*Prachára*) are secret and undetected by others. Hence the word has come to mean 'Secret emissaries, and spies.' These

tion* should hold counsel regarding some secret plan or affair with his ministers skilful in offering advice.

Q. A king conversant with the nature of counsel† reaps prosperity easily, and one of a contrary nature even if he be independent is put down by his learned (rivals).‡

R. Just as Rakshasas destroy a sacrifice in which the *mantras* (sacred hymns) used are attended with flaws, so his enemies destroy a king from all sides whose *mantra* (counsels) is bad.§ Therefore one should be very careful about his counsels.

S. Counsel about state affairs should be held with trustworthy|| as well as learned¶ persons. But a trustworthy fool, so also a learned but untrustworthy person should be avoided.

T. (In matters of counsel) a king should not deviate from the *Shastra*-approved path, by which pious men of the past, whose actions were ever crowned with success and who ever trod the road of rectitude, travelled to success.

---

will keep the king informed of the state of affairs in his own as well as in his enemies' dominions, thus helping considerably in arriving at right conclusions in his deliberations.

* *Mantrajna* means one who know *Mantra*; this last word has been explained elaborately by the commentator. Any secret consultation about the interests of the kingdom is called *Mantra*.

† The text word means lit: "one who knows how to hold consultations and how to profit by them."

‡ The original word is *Vidwatvi* which means "by the learned." For *Avabhuyate* some read *Avadhuyate*.

§ The Rakshasas being evil doers are as a race inimical to the performance and spread of religious acts. They watch opportunities for doing evil and whenever there is the least flaw in the *Mantras*, &c. of a sacrifice, they speedily destroy it. There is a pun upon the two meanings of the word *Mantra* here.

|| *Apta* may also mean, a relative or one in some way related to the king. This meaning is also applicable here.

¶ By 'learned,' the commentary means 'sound politicians.'

U. A monarch, who disregarding the rules contained in the *Shastras** suddenly† falls upon a foe, never returns without feeling the sharp edge of this latter's sword.‡

V. The power of good counsel is superior to powers of energy and dignity.§ Witness the case of Kâvya|| who though possessed of dignity and energy, was foiled by the priest of the celestials¶ by means of his power of counsel.

---

* The phrase in the orignal lit: rendered would be—going astray from the foot-prints impressed in the Shastras; this indeed is metaphorical.

† That is, without mature deliberation.

‡ That is, 'feels to his great pain the sword-cuts of the enemy which means nothing short of death.' There are several changes of reading in this Sloka, which for their minority we omit to note.

§ The author now lays stress on the superiority of the *Mantra Sakti* over the other two *Saktis, viz., Prabhu* and *Utsàha*. *Prabháva* is explained by the commentator to mean 'power originating from the possession of an efficient army and a solvent treasury.

|| Kavya is another name of Sukra who was the preceptor of the Asuras (Vide note to Sloka 8 Section I).

¶ The allusion referred to is as follows :—In their long warfare with the Asuras, the gods were oftentimes worsted and rendered quite helpless. But such of the Demons as would be slain in battle were restored to life by Sukra, their preceptor, by means of his *mantras* or mystic charms, which he alone possessed. Seeing this, the preceptor of the gods resolved to secure this charm if possible, and so he sent his own son Kacha to Sukra in order that he might learn it from him by becoming his pupil. So Kacha went to Sukra; but the demons fearing lest he should master the lore, murdered him and mixed his ashes with Sukru's beverage and offered him as a drink to their preceptor. Kacha was drank in by Sukra. But at the intercession of his daughter Devayani, who had fallen in love with the youth, Sukra promised to restore Kacha to to life. He instructed Kacha in the mystic charm, when he was within his bowels and then ordered him to come out. Kacha accordingly came out tearing open the abdomen of his preceptor who died in consequence. But now Kacha restored him to life by means of the same charm he had learned from him. Kacha then returned to the gods and used his learning in their benefit. Thus Vrihaspati by his power of counsel got the better of Sukra. The last portion of the history as given

30. A lion untaught in the lessons of polity kills the elephant only through his superior physical strength.* And an intelligent and learned† man succeeds even in taming and subjugating hundreds of such lions.‡

31. An act maturely deliberated upon by learned men, who can read§ a coming event (from a distance) and who always reap success by the employment of commendable means, can never fail to bear fruit.

32. By proper means,‖ a king should desire to obtain his ends; considering (the advantages or otherwise of) the times, he should fall upon an enemy.¶ Over-much reliance on valour and energy** often-times becomes the source of repentance.††

---

by the commentator is not to be found in the mythologies. It is said that when Kacha was restored to life he resisted the advances of Devayani, Sukra's daughter, who thereupon cursed him saying that the charm he had learnt would be powerless at his hands.

* The first of the sentences is intended to impress upon the readers mind the strength and brute force of a lion. These are of no avail against the cultured intelligence and cleverness of a man who foils them by means of his schemes &c.

† That is, one who is possessed of *Mantra Sakti*.

‡ The first part of the sloka bristles with bad readings, for which the commentary reads,

"*Asikshitanayas Singha Hantivam Kevalam Valát,*"

This reading we have accepted.

§ The word in the text is "who can see."

‖ The original word is *Upáya* which means, the measures of policy to be used against a foe, viz conciliation &c (vide an earlier note).

¶ The commentator explains, 'should march against him.'

** The original phrase lit: translated would be, "one who knows the taste of only one liquor viz *Vikrama* or power."

†† What the author means to say is, that mere power, energy or valour, whatever it might be called, is not sufficient to secure success in any undertaking. The advantages of time and policy cannot safely be overlooked; those who overlook them and think that unaided *Vikrama* will give them success, and act accordingly, reap only grief and disappointment for their pains.

33. A distinction must always be made between what is capable of being done and what is not so, by the light of a serene intelligence. The butting of a elephant against a rock, results only in the breaking of its tusks.*

34. What† fruit save distress can there be in store for him who undertakes an impracticable act? What mouthful, indeed, can he expect to get, who tries to snatch a mouthful from (empty) space?‡

35. Fall not on fire even like (foolish) insects! Touch only that which can be touched (with safety)! What indeed does an insect falling on fire reap but (thorough) burning!

36. The dangers attending the acts of one endeavouring, out of foolishness, to get things difficult to obtain, are sure to bring sorrow in their train.§

37. By the employment of knowledge proportionate to the thing to be known,|| a person whose steps are well-calculated,¶ attains to the pitch of prosperity as high as the highest summit of a mountain.

---

* What the anthor means is this that before undertaking a thing a king should judge whether it is at all capable of being done or not. To try to do an act incapable of being done, is as useless and attended with danger, as the butting of an elephant with its tusks against a rock.

† This Sloka virtually consists of three Slokas, its two lines being, the first and last of a series of Slokas; four lines have been omitted after the first line here. We translate the three Slokas in order to preserve the continuity of thought; the numbers of the Slokas change accordingly.

‡ The second line as given in the commentary literally rendered will be "How can he who wants to taste space, have a mouthful." A man trying to bite off a portion of space can have no mouthful.

§ A man trying to get things difficult to obtain, surely repents for his mad endeavours afterwards.

|| The commentary reads *Bodhyánugatayà* for *Bodhànugataya*. The original lit: rendered will be "by intelligence guided by knowledge or prudence."

¶ The original lit; translated will be, as the commentator says, 'one whose footsteps are pure.'

38. The status of royalty is a thing very difficult to ascend to and is done homage to by all persons. Like sacerdotal dignity,* it is blotted with stains at any the slightest transgression.

39. Acts (such as acquisition and preservation of territory) undertaken by kings conversant with the nature of *Asanas*, in perfect conformity to the rules of polity, ere long, like (good) trees† yield desirable fruits.

40. An act duly (in conformity to the prescribed rules) undertaken, even if it fails to bear fruit, does not become so much the cause of distress as the one begun out of foolishness.‡

41. When an act commenced in the right way is followed§ by results contrary (to all expectations), the performer is not to blame, in as much as his manliness there is handicapped by fate.‖

42. In order to secure success, a man of pure intelligence should (in the first instance) put forth his exertions, the rest lies with Fate which can cut him short at any stage.

43. A wise *Vijigisu* after critically reviewing his own

---

* The Sanskrit word is *Brahmanya* or the character or position of Brahmana.

† The word in the text is *Vana* or forest.

‡ What the author means is this—a foolish act brings greater sorrows on its performer than the one which though ultimately barren has been commenced in the proper manner.

§ For *Atut* the commentary reads *Ati* which change is in dispensably necessary ; this part lit : rendered will be "If when only commenced, an act meets with reverse results."

‖ This part literally translated will be, "whose manliness is separated from him by Fate." After this, one Sloka is again omitted of which the translation is given below :—

"Just as a chariot cannot move on one wheel, so Destiny unaided by human exertion can yield no fruit." Luck and labour must go hand in hand ; the one apart from the other is a dead stock.

condition* as well as that of his enemies, should set out on an expedition. This—that is to know his own as well as his foe's strength or weakness, is to be conversant with the essentials of good counsel.

44. An intelligent politician should never do an act that would be totally barren, or attended with great dangers; or about the success of which there would be any doubts, or that would bring inveterate hostility in its train.

45. An act unblamable at the time of its being done and in all times to come, pure and performed in the proper manner, and bestowing innumerable blessings (both here and hereafter),† such an act is always praised by the pious.

46. An act that would be attended with uninterrupted good and that would bring no blame on its performer, such an act should be engaged in, although for the time being it might not be agreeable.‡

47. To crown an act with success, it is always better to have recourse to one's knowledge of means, from the very beginning. Sometimes one who is always successful§ may have recourse to the conduct of a lion.||

48. The acquisition of wealth¶ from wicked persons

---

* The things he is to look to are, as the the commentator says, his three *Saktis*, the advantages of the season and soil, the signs of coming victory or defeat indicated by planets, birds &c.

† Literally translated will be—bringing a chain of good.

‡ The commentary explains this portion otherwise, it says:—'although for the time being it does not bring any friendship with it.'

§ The original word lit: translated would be, "who is the friend of success."

|| That is 'violent means.' The author means to say that knowledge is a more powerful agent than violence in bringing about success. But sometimes 'violence' may be used also. There are several minor changes in reading suggested by the commentator.

¶ The word is *Sampat i. e.* wealth in the shape of territory or treasures or any thing else.

by precipitate assault* is ever difficult. But with the help of the measures of policy, one can plant his feet even on the head of an infuriate elephant.†

49. Here (in the earth of ours) there is nothing that is incapable of being achieved by the learned and wise.‡ Metals (such as iron &c) are known to be incapable of being penetrated; but by suitable (scientific) measures (heating &c) they also are liquified.§

50. A (unsharpened) piece of iron carried on the shoulder does not cut it at all. But as soon as it is sharpened a little, it is turned into a means for fulfilling desirable|| ends (such as, slaughter of foes &c).

51. That water extinguishes fire is a fact well known on earth. But assisted by the employment of proper measures, fire can also desicate water up.¶

52. Poison is incapable of being taken internally and when it is taken so, it produces fatal results. But even poi-

---

* Without taking into consideration the nature of the Season and Soil. The author means that rash, inconsiderate attacks are seldom attended with success.

† This sloka is differently read in many other texts.

‡ Lit: there is no such thing that is beyond the abilities of the wise as regards its performance.

§ The refrain is the same as before, that policy is better than violence. *Avedyam* may have another meaning *vis* diamond. The translation then will be, "even metals and diamonds (the hardest of things known) are melted by proper measures.

|| The appropriateness of the Sloka in this connection may be questioned. Although it seems out of place, its bearing to the present discourse is thus sought to be established by the commentator. So long as the piece of iron is unsharpened *i. e.* so long as no measuse has been taken to turn it into usefulness, it cannot cut, but as soon as by some means or other it is sharpened, it becomes a very useful weapon. It is in the means employed to turn it into usefulness lies the true worth of the thing.

¶ The text omits this Sloka.

son being mixed with other things and ingredients is turned into and used as a medicine.

53. To know what is unknown,* to decide and resolve upon what is already known, to dissipate the doubts about any doubtful subject and to know the rest of a thing when only a part of it is known,—these should be the duties of ministers.

54. Abiding by the rules laid down by wise politicians, a person should never contemn or despise any body. He should hear every body's words for culling salutary counsels out of them.

55. The acquisition of unacquired things, and the protection of things already acquired,—these are the two fields in which the ingenuity and prowess of the *Vijigisu* should be exercised.

56. The magnificence and luxuries a successful sovereign are really a beauty, but these are mockeries in respect of a king who has never been successful (victorious over his foes).†

57. ‡The king, who arrogant and foolish in his acts, crosses his own ministers, is himself soon crossed§ by his enemies, his counsels being totally futile.

58. The seed of counsel should be carefully preserved, inasmuch as it is the seed of kings.|| The destruction of the seed of counsel¶ is always followed by the destruction

---

* The minister should collect information regarding unknown things by means of spies and secret emissaries.

† This and the previous Sloka are not to be found in the original before us. The first line of the first Sloka is sometimes differently read.

‡ The translation is free.

§ That is, as the commentator says, defeated and despoiled of his kingdom.

|| Counsel is here compared to a seed out of which the tree of royalty grows.

¶ Which means, the betrayal or breach of counsel.

of the kings; while it preservation preserves them excellently.*

59. Himself acting like a lion and conversant with policy, the monarch's acts should only be known to his family members, when they are in a fare way of being done, and to others when they are already accomplished.†

60. The wise hold as commendable such counsel that is desirable, that does not entail future sorrow,‡ that yields a series of good results in long succession§ and that does not extend over a long period.||

61. A *Mantra* or counsel is said to consist of five parts *viz.*, support, means to ends, division of time and country, averting of calamities and final success.¶

---

* That is the preservation of strict secrecy regarding counsels is of vital importance in the preservation of a kingdom.

† The commentator explains:—A lion, when enraged, invisibly concentrates all its energy before it takes the final spring. So also should a king do. The author means to say the movements and plans of a king should not even be known to the members of his own family before they are actually put into action. Strict secrecy should be imposed here and in all other matters of state.

‡ That does not become the cause of future repentance.

§ The commentary here substitute *Anuvandhifalaprada* for *Anuraktifalaprada*, which latter means 'good results in the shape of the good will of the subjects.'

|| A counsel extending over a long period is in greater danger of being betrayed than one extending over a short while.

¶ What the author means is that when any deliberation or counsel is to be held regarding any undertaking, these things namely the support in the shape of men, munition and magnificence, the means, the advantages or otherwise of time and territory, the advent of any unforeseen event and final success, should be given the best considertion to. The king should see whether he is well supported, whether his means are efficient enough, whether the advantages of soil and season are in his favor, whether there is change for any untoward event to cut him short and whether there is any doubt about the final success. The fifth or last part is not mentioned in the text.

62. When an act is at all undertaken, it should be duly accomplished; when it has not been begun, it should be at once taken in hand; and when it is accomplished, its results should be made permanent and enduring by commendable means.*

63. Persons, conversant with the nature and importance of counsel,† should be directed to hold consultation about the measure to be employed for performing a certain act;‡ and that measure regarding which is their minds agree, should be had recourse to, as soon as possible.

64. Acts regarding which the minds of the counselors agree§ and do not entertain any misgiving,‖ acts which are not blamed by the pious,—only such acts should be undertaken.

65. When any counsel has been duly resolved upon by the ministers, it should again be seriously weighed by the king himself (in order to avoid flaws and faults). A wise¶

* The author her specifies the primary duties of ministers. They should direct the accomplishment of all undertakings; they should take new undertakings into hand; they should turn into advantage works or acts already done.

† The original word as explained by the commentator, includes, ministers, spies and emissaries of kings.

‡ The text word is *Káryyodwésés* which the commentator thus explains—"the door by which such business, as ruling of the earth &c., comes." What he means to say is that spies and ambassadors and ministers should watch the movements of the foe and the *Udásina* &c., and at the right moment should fall upon them, employing measures, agreed upon by all. We take the word to mean, the means to an end. The translation is free.

§ That is "where there is no difference of opinion."

‖ It is believed that the mind can intuitively become aware of the probable failure of an undertaking. It feels hesitation and there is some sort of a trepidation in it.

¶ The text word is *Tatwajna* for which the commentator substitutes, *Mantrajnas* or sound counselor.

monarch should so conduct himself as not to prejudice his own interests in the least.

66. Ministers, for the advancement of their own interests, desire a prolonged campaign. A king that protracts his business over a considerable length of time, becomes a puppet in the hands of his ministers.*

67. Cheerfulness of the mind, earnestness, the quickened condition of the sense-organs,† united action with the supporters and allies, and a prosperous state of affairs, these are signs that indicate coming success.

68. Rapidly-working, uninterrupted antecedents, prolific of sources of prosperity, are antecedents that foretell the success of an undertaking or act.

69. A counsel should be again and again discussed (before it is finally disposed of); it should strictly be preserved (kept secret) with scrupulous zeal. A counsel carelessly kept, being prematurely divulged, destroys the king (concerned) even like fire itself.‡

70. A counsel that has not yet found its way among the people, should be mutually preserved (by the king, the ministers, spies, &c.) A counsel that is not scrupulously preserved, is given publicity to, by the friends and relatives (of the counselors).§

---

* This part is freely translated.

† This is brought about only when a man expects something which will be pleasing to him. When some adverse result is expected the senses become dull and apathetic.

‡ This sloka is substituted in the commentary for sloka 64 of the text.

§ It is no use trying to keep a cousel secret that has once been given air to. The counselors concerned should help one another in preserving its secrecy. It should not be trusted even to a friend or a relative, who in his turn may also communicate it to his friend. Thus it will be trumpeted over the town and reach the enemy's camp. This sloka is omitted in the text.

71. Inebriation, inadvertence, anger,* talk during sleep, courtezans (cherished with too much confidence)† and creatures who are despised or looked upon with indifference,‡ these sometimes divulge a counsel prematurely.§

72. A king should hold counsel in a place on the roof of his palace or in a forest where there are no pillars (to resound the conversation), no windows (to let the speeches go out) and no nook or corner (to conceal an inquisitive eves dropper).|| He should also see that he is not watched by any body.

73. A room which has no loop-holes or out-lets, which is situated in a secluded spot, where there is no fear of overhearing enemies, or no strong breeze, or no pillars or no frequent coming and going of men,—in such a room, a prosperous king, having purified himself¶ should hold his councils.

---

* The text word is (*káma*) which the commentary substitutes by *Kopa.*

† Another meaning is possible viz wives having masterly influence over their husbands *i.e.*, females whose husbands are henpecked.

‡ These creatures are never suspected of being able to take notice of any thing. So, one talks carelessly before them; stories are said of parrots and other birds, which hearing a man talk, imitate him, and as soon as a stranger steps in, repeats his words. Indian tale-parrots are said to possess intelligence equal to that of men.

§ The author wants to say that when a man is extremely drunk, or when he is careless, or when he is angry, or if he has the habit of talking in sleep, he is liable to disclose his counsels against his will. A courtezan, or a female too much confided upon, often gives air to a secret, which her lover out of fondness might have told to her.

|| For the text word, the commentator substitutes, *Nirbhinnántarasamsrayé* which reading we have accepted.

¶ Purification of the body before going to do something important, is considered to add to the powers of the mind, which belief can not be looked upon as purile in view of the subtle and inexplicable relation between the material and the psychical. This sloka is omitted in the text.

74. Manu says, twelve, Vrihaspati says sixteen, and Usanas says twenty, ministers should form a cabinet.*

75. Others again say that as many good and deserving counselors as are available (lit: possible), should be admitted into the cabinet.† Duly entering the cabinet and with mind (attention) undivided, a king should hold counsel for facilitating the success of an act or understanding.‡

76. Some say that for a particular act or mission, a king should engage ministers to the number of five, seven or more, all severally entrusted with several portions or charges.§

77. A king seeking his own welfare should discuss the subject of a consultation severally with each of his ministers; after which, he should take into his serious consideration (or weigh in his judgment)‖ the opinion of each by itself.¶

78. A king should, after having weighed the opinion of other counsellors, act upon that counsel that should be proffered by a highly intelligent, well-wishing and numerously-supported minister who ever acts in conformity to the Shastras.

---

* *Mantra* in the last compound word of the text is a misprint for *Mantri*.

† This part is freely rendered for lucidity's sake. What the author says is that there is no hard and fast rule regarding the number of ministers to be taken into consultation. Really deserving men should be selected and heard.

‡ For *Yathâ* in the first line and *Karyyasidhi* in the second, some read *Tathâ* and *Karyyabhudhi*.

§ What the author means is this. Several ministers should be entrusted to carry on particular work. The portions of the work should again be divided among them according to their capabilities. In one word, the writer advocates the principle of "Division of labour" here as elsewhere. This sloka does not occur in the text.

‖ Lit: "Enter into" hence, comprehend &c.

¶ The first line is vicious, for which the commentator substitutes:

Akaikena hi Kàryyáni Subichâryya punaspunas.

79. Having once formed a resolution,* never let the proper time for carrying it into action pass away. But when in some way or other, that time is past, the resolution should again be formed anew in due manner.

80. An intelligent prince should never let slip the season for doing any action, for, combination of circumstances favourable to an act, is to be found very seldom.†

81. Following the footsteps of the pious, an intelligent king should carry out his projects in proper season. Exerting in the right way and in the right time, he enjoys the delicious fruits of his actions.

82. Viewing carefully the dark and the bright side of his project, a king, with the advantages of time and place in his favour, and supported by his faithful allies, should fall upon things (such as town and villages) calculated to conduce to his aggrandisement. He should never be rash in his acts.‡

83. A rash prince, without judging the strength or otherwise of his foes, and arrogantly thinking "I am the most powerful" and disregarding the (salutary) counsel of his ministers, attacks his enemies only to meet his own fall; such a prince is narrow-minded and impudent and knows not what he does.

84. He only who mistakes evil for good and whose understanding is shallow, disregards the counsel of his ministers. A rash king attacking rashly, is soon entangled in inextricable difficulties.

85. Thus an energetic monarch betaking to a course of

---

* Lit: "having once decided upon a certain counsel" i.e., when a definite conclusion has been arrived at, regarding a counsel.

† The author here points out the soundness of the saying—"Delay is dangerous."

‡ The translation is a free one. Several minor changes of reading is noticed in the commentyar.

true policy, should, by the power of his counsel* bring into subjection his foes resembling vicious snakes.

Thus ends the eleventh section, the dissertation on counsels, in the Nitisara of Kamandaka.

SECTION XII.

—o—

1. HAVING previously held the necessary counsel a wise† king should depute to the monarch against whom he intends to march, an ambassador confident of his special abilities,‡ whose selection would be approved by the cabinet.§

2. A person, dauntless,|| accurate in memory, eloquent, accomplished in arms and in the *Shastras*, and well-exercised in all sorts of works, such a person only deserves to be a king's ambassador.

3. Ambassadors are said to be of three kinds, *viz.*, those invested with full powers; ¶ those with restricted powers** and those merely carrying the errands of their masters.†† In

---

* There is a pun on the word *Mantra* which means both counsel and charms and incantations for taming snakes.

† Lit: "Skilful in counsel."

‡ Lit: "Proud of his missionary powers." The text is vicious, for which the commentary gives *doutyabhimàninam*.

§ Another meaning is suggested by the annotator *viz.*, one among the ministers who selected by the rest.

|| The original word is *Pragalva*.

¶ That is a plenipotentiary, such was Krishna when he was deputed by Yudhisthira to negotiate with king Dhuryodhana.

** This class of ambassadors, as the commentator says, can do nothing of their own accord. Thier conduct is prescribed for them by their soveriegn, whose orders they are unable to put aside.

†† These are ordinary messengers who merely repeat what they are instructed by their masters, and nothing more or less.

respect of rank, the latter are inferior to the former respectively, in consequence of the smallness of the powers vested in them.*

4. In accordance with the commands of his masters, an ambassador, after (mature) deliberation as to the effect† of his contemplated measures upon the dominions of his king, and on those of his enemies, should go to (visit) these latter one after another.

5. He should befriend the frontier‡ as well as the forest tribes, and should find out the inland and navigable communications and easy routes, all for facilitating the unimpeded progress and march of his (master's) army.

6. He should not enter the enemie's city or the court without knowing its whereabouts.§ He should, for accomplishing his purpose, wait for opportunities, and when permitted, enter the foe's territory.

7. He should inform himself about the stability of the foe's kingdom, about his forts and castles and their defences and defects, and also his army, allies and treasuries.

8. He should deliver the orders of his master, word per word, even if weapons be raised (to smite him down).|| He should also apprise himself of the loyalty or

---

* The last portion is not so clear. What the author means seems to be that in respect of rank a plenipotentiary is superior to an ambassador with limited powers and so on. But this is self-evident.

† For this compound some substitute *Swaleàchyapara vâkyânâm*, which means 'his own as well as others' words.' This change of reading is not necessary.

‡ The word in the text is a misprint for *Antaspàla*.

§ Two explanations of the text-word are given in the commentary. The one embodied in the translation is not, as it appears to us appropriate; the other is 'unknown and unperceived by the enemy.' This strengthens the antithesis in the last portion; what the author means is this,—that an ambassador should not like a spy covertly enter an enemies dominions but would do so with his open permission.

|| What the author means is that the ambassador should not lie even

disloyalty of the enemy's subjects (by watching their movements of the face and hands &c).

9. He should not let any one else know the disaffection* of the enemy's *prakritis* (subjects) towards their master, but should himself, unpercievably do what he would think fit to do.†

10. Even when questioned on the subject, (by the inimical sovereign) he should not speak anything about the disaffection (or weakness) of the *Prakritis* of his own lord, but should in flattering‡ language say—"Your majesty knows everything well."

11. He should eulogise the enemy in four ways—by comparing him with the V*ijigisu*, (*i.e.*, the ambassador's masters) in respect of his high lineage, his fame, his substantiality, and his commendable deeds.§

12. Coming into contact with the treacherous|| element of the enemy's state under the pretence of instructing them in the four branches of learning and the five arts, he should (with their help) know the former's movements as also which party could be easily weaned over.¶

---

when his life is threatened; it is his duty to deliver the message he has been entrusted with, without the slightest mutilation.

* The text-word lit: means—'falling off' hence 'want of allegiance' &c.

† The author means this, that when an ambassador comes to know that the enemy's *Prakritis* are not what they should be, he should not let the fact take the air, but should himself take advantage of it and covertly do what would be conducive to the good of his master.

‡ It may also mean 'modest, humble'; the translation is free.

§ The author intends to say that to ingratiale himself into the favor of the foe, the ambassador should praise him saying that he is in no way inferior to the *Vijigisu* his master. For *Falena* the commeentary reads *Kulena*, which reading we have accepted.

|| The original word means 'one receiving wages from both sides.' Hence one who is a hypocrete and treacherous.

¶ Or it may mean 'where dissension could be easily sown.' The explanation given in tne commentary supports this view.

13. He should keep up communications with his own secret agents' remaining disguised as ascetics in pursuit of knowledge in *Tirthas*,* *Asramas*,† and *Surathánas*.‡

14. He should point out to the alienable party (in the enemy's country) his own master's manliness,§ high lineage prosperity (affluence), forbearance, great energy, magnanimity and gentility.||

15. He should put up with insulting language and avoid the influence of anger or lust (on all occasions).¶ He should not lie down (to sleep) with others**; he should keep his own purposes strictly secret, but know those of others.

16. An intelligent ambassador should not be depressed and hopeless regarding the accomplishment of his projects, although he would have to wait a considerable length of time. But by various tempting offers and baits (to the subjects and

---

* *Tirtha* ordinarily means a holy place. Here it means specially a place where two or more sacred rivers fall into one another, and which in consequence, becomes a place of pilgrimage.

† *Asrama*—is the place where ascetics, dwell; hermitage &c.

‡ *Surasthàna*—lit: a place of a god; hence a sacred place where temples are built and images of gods enshrined and consecrated. This is the reading of the commentary for *Asrayasthâna*.

§ For *Santâp* the commentator gives *Pratâp*.

|| What the author means is this that as soon as the messenger or whatever he may be called—finds that there is a section among the enemy's subjects that may be weaned over, he will at once begin to work by pointing out the superiority of his own employer over their sovereign in every respect. The word 'alienable' has been used for the word *Vedya* which lit: means that which may be easily penetrated, or separated from its main stock.

¶ For, in anger and in lust a man looses himself, and knows not what he does.

** The author prohibits this, as he thinks that the messenger may be a sumnumbulist and he may speak out his mind during sleep.

officers of the enemy), he should study the passing times.*

17—19.—If during these days that pass away unprofitably, he does not find any defect† in the administration of the ruler of the earth (the enemy), the ambassador—if he is a sound politician and earnestly desirous of the advancement of his own party (king)—should wait (patiently) for advantages of time and place, during a period when the enemy (disgusted with his own idleness) would himself intend to undertake something, such as, the provocation of his own *Pársnigráha*, the pacification of the disaffected section of his subjects, the storing of his forts with stocks of food grains and their repairs.‡ He should console his mind with the thought that the foe would, of his own accord, march against his (ambassador's) master, and he should endeavour accordingly.§

20. When day after day the time for action is deferred, an intelligent ambassador should consider, whether or not the enemy is procrastinating, only to let the opportunity for his (ambassador's) master to attack him (enemy) slip away.‖

---

* What the author means is that delay should not deter an intelligent messenger. He should make the best use of that time by studying the state of the enemy's *Raj* in various ways.

† Anothor meaning is possible *viz.*—if any calamity overtake the enemy, affording a good opportunity for his rivals of fall upon him.'

‡ During the progress of any of these undertakings, the ambassador has every chance of lighting upon some secret or of getting hold of some thing likely to be beneficial to the interests of his own master.

§ The author means to say that if the ambassador finds no flaw in the enemy, he should not despair but content himself with the thought that even the enemy himself may one day march against his master, when the informations gathered by him would be turned to profit.

‖ The translation is free. The author means in case to say that the ambassador finds the enemy deffering every thing to a future period, he should seek an explanation of this conduct in another direction *viz.*, whether or not the enemy is gaining time to deprive his rival of the advantages of a seasonable attack. When once the proper time slips away, the opponent will have to await long for another such opportunity.

21. When it will be evident that the time for action has arrived, he should go back directly to the kingdom of his lord; or remaining there (in the enemy's territory), he should communicate to his master all the important points of his information.

22—23. To find out the foes of the enemy, to alienate his allies and relatives from him, to know (exactly the state of) his forts, finances and army, to determine the course of action to be taken, to wean over to his (ambassador's) side the governors of the provinces of the enemy's territory, and to know all the particulars of the route (country) through which march (against the enemy) is intended,—these are said to be the duties of a *Duta*.*

24. A ruler of earth should harass his enemy by means of his own *Dutas*†; on his own part, he should be perfectly aware of the movements of the enemy's *Dutas*.

25. A person skilled in the interpretation of internal sentiments by conjecture and by external gestures, accurate of memory, polite and soft in speech, agile in movements, capable of bearing up with all sorts of privations and difficulties, ready-witted‡ and expert in everything,—such a person is fit to become a spy.

26. Sly spies disguised as ascetics, traders or artisans should go about in all directions§ apprising themselves of the opinion of the world (*i.e.*, the subjects or the public at large).

27. Spies well-informed in everything (*i.e.*, important topic or question of the times), should every day come to

---

* Hitherto we have been rendering *Duta* into 'ambassador,' but really *duta* is more generic—comprising scouts and spies within its meaning. It means, 'any one deputed to do something.'

† These *dutas* penetrating through all the secrets of his counsel, would cause the enemy considerable anxiety.

‡ That is, possessing presence of mind;

§ The commentator says 'in the *mandala* of the twelve kings.'

and go away from (*i.e.* communicate with) the ruler of earth, for they are the eyes of the king, that enable him to look at distant things.*

28. In order to penetrate into and divulge the secret of secrets of the enemy, one (a spy) should cautiously and covertly watch his (enemy's) movements. A ruler of earth, having the spies for his eyes, is awake even when he is asleep.†

29. A king should have all his and his enemy's dominions pervaded with spies who resemble the sun in energy and the wind in their movements‡, and whose selection is approved of by the public.

30. Spies are the eyes of the ruler of earth; he should always look through their medium§; he that does not look through their medium, stumbles down, out of ignorance, even on level grounds‖; for he is said to be blind.

31. Through the medium of his spies, a king should know the growth and advancement of his rivals' prosperity, their movements in all circumstances, and the purposes and

---

* The text lit: rendered would be—"for they are the king's eyes that remain at a distance"! The author means that the spies are the medium through which a king perceives things that being away from his own sight, cannot be directly perceived by him. The idea of describing spies as the king's distant eyes is a very favorite one with the Sanskrit poets.

† What the author means is this that although the king sleeps yet his emissaries are wide awake and are working; so when he wakes up he will come to know everything important that may have transpired during his sleep.

‡ That is, who act and move in as imperceptible a manner as the wind.

§ That is, whatever, he should do, should be done in consultation with the spies who always look to the state of affairs for him.

‖ That is, even in the performance of ordinary work. Just as a blind man stumbles even on level grounds, so does a king meet with difficulties in all undertaking when he does not use the spies as his eyes.

intentions* of their subjects (lit: of those who inhabit their dominions).

32. Emissaries are said to be of two kinds—*viz.*, secret and public. Secret emissaries have been particularized above; a public emissary is called a *Duta* or an ambassador.†

33. Guided by his spies, a king should proceed to any work, like *Ritvijas*‡ in a sacrifice being guided by the *Sutras*.§ The spy-service is to said be well-established when the ambassador is kept well-informed by the spies.

34. A *Tikshana*,‖ a religious mendicant, a sacrificer or a person of purest character—these are the disguises (under which spies roam through a king's *mandala*)¶; when they (the spies) are thus disguised, they do not recognise one another.

35. For the successful termination of their missions, a site for the habitation of the spies should be selected, where there is a constant conflux or gathering (of people). There the spies should stay being duly served and looked after.**

---

* Literally 'what they want.'

† The author includes ambassadors under the category of 'spies' or *charas*—which etymologically means those who walk through the king's dominions (*mandala*). The difference between a *Chara* and a *Duta* is that one is a secret agent while the other is a public one.

‡ *Ritvijas* are the priests who officate at sacrifices; ordinarily four are mentioned *viz* the *Hotri*, the *Udgàtri*, the *Adhvaryu* and the *Brahman*; at grand ceremonies sixteen are enumerated,

§ That part of the *Vedas* containing aphoristic rules for sacrifices and other ceremonies.

‖ Lit: pungent, sharp; here a person of fiery or passaonate temparament. Probably there was a class of ascetics of this description.

¶ What the author means is this that the spies ordinarily simulate the appearances of these persons, when they roam through the enemy's territory in order to hide their identity.

** The last line of this Sloka is extremely vicious in the text; for which the commentary substitutes:—

'Tisteyuryatra Sanchdrds paricharyyábabdhinas,'

which we accept.

36. In the residence of the spies there should stay persons disguised as traders, merchants* husbandmen, convent-heads, (religious) mendicants, professors (of religion); pure-hearted (ascetics), and mercinaries.

37. Spies skilled in studying the hearts of men, should be posted in the territory of all kings who are within the *mandala* of the *Vijigisu* or within that of his enemy.

38. The king that does not know (watch) the movements of the kings of his own *mandala* or of those of his enemy's *mandala*, is said to be asleep† although he is wide awake, and he never wakes up from such sleep of his.

39. (Through his spies) a king should know (watch) those (enemies) who have reason to be exasperated with him and also those who are so without any reason whatever‡; he should by secret measures of punishment (assassination &c.) do away with those among his own household, who are seditious and angry§ with him without any cause whatever.||

---

* For *Vala* of the text the annotator gives *Vanik*, and explains it to mean a 'foreigner.'

† There is a pun upon the words *Jâgran* and *Susupta* here. The author means, a king ignorant of the movements of his rivals is as good as one asleep, although he may literally be awake and working. Such carelessness results in his being subjugated; and his inactive nature can never in future throw off the yoke of thraldom.

‡ The author distinguishes between classes of foes—those who are born enemies and those who are made so by some cause or other, such as the withholding of a promised thing &c.

§ This is strictly literal—the meaning is—disaffected towards him although they have never been maltreated.

|| It sounds absurd that we may have enemies although we have never done anything to create one. The commentary cites a Sloka here in order to clear any doubts on the point; the translation of the Sloka is as follows:—"When even an innocent *Muni* (sage) does his own duties, he creates thereby three parties—*viz.*, friends, foes, and neutrals."

40. Those who have reasons to be exasperated with the king, should be conciliated by gifts and the bestowal of honors &c., and then the king should live together with them, having thus subjugated them (won them over to his side); and in this way he should amend his own faults* (which might have given his enemy a hold).

40A. He should preserve the peace of his kingdom by giving the wicked and the seditious (*i.e.* the disturbing element) the snub they deserve. With all his endeavours, he should mend his weakness by conciliation, gift or (bribery).†

41. Taking advantage of the slightest laches of even the most powerful enemy, a king should cause his (enemy's) kingdom to sink completely (in the sea of distress and destructions), even as water causes a drinking cup to sink down in it by entering it through even the smallest hole.

42. Persons simulating to be idiots‡, or deaf, or blind or dumb or eunuchs, and *Kiratas*§ and dwarfs, and hunchbacks and such other agents||.

43. And (disguised religious) mendicants and *Charanas*¶ and maid-servants and men versed in all arts and acts, should gather undetected**, the informations regarding a king's household.

44. (Persons disguised as) bearers of the royal Parasole

---

* Lit: 'And thus should he fill up the gaps *i.e.*, holes or weak points of his administration.

† This Sloka is omitted in the text. The commentator explains the last part thus—the anger and disaffection of the subjects and servants are as it were the breach through which the enemy effects his entrance.

‡ The word is *Joda*, which the commentator takes to mean—'deaf and dumb.'

§ The most degraded class of mountain tribe obtaining in ancient India.

|| The commentary here reads *KàraCas* which means 'those versed in fine arts.'

¶ Lit: A wandering singer or actor.

** Lit: "unseenly."

yak-tails (lit: fans), pitchers, and palanquins, and horse-boys and grooms and other such servants, should keep information about the doings of the high state officials.

45. The cooks,* the bed-room servants, the *vigakâs*:—the Valet de chambre,† the attendants at the table, the shampooers,

46. And the orderlies entrusted with serving up water, betels, flowers, perfumes and ornaments, these and others like them that always keep near the king, should be made instrumental in administering poison to him.‡

47. Cool-headed spies should study the conduct (of all the high state officials) through signs, gestures,§ bodily appearances, the secret tokens they use and the letters they write.

48. Spies versed in all acts and in all arts, assuming various disguises, should roam (in every part) of a *mandala* imbibing public opinion like the solar rays imbibing moisture from the earth.

49. An intelligent *Vijigisu* conversant with the *Shastras* and the ways of the world, should be cognisant of the fact that as he through his spies (lit: by some means) strives to play his enemie's false, so these latter also try to pay him back in his own coin, by engaging|| spies to watch over him.

Thus ends the twelfth section, the rules regarding embassies and the spies, in the Nitisâra of Kamandaka.

---

* Lit: "those who prepare highly seasoned dishes."

† That is spend thrifs.

‡ The last line is vicious in the text—the eommentary gives, *Karttavya Rasadà* which reading we accept.

§ For *Murchchita* of the text the commentary gives *Mudritais.*

|| For *Viyujyamâna* the commentary reads—*Niyujyamâna.*

SECTION XIII.

1. WHEN a monarch would, from the daily reports of the spies, come to know of the failure of his embassy to the foe, he should set out with hostile intentions against this latter, according to the prescribed rules of march, relying on his own keen intelligence as his only guide.*

2. Like fuels† producing fire, a keen and resolute understanding dominated over‡ by equanimity and perseverance, produces many happy results.

3. Just as metallic ores§ are sure to yield the precious gold, and the churning (of the curd) butter, so, earnest endeavour supported by intelligence and perseverance is sure to be crowned with success.

4. An intelligent and energetic king possessed of the *Prabhusakti*||, becomes the excellent receptacle for all prosperity, even as the mighty main is for all waters.

5. Like wealth of waters preserving the lotus, it is intelligence alone that preserves the royal prosperity; and this prosperity is carried to magnificence only by energy and perseverance.¶

---

* *Purassara* literally means—'that which walks before'; hence a 'guide.' The sloka bristles with bad readings, and but for the emendations of the commentary, it would have been impossible to make out any meaning. The correct text would be :—

Anvaham Characharyyâbhirvifalé Dutachéstité
Yàyâdyathoktayânastu Sukshma vudhipuvassara.

† The text-word *Aranee* literally means two pieces of *Sami* wood used for kindling sacred fire by a attrition.

‡ That is,—governed.

§ The original word is *Dhátu* which the commentator takes to mean earth, stones and other worthless things obtained with crude minerals.

|| Vide note to sloka 1 and 22, Section I.

¶ The commentary adds—"even as the lotus is caused to bloom fully by the influence of the wind and the solar rays."

6. Prosperity never leaves an energetic king* who follows the dictates of his intelligence, even as its shadow never leaves the body; but it goes on increasing (every day).

7. Like rivers flowing into the ocean, prosperity ever flows dowu on a king,† who is free from the influence of the *Vyasanas* and is indifatigable, highly energetic, and intelligent.

8. An idle king whose mind is affected by the influence of the *Vyasanas* is, in spite of his possessing many good qualities and a (keen) intelligence, cast off by (the goddess of) prosperity, even as eunuchs are cast off by women.

9. By constant activity he should add to his everything (*i.e.*, prosperity, happiness, &c.), even as fire is added to by the putting of fuel in it.‡ Even a weak king, if he is ever energetic, reaps nothing but prosperity.

10. For enjoying prosperity which is like a faithless lady,§ a king should ever, with all his manliness, desire activity, and should not behave like one impotent.

11. An ever-energetic king by having recourse to the *Sainhee Vriti*‖ should bring prosperity under his own control as if dragging her by the hair, like a man dragging his wicked wife.

12. Without planting his feet on his enemy's head graced with crowns adorned with diverse kinds of gems and and jewels, a person (king) cannot reap prosperity (lit. blessing).

13. Where can there be any happiness (for a king),

---

* The reading *Utsâhasampannân* is vicious;—read *Utsàhasampannât.*

† Literally, the translation would be "prosperities enter into him like rivers entering into the ocean."

‡ The author's meaning seems to be this that the more you add fuel to the fire the more its flames blaze forth; so, the more a king exerts himself, the more does he advance on the ladder of prosperity.

§ Prosperity is compared to a faithless lady, for it is never steady with a man.

‖ Lit: 'lion-like conduct' *i. e.* ever active and manly conduct.

unless the deep-rooted tree—his enemies—be eradicated by the mighty elephant—his intelligence—goaded by the guide—his earnest endeavours!

14. Prosperity can only be brought home (captive) by a strong arm, resembling the graceful trunk of an elephant and glittering with the dazzling lustre of an easily drawn sword (that it wields)!

15. A high-minded person desirous of ascending to a great height (in the ladder of prosperity), plants his feet higher and higher, whereas a low-minded one apprehending fall and destruction, plants them lower and lower.

16. Like the lion planting his paw on the head of an elephant, one (a king) possessed of great energy may plant his foot on the head of another excelling him much in bulk.*

17. Fearless like a serpent, a king should make such display of his magnificence as to strike terror into the hearts of his foes. According to the measure of his strength, he should undertake the chastisement of his foes.†

18. A king should fall upon his foe first having removed the cause of disaffection of his people.‡ These causes are bred by the absence of good and the following of offensive policies of administration, as also by adverse Fate.

---

* The authors means:—A highly energetic and active monarch is capable of subjugating even a foe whose territories are more wide-spread than his own.

† Although the author exhorts in favor of constant activity, yet he warns kings against rashness. Before undertaking an attack, a king should judge his own strength in comparison to that of his foe. Energy of course goes a great way in securing success; but it cannot work miracles.

‡ *Prakritivyasana* lit: means the *Vasyana* or defect in his *Prakritis* or the constituents of his government.' What the author means is that before going to fight with an external enemy, a king should put down the causes that tend to procuce internal enemies, and to breed civil fueds.

19. *Vyasana** is so-called for it retards the material well-being (of a kingdom; (one a king) under the influence of the *Vyasanas* goes down and down (the depths of degradation); and therefore the *Vyasanas* should be avoided (as much as possible).

20. Fires, floods, famine, prevalence of diseases, and plague and pestilence—these are the five kinds of the *Vyasanas* (calamities) that proceed from Fate; the rest come from human sources.

21. The evils proceeding from Fate should be averted by means of manly efforts and the celebration of propitiatory rites; and a king knowing what should be done, should remove the evils coming from human sources by his energeticalness and adoption of wise measures of policy.

22. From the king (*Swamy*) to the allies†—all these constituents form the *Prakriti Mandala*, (or government). I shall now in due order, enumerate their functions and their frailties.

23. To hold counsels,‡ to secure the results of counsel,§ to direct others in the performance of actions, to ascertain beforehand the effects (good or bad) of future events and occurrences, to look after the income and expenditure (of the kingdom), to administer justice,‖ to subjugate enemies,

24. To avert threatening evils and calamities, and to protect the kingdom,¶—these are the functions of a minister. But a minister when he is under the influence of the

---

* Etymologically means that which throws back (the good or the progress and prosperity of a kingdom).

† Vide *Supra* Sloka 1. Section IV.

‡ The word *mantra* includes all operations—from the initial proceedings of a consultation to the attainment of a certain result.

§ *i. e.* to acquire and preserve territories &c.

‖ Lit: to "mete and dole" laws; to inflict punishments according to the offences.

¶ For *Rājarajyāvisechanam* the commentary give as, *Rājarajyāvirakshanam*

Vyasanas (vicious propensities) fails in all these (functions of his).

25. A king whose minister possessed by the *Vyasanas* is weaned over (by the foe),* becomes incapable of resisting the enemy by the application of the measures of policy, like a bird incapable of flying when its wings are cut off.

26. Gold, corn, cloths, conveyances and all other such things (that the king enjoys), arise from the (prosperity of the) people.

27. The people promote the trade, commerce, cultivation and other such means that conduce to the prosperity of a kingdom.† These totally depend on the people. Therefore, when the people are in danger (or under the influence of evil propensities) no success can be achieved.

28. Castles are the places of refuge for the people in times of danger; they are protections for the troops and the treasures; with a view to take refuge into them, the citizens (seek to) oblige their rulers (by gifts, presents, &c.)

29. That which is a means for carrying on *Tushni* warfare, that which affords protection to the people (in troublous times), that which can take in friends and foes alike and that which is a check against the attacks of the neighbouring forest tribes—is called a Durga (castle).§

30. A king safe within the recesses of his castle (or a king possessing numerous castles) is respected both by his

---

* Several important change of reading are to be noted here. For *Amatyâis vyasanopatais hriyamâno* read *Amâtyê vyasanopêtê hriyomânê* and for *Asakta ebotpatati* read *Asakta ebotpatitam.*

† The original word is *Vàrtà* which lit: means,—the occupation or profession by which one earns his livelihood. We have rendered the the word freely.

‡ When a king concealing himself in his castle in a manner undetected by the enemy, suddenly falls upon the latter, such a sort of assault is called *Tushni Yudha.*

§ *Durga* etymologically means that which is approached or taken with difficulty.

own and his enemy's partizans. But when *Durga-vysana* exists none of these exists.*

31. The act of maintaining dependents, acts of munificence, (personal and other) decorations, purchasing of conveyances (horses and elephants), stability (of the kingdom), facility for sowing dissension among the enemy (and his allies), repairing of castles,

32. Construction of bridges and cause-ways, trade and commerce, the acquisition of friends and allies and the love of the people, and lastly, the accomplishment of rightious and desirable acts—all proceed from the treasure (*i. e.* all these depend entirely on a solvent financial condition.)

33. "The foundations of royalty are laid in the treasures"—this is a popular saying well-known in all regions. A ruler of men whose treasury is in danger (of being insolvent) loses all prospects of success in the above-mentioned acts.

34. A king with a solvent treasury increases his forces reduced (in consequence of wars), and he naturally wins the good-will of his people. He is even respected and served by his enemies.

35. To add to the number of friends and foes, and to the amount of gold (*i. e.* wealth and the territorial possessions of a kingdom), to accomplish with alacrity acts deferred to an indefinite future, to protect what is acquired or gained,

36. To destroy the army of the foe, and to save the forces of its own side,—all these acts proceed from the army. So when the army is under the influence of the *Vyásanas* (*i e.* when it is defective), these (the above-named acts) run to ruin (*i.e.* are never accomplished with any degree of success).

37. The foes even of a king possessing an efficient army, are turned into his friends (seek his friendship). A king possessing a large army, rules the earth (unmolested) after having (properly conquered it).

* That is, when castles are not repaired and properly looked after, the king and his people lose all respect and chance of safety.

38. A faithful ally restrains others throwing off their allegiance, and destroys the enemy. He serves the king (to whom he is allied) by risking his own dominions, treasures troops and his life even.

39. By ties of mutual affection, he succeeds in securing numerous other friends and allies. When therefore the ally is under the influence of the *Vyasanas*, his function is no longer duly discharged.

40. A true ally promotes the welfare of his allied king, without expecting to be remunerated in return. A king having (faithful) allies, succeeds with the greatest ease, even in most difficult undertakings.

41. Pursuit of knowledge, protection of the *Varnas* and *Asramas* of his own kingdom, ability of using pure (unpoisoned) weapons, accomplishment in all the modes of warfare,

42. Habits of hardiness, knowledge of the implements of war (offensive and defensive) and of the characteristics of acts (such as, testing the strength of armours &c), ability for riding properly on horses, elephants and chariots,

43. Skilfulness in wrestling, the art of clearly seeing through the purposes of others (lit: entering into other's heart), crookedness with the crooked, and honesty with the honest,

44. Consultations and reconsultations (with the cabinet, regarding a certain project), preservation of the secrecy of counsels, healthiness (of the mind), disregard of (such modes of policy as) conciliation, gift or bribery, and application to (such modes as) sowing dissensions and inflicting punishments,

45. Knowledge of the movements and intents of the commanders and other officers of his troops, and of the counsellors, ministers and priests, imprisonment of the wicked (among the above-named officers),

46. Observation of those who come to and go away from him as ambassadors, the removal of the calamities that

threaten the people, and the appeasing of the angry or disaffected element (of the state),

47. Obedience to the preceptors, bestowal of honours and respects on those worthy of them, administration of justice, suppression of the disturbing factor of the kingdom (lit: the taking out of the thorns of the state, such as the thieves, robbers, murderers, &c.,

48. Knowledge of what exists and what does not, examination of what is done and what is left off undone, investigation as to who is satisfied and who dissatisfied among his dependents,

49. Complete acquaintance with the movements, (and character) of the *Madhyama* and the *Udásina** and the act of turning this acquaintance to means for establishing firmly his own rule, (or to means for the success of his undertakings), acquisition of allies and the chastisement of the enemies,

50. The protection of his sons and wives and his own-self, entertaining amicable feelings towards his relatives and friends, the promotion of such measures of revenue on which his own material progress depends,

51. Infliction of hardships on the wicked, and to afford facilities for the advancement of the honest, abstinence from doing injury to any being, and the avoidance of sin or unrighteousness,

52. Prohibition of evil deeds and the promotion of good ones, the giving away of things fit to be given, and the accumulation of those that should not be parted with,

53. Withholding of punishment from those who do not deserve them, and the infliction of them on those who rightly merit them, acceptance of things acceptable and the rejection of those unacceptable,

54. Performance of fruitful deeds, and the rejection of

* Vide Supra note.

fruitless ones, the just levying of taxes and their remission in bad seasons,

55. The preferment of high officials of state, and the removal of those who deserve dismissal, pacification of calamities (such as famine, pestilence, &c.,) and the establishment of friendliness among his servants,

56. To know what is unknown, and to be assured of what is known, to undertake good acts, and to see to their ends acts undertaken,

57. Desire for acquiring what remains unacquired and facilitating the advancement of what is acquired, and the proper consignment of a thriving object to the care of a deserving person,

58. Suppression of wrong and the following of the paths of rectitude, and (lastly) the doing of good to one who does good to him,—these are the functions of a ruler of earth.

59. An energetic king following the paths of true policy, leads to eminence these and his government and ministers; but influenced by evil propensities, he leads them to destruction.

60. But when a king becomes busy in the performance of religious deeds and in acquiring wealth, or when he is demented, all these functions ought to be discharged by his ministers.

61. Excessive harshness in the words spoken and in the punishments meted out, defect in the administration of finance, inebriation, (excessive love for the company of) women, and for hunting, and gambling (at the dice),—these are the *Vyasanas* of a king.

62. Procrastination, sluggishness, conceit, carelessness, cultivation of (other's) ill-will,—these and those enumerated above (*viz.*, the *vyasanas* of the king), are the *vyasanas* of the ministers.

63. Excessive rain, want of rain (drought), locusts, rats, mice and parrots (and other such corn-destroying agents)

unjust taxation, confiscation of the properties of the people, foreign invasion and depredation, and thieves, and robbers,

64. Abandonment of the king by his forces and his favourites, distress brought about by the prevalence of diseases, and the death of cattle, and the ravages of the murrain,—these are the *vyasanas* of the kingdom.

65. Disorder and decay of the implements of war and of the ramparts and ditches, want of weapons in the arsenal, and failure of the stock of food and fuels,—these are the *vyasanas* of the castle.

66. Extravagance, outlay (in different projects), misappropriation (by the officials and servants), want of accumulation, robbery, and remoteness (of the flowing in of money),—these are said to be the *vyasanas* of the treasury.

67. To be besieged (by the enemy), to be surrounded on all sides (by hostile forces), to be disgraced, to be deprived of a being duly honoured, to be disaffected (or badly paid), to be diseased, to be fatigued or over-worked, to be returned from distant lands, to be newly recruited,

68. To be reduced in unmber, to be deprived of its leaders, to have its brave warriors killed, to be excited with hopes and disappointments, to become faithless,

69. To have women with it, to be scattered over different countries, to have thorns (*i. e.*, spies &c., set by the foe) in its ranks, to be torn by dissensions, to be sent to fight in foreign *Mandalas*, to be undisciplined,

70. To have its senior officers enraged,* to be commanded by men differing in opinion, to have foes in its own ranks, to be united with the enemy, to be careless of its own intersts and those of the allies (of its monarch),

71. To be cut off from the supplies of food and the support of allied troops, to be destitute of shelter (wherein to

* The word in the text is *Krudha-maulam*. *Moulam* as explained by the commentator, means soldiers who have served the royal dynasty from generation to generation.

secure the families and properties of its soldiers), to hazard battles without the consent of its master, to put forward different excuses (for its delinquencies),

72. To have bad *Parshnigráhas,* and to be ignorant of the country (where it is dispatched)—these are said to be the *vysanas* of the army. Of these some are irremediable and some remediable; of this, I am speaking presently.

73. When relieved or set free, a beseiged force, becoming highly efficient may fight; and an army surrounded on all sides and without any egresss, must also fight (out its own way).

74. An unhonored army when duly honoured, will fight; but a dishonored army, with its fire of indignation burning, will never do so.

75. An army badly paid will fight, when it is duly paid up to date; but a diseased and disordered (inefficent) one, will not do so; for then, it will be defeated.

76. After enjoying proper rest, an overworked and fatigued army will again face the compaign; but an army returned from distant lands with its energy drooping, becomes incapable of using weapons (*i.e.* active service,)

77. A newly recruited force will fiight when united with older regiments of the realm; but an army with its brave warriors killed and reduced in number will not fight.

78. A routed army, supported by brave heroes will again face the battle; but an army, with its leaders slain and its vanguard slaughtered, will turn away from the fight.

79. When its hopes are realised and its disappointments removed, a force will not fight, for then, there will be nothing inducing it to risk a battle. When confined within a small area, an army will not fight, in consequence of the narrowness of the field.

80. An army at first beseiged and then set free, will fight when equipped with the implements of war (horses, conveyances and weapons); and an army having women

with it* becomes capable of fighting when the women are removed.

81. An army scattered over different kingdoms, and away from home, will not fight (heartily); and one with the thorns (spies &c.) set by the enemy within it, becomes incapacitated for active service.

82. An army torn by dissensions, with its soldiers opposing one another, does not fight (is unfit for battle); so also an army despatched to a foreign *mandala* or realm (does not fight).†

83. An army that had not travelled to foreign lands, and one that has fled away, cannot fight. An army that has served the forefathers of a king, will not fight, when it is enraged; but when satisfied, it will fight (most gladly).

84. An army hemmed in on all sides by the foe and confined in one place, cannot fight; and troops whose camp is assailed by the enemy also become incapable of fighting well.

85. An army with the enemy within its ranks, will not fight; but when these thorns (the foes) are removed, it will fight; an army though corrupted by the enemy, will fight, if led by courageous warriors.‡

---

* The original word is *Kalatra Garvam*—which means 'to have women within it.' The commentator explains *Kalatra* as *Kulastri* or ladies, —his meaning being, that when the wives and families of soldiers are allowed to travel with them, they fight reluctantly, ever watchful for saving their lives whose importance is enhanced as they look upon their objects of affection. But when these latter are far away, the soldiers in the excitement of the battle, totally forget them and fight heedless of their lives, thus paving the way of victory for their king.

† The commentator explains—for it is worn out with the fatigue and hardships of the journey.

‡ The texts of Slokas 84 and 85, are vicious, the commentator gives the following two for them.

84. Misram Satrubhirékastham tadàkrántatayá kshamam,
Sotrorupanibistam Yat sámarthyánnàksham Yudhi.

86. An army is said to be neglectful of its own interests when in times of danger it remains inactive. An army engaged in serving an ally in consequence of its excellent advantages regarding time and position, cannot be properly used (in any other purpose).

87. The supply of food and clothing is called *Bibadha* and *Asára* means the troops of the allies. An army cut off from the supply of food and clothing and from the support of the troops of the allies, cannot fight.

88. The troops that have no shelter (to secure their families and properties) will fight when shelter is provided by the citizens for them. An army that acts without the orders of its master, is not attached to him (is faithless), and will not fight.*

89. An army becomes leaderless when every one in it, is his own master, (and no one is accepted as leader); such an army is incompetent to fight; so also, a disabled army and one with a bad *Parshnigraha*, are incapable of fighting.

90. An army ignorant of the state of affairs (about it) is said to be blind, and for this reason, it is incompetent for fighting.† These are the *Vyasanas* of the army; carefully looking into them,‡ a king should undertake a war.

91. An ally is said to be the under the influence of the *vyasanas* when he is suffering from the afflictions of Fate, or is assailed on all sides by the forces of the foe, or is possessed of the defects arising out of lust and anger, which have been enumerated above.

92. Beginning with the king, of the seven constituents of

---

85. *Dusyayuktam na yudhyéta, Yudhyetodhritakantakam,*
Pradhāna Yodha samguptam, Dusyamchápi Samutpatét.

* This part is understood. The commentator supplies a different reading, which we do not accept.

† The text is vicious; the commentator gives,
Adésikam Smritam hyandham, tanmulatwát Kriyákshamam.

‡ For when they exist, no endeavours can bring about victory.

a government that have been described above, the *vyasanas* of each preceding constituent is graver than the one following it.*

93. A king should be cognisant of all these *vyasanas* of the members of his Government; and he, without letting the right opportunity slip away, should exert himself in removing them to the best of his powers, intelligence and endeavours.

94. A monarch desirous of the welfare and prosperity of his government, should not overlook, out of error or arrogance, the *vyasanas* that may overtake the *Prakritis*. He that neglects the *vyasanas* of his *Prakritis*, is, ere long, defeated by his enemies.

95. Weighing gravely what should be done, a king should apply himself to the performance of his duties. Endeavouring his best, he should see the end of all his undertakings. A ruler of earth, the constituents of whose government are purged of all their defects and drawbacks† through his wise policy, enjoys for a long time, the three objects of existence.‡

Thus ends the thirteenth chapter, the description of the vyasanas and the means for remedying them, in the Nitisar of Kamandaka.

---

* The original Sanskrit construction would admit of no other rendering. The meaning is, that the *Vyasanas* of the king are prolifi cof greater evils than the *vyasanas* of the ministers, and so forth.

† The text word lit: rendered would be "whose holes are filled in with wise policy."

‡ The objects are, *Dharma* or virtue, *Artha* or wealth, *Kâma*, or objects of enjoyment.

SECTION XIV.

THE *Prakritis*, beginning with the minister and ending with the ally, are said to be the constituents of a government. Of all the weaknesses of the government, the gravest is the weakness of the ruler of earth.

2. A monarch free from all weaknesses, is capable of redeeming the weaknesses of the government; but a prosperous government can not rescue its head (the king) from his weaknesses.

3. A king who does not possess the eye of political knowledge is said to be blind; it is better to have such a blind king than one, who though possessed of such eyes, transgresses the path of rectitude out of pride or carelessness.

4. Such a blind monarch may be rescued from ruin by his ministers skilled in giving advice. But when a king, though possessed of the eye of political knowledge blinded by pride, he completely ruins himself.

5. For these reasons, a king possessed of the eye of polity, following the advices of his prime minister, should avoid the weaknesses that mar (the realisation of) virtue and wealth.

6. Too much harshness in speech and in the punishments meted out, and unjust seizure of property and withholding of what is due,—these are said by those conversant with the nature of weaknesses, to be the three weaknesses arising out anger.

7. Excessive indulgence in hunting, gambling (at dice), women's company and drinking—these are said by those understanding the meaning of weaknesses, to be the four kinds of weaknesses bred by lust.

8. Among men, harshness in speech causes great trouble and is prolific of much harm; it should therefore not be practised. On the other hand, a king should win (the good-will of) the public by his sweet and mellifluous speech.*

9. He that by fits and starts, often speaks too much in anger, causes thereby much anxiety to his subjects, like a fire shooting numerous sparks.

10. Sharp daggerlike words penetrating into the core of the heart and cutting to the quick, excites a powerful person ;† and thus excited, he turns into an enemy.

11. A monarch should not excite the public by harsh words; he should be sweet in his speech; even a miserly monarch, acting in a kind and friendly manner, is (faithfully) served (by the people).

12. The shbjugation of the unsubjugated and their chastisement, is called *Danda* by the wise‡. One should deal out *Danda* according to the rules of polity; for, infliction of punishments on those deserving them is praiseworthy.

13. A king hard (cruel), in the infliction of punishments excites (fear in the heart of) the people; thus troubled, they seek the protection of the enemy.

24. In this way affording shelter to the people, the enemy rises to power; and a powerful enemy causes destruction. For these reasons, a monarch should not excite (the anxiety of) his subjects.

---

1 This Sloka contains many vicious readings;—for *Pàrusya* read *Pârusyam* and for *Loka* read *Loké*.

2 The first part of the last line of this Sloka is bad, for which the commentator supplies :—

Tejasvinam dipayati.

3 The word *Sarbhi* in the text is a misprint for *Sadbhi*. *Danda* is the last of the four expedients of foregn policy (vide *Supra*).

15. Rulers of earth doing good (kindness) to the people grow in prosperity; their growth depends on the growth of the people, and their ruin on these latter's ruin.

16. Except in the case of the dispoliation of the kingdom, a king should avoid the infliction of the capital punishment, even in the gravest of offences. In the aforesaid instance only, such punishment is commendable.*

17. The expenditure of a considerable amount of money in order to exculpate a culpable offender, is said to be *Arthadusana*† by those conversant with the essentials of polity.

19. The jostling of the conveyances, their destruction; the sufferings caused by hunger, thirst, fatigue, exertion, cold, heat and the wind;

20. The infliction of much distress arising out of *Yána-vyasana* on the army; heated, sandy and thorny soils;

21. Injuries done by collision with trees, scratches from thorns and plants; difficulties caused by rocks, creepers, trunks of trees and earthen mounds;

22. Capture or death‡ by the hands of foresters and foes hidden behind rocks, or in the beds of rivers or inside under-woods and copses;

23. Assassination by his own troops weaned over by the enemy; danger of falling a prey to bears, serpents, elephants, lions, and tigers;

24. Choking of the breath by the smoke of the forest-conflagration; and mistaking the way or direction and the consequent wandering—these are said to be the *Mriga-*

---

* For *Juktadanda*, the commentator gives *Tatra danda*, which appears to be an emendation true.

† The word lit: means some flaw in the collection and expenditure of money—*Arthadusana* occurs when money is unjustly collected or unnecessarily expended.

‡ *Pariklésai* is a misprint for *Pariklésa*.

yávysana (or the evils attending too much indulgence in hunt) of rulers of earth.

25. Indefatigability, physical exercise, the cure of phlegm fat and indigestion, and excellent sureness in shooting arrows at moving or steady aims,

26. These are spoken of by others to be the goods proceeding from hunting; but this view can not be accepted. The evils of hunting are almost all of a fatal nature. So, hunting is a great *Vyasana*.

27. Indigestion and other such physical complaints may also be cured by constant healthy exercise on horseback; and sureness in shooting arrows at moving aims, can also be mastered in other ways.

28. But if a king is ardently desirous of (enjoying the pleasures of) the hunt, let a beautiful park be constructed at the precincts of the town, for his sports.

29. The park should be surrounded on all sides by ditches and walls incapable of being crossed or leapt over by the game. In length and breadth it should extend to half a *Yojana* (or about eight miles).

30. It should be situated near the foot of a mountain or the bed of a river, and should abound in water and soft green grass. It should not contain thorny plants and copses, and should be free from poisonous trees or plants.

31. It should be decorated with beautiful and well-known trees loaded with blossoms and fruits and spreading cool, pleasing and thick shades.

32. The burrows, pits, and cavities should be filled up with dust and gravel, leaving no chasm or declivity in the soil; and it should be levelled by the removal of trunks of trees, earthen mounds, and rocks, &c.

33. The lakes and other expanses of water inside the park, should be freed from sharks, crocodiles, &c., and they should be deep, and adorned with diverse acquatic flowers and birds.

34. The park should abound in such game, as she-elephants and elephant cubs, tigers with their teeth broken and claws pared off, and horned beasts with their horns cut off.

35. It should be beautified with creepers crested with flowers and blossoms within easy reach, and should be adorned with nice little plants growing on the sides of the ditches.

36. Outside the park, the fields stretching to a great distance, should be levelled and cleared of trees. The park itself should be inaccessible to the forces of the enemy, and thus afford a feeling of safety and comfort to the mind.

37. Such a park when guarded by hardy and resolute guards, faithful in allegiance and capable of reading the hearts of spies, becomes the source of immense pleasure to the monarch.*

38. Strong and hardy men well-versed in the art of hunting, should for the sport of the king, introduce into the park various kinds of game.

39. A king, capable of bearing up against the fatigue of a morning walk, should enter into the park for sport accompanied by his faithful and favourite attendants and without detrement to any other function of his.

40. When the monarch enters the park for sport, then outside it, sentries, should be placed, ready and arranged (for action) and watching the boundaries far and distant.

41. The king pleased with the sport, would then reap those good results that have been said by the wise to proceed from hunting.

42. Regarding hunt, these are the rules that I point out. Transgressing these, a king should not go about hunting like a common professional hunter.

---

* The Sloka bristles with bad readings. For *Tadbanàn* read *Tatbanam*, and for *bhuribhutayé* read *bhutayébhavet*.

43. Speedy flowing out (loss) of money in spite of all care to preserve it, untruthfulness, feelinglessness (cruelty), anger, harshness in speech,*

44. Covetousness, neglect of righteous ceremonies, discontinuance of (commenced public) works, separation from the company of the good and union with the wicked,

45. Certain draining of the treasury, endless hostility (with the defeated party), feeling of destitution when still there is money enough (to meet the requirements of the game), and a sense of affluence when indeed there is no money in the fund,

46. Anger and joy at every moment, remorse at each step, distress at each moment, and questioning of the witness at every doubtful cast of the dice,

47. Disregard of such (indispensable) acts as bathing, cleansing of the body, and of sexual enjoyment, want of physical exercise, weakness of the limbs and the body, overlooking of the precepts of the *Shâstras,*

48. Retention of the discharge of urine, sufferings from (the pangs of) hunger and thirst,—these are said by persons versed in polity, to be the evils of gambling.

49. Even Pāndu's son Yudhisthira† that very virtuous

---

* Lit :—"Words cutting like the dagger."

† The story of king Yudhisthira's gambling with Duryodhana is contained in the Mahabharata. These two were two cousins, one ruling in Hastinapur and the other in Indraprastha. Duryodhana who was jealous of the prosperity and advancement of Yudhisthira, invited him to a game at dice (of which Yudhisthira was particularly fond), hoping thereby to rob him of all his possessions. In that gambling match Duryodhana who was ably assisted by his maternal uncle Sakuni, won from Yudhisthira everything that he staked till the infatuated gambler staked himself, his brothers, Droupadi (his wife) herself, all of whom shared the same fate, and as a condition of the wager were forced to serve the Kouravas. But afterwards, Dhritarastra, Duryodhana's blind father, relented and set them free.

and learned monarch resembling a second Lokapāla,* lost his lawful wife in wicked gambling.

50. The very powerful monarch Nala having lost his prosperous kingdom (as a wager) in gambling, abandoned his lawful queen in the woods, and afterwards did the work of a menial.†

51. Prince Rukmin of golden complexion, who was equal to Indra himself and a bowman whose match was not to be found on earth, even that prince met with his destruction through the evils of gambling.‡

52. The foolish Dantabakra, the ruler of Kousikarupa, had his teeth broken, in consequence of excessive indulgence in gambling (at dice).§

53. From gambling causeless hostilities proceed; through gambling love and affection wither away; and as a con-

---

* The *Lokapālas* are the divine Regents that are supposed to rule over the quarters of heaven.

† Nala was a very noble-minded and virtuous king. He was chosen by Damayanti, inspite of the opposition of gods, and they lived happily for some years. But Kali a god, who was disappointed in securing her hand, resolved to persecute Nala, and entered into his person. Thus affected, he played at dice with his brother, and having lost everything, he with his wife was banished from the kingdom. One day while wandering through the wilderness, he adandoned his almost naked wife and went away. Subsequently he was deformed by the serpent Korkotaka and thus deformed entered the service of king Rituparna as a horse-groom under the name of Vahuka. Subsequently, wich the assistance of this king, he regained his beloved and they led a happy life. *(Apte).*

‡ Rukmin was the brother of Rukmini Bhismaka's daughter, one of the wives of Srikrishna. The allusion is obscure; the commentary only says that Rukmin was slain by Valabhadra, Krishna's elder brother, in consequence of a quarrel arising out of a game at dice.

§ Here also the commentary is not elaborate. It is said that Dantabakra also played at dice with Valabhadra, who some how or other was enraged, and broke his teeth with a blow of the dice. The allusion is obscure.

sequence of gambling, dissension is sowed even among strongly united parties.

54. For these reasons, an intelligent monarch should avoid gambling which is productive of evils only. He should also prohibit other proud rulers from challenging* him to a gambling match.

55. Delay in the discharge of duties, loss of money, and the abandonment of virtuous deeds, provocation of the *Prakritis* caused by the king's continued absence in the seraglio,

56. Divulgence of the secrets (by the women with whom they are fondly confided), inducement to commit culpable deeds, jealousy, intolerance, anger, hostility and rashness,

57. These and those enumerated above, are said to be the evils arising out of excessive fondness for the company of women. Seeing this, a monarch desirous of the welfare of his kingdom, should shun the company of women.

58. The energy of the low-minded who are ever hankering after a look at the face of women, dwindles away with their youth.

59. (Aimless) wandering, loss of self control, senselessness, insanity, incoherence in speech, sudden illness,

60. Loss of energy, loss of friends, perversion of the understanding, intelligence and learning, separation from the good and union with the wicked, coming across misfortunes,

61. Faltering steps, tremor of the whole body, giddiness (lassitude), excessive enjoyment of women,—these are the evils of the indulgence in drinking, which have been strongly denounced by the wise.

62. The Vrishnis and the Andhakas of illustrious fame, endowed with power and learning and good behaviour, met

---

* For *Samábbhayam* the commentary gives *Samáhuyam* which reading we accept.

with their destruction in consequence of the evils of drink.*

63. The illustrious Suka the son of Bhrigu, that best of asceties who was equal to his father in intellegence, ate up through excessive intoxication, his very favourite disciple (Kacha).†

64. A person intoxicated with drink, does anything and everything indiscriminately; and in consequence of his indiscriminate conduct, he is excommunicated (from public society).

65. Beautiful women and drink, may be enjoyed within the bounds of moderation; but a learned king should never indulge in hunting and gambling, for these are full of greater dangers.

66. These are the seven kinds of rampant evils retarding the material prosperity of a kingdom, that have been enumerated by those who are conversant with the science of omens and prognostics. The presence of one of these (in a sovereign) is enough to cause his immediate ruin, not to speak of the simultaneous presence of all!

67. These seven kinds of *vyasanas* ending in evil, increase the longing of the senses for their respective objects of enjoyment, and destroy the superiority, wisdom, and excellence and the evergrowing prosperity even of those who are endowed with intelligence equal to that of the Gods.

68. The enemies of a king always under the influence of the *Vyasanas*, defeat him, and themselves become invincible;

---

* The Vrishnis and the Andhakas, were the two offshoots of the Yadu dynasty. When at *Probhasa*, they drank too much, and then slew one another through excessive intoxication. The story is contained in the Mahabharata.

† Kacha was Vrihaspati's son. He went to Sukra to master the secret lore of reviving the dead. But the Asuras becoming jealous of him, slew him, and when Sukra was intoxicated, offered Kacha's cooked flesh to him. He ate up without knowing what he was eating. For a fuller story, vide *supra*.

but the wise monarch who is free from the influence of the *Vyasanas*, vanquishes his enemies, and himself becomes unconquerable.

Thus ends the fourteenth Section, the seven kinds of Vyasanas. in the Nitisara of Kamandaki.

SECTION XV.

1. FREE from the influences of the *Vyasanas*, and fully possessed of the matchless regal powers, a ruler of men desirous of victory, should set out against his wicked enemy suffering from the influence of the *Vyasanas*.

2. In almost all cases, the wise advise military expeditions against the foes, when these are overwhelmed with calamities; but when a king is confident of his own powers and is in highly prosperous state he may fall upon the foe, though this latter may not be afflicted by the *Vyasanas*.

3. When a monarch would be sure of his ability to forcibly slay even his foe swelling with powers, then (and then only) should he start on a military expedition, inflicting injuries, such as loss and distress, on the latter.

4. A king should first set out to conquer that part of the enemy's territory which teem with the wealth of corn and is thus a thing to be sought out. It is considered sound policy tô deprive the enemy of his supply of food by the destruction of the corn, and thus to add to the strength of a king's own army.

5. His rear safe and secure and avoiding dangerous countries in front, a cool-headed king, cognisant of the movements of the foe, should enter such territories of the enemy

where there would be no difficulty on the route for the supply of food and the support of the allies.

6. Indefatigable and fearless, an intelligent monarch well-provided with food and drink and with detachments* ready for action, should march through all places—level countries, uneven tracts and low lands,—being always guided by a reliable vanguard.

7. In summer, a monarch should march through woods abounding in waters, in which the elephants of the army may perform their ablution; for, if they do not get water (for washing their huge bodies), leprosy will affect them, owing to the severe heat of Summer.

8. An internal heat burns inside the bodies even of elephants employed to perform easy work; this heat when increased by the toils of heavy work, soon kills them (elephants).

9. When there is want of sufficient water in Summer, all creatures are reduced to great distress,† and elephants when they are deprived of drinking water, soon become blind, in consequence of the heat that scorch their bodies.

10. The kingdoms of the rulers of earth, rest on elephants resembling in effulgence masses of blue clouds, from whose temples the fragrant ichor exudes‡ and who are capable of rendering asunder rocks with the stroke of their tusks.

11. One elephant, duly equipt, trained in the ways of war and ridden by the bravest of persons, is capable of slaying six thousand well-caparisoned horses.

12. Armies having elephants in them, are sure to achieve success on water, on land, in narrow defiles crowded with trees, on ordinary, even or uneven grounds, and in such

---

* *Gulma* means a detachment of troops consisting of 45 foot, 27 horse, 9 chariots and 9 elephants.

† Lit: 'the last state of existence.'

‡ For an explanation of *Dàna*, Vide *Supra* note to Sloka 2, Sec. VII.

acts as creating breaches in the ramparts and towers (lit: *harmya* is a mansion).

13. For these reasons, a king should march slowly and without causing fatigue to his troops, through such countries where there are routes on which there is plenty of food and drink, and where there is no danger or difficulty—there by increasing his own efficiency.

14. Even the smallest of prosperous enemies causes great difficulty from behind. So, coolly reviewing his condition, a king should undertake military expeditions. He should not ruin what he possesses, for what is uncertain.

15. Difficulties at the back, and success in the front, of these, the former is of greater moment (and deserves early attention.) Those (kings) who transgress this principal (*i.e.* act otherwise), enlarge the holes (defects of their administration). For these reasons, weighing these things well, a king should set out on an expedition.

16. When a monarch is strong both in his front and his back (*i. e.* when he is capable of subjugating his foes both in front and rear) then only should he launch upon an expedition bearing great fruits. Otherwise, marching forward with the enemy at his back unchecked, a king suffers signal loss in the rear portion of his army.

17. On setting out on a expedition, a king should place in the van, an army of many detachments, whose ranks teem with many brave heroes. There is unity in an army of great heroes, and unity (*i.e.* united army) is unconquerable by the enemy.

18. When a foe must be marched upon, an energetic king should not be afraid of the difficulties that may be at his rear; he should depute in the front his commander-in-chief or the prince with a portion of the army (and himself remain to watch the foe in the rear).

19. Of internal and external defects, the internal is graver—(*i.e.* should be first attended to). Amending the

internal ones and providing necessary measures for the (removal of the) external ones, a king should set out on an expedition.

20. The priests, the ministers, the princes and the noblemen—these are the principal leaders of the army ; their disaffection of which no sign is outwardly perceivable, and which is caused by some change of policy,* is said by the sages to be internal defect.†

21. The other kind of disaffection of which the fury is outwardly perceivable, is the disaffection of the frontier guards, foresters and border tribes. When this sort of disaffection is generated, a king should meet it, assisted by their ministers and counsellors of skilful ways (weaning them over to his side).

22. Internal disaffection should be pacified by such measures of policy as conciliation, gift &c, and external disaffection by the causing of disunion and dissension among the disaffected party. A wise monarch should pacify disaffection in such a manner that the disaffected do not resort to the enemy's side.

23. The loss of men and munition is said to be destruction; and the loss of money and corn (food) is said to be drain. A wise and prudent king should never betake to a troublous policy prolific of (such) destruction and drain.

24. He should follow such policies as are sure to be crowned with success and attended with much beneficial results, and whose termination would not be delayed and future effects would be conducive of much good. But he should never resort to such troublous policies which involve the evils of destruction and drain.

---

* Lit :—proceeding from *Mantra* or counsel.

† *Prakopa* lit: means the morbid irritation or disorder of anything ; it is usually preceded by such words as *Vât*, *pitta* &c, which are the humours of the body.

25. Attempt to accomplish what are incapable of being accomplished, want of attempt for what are capable of being accomplished proceeding out of imprudence, and attempt in inopportune moments for what are capable of being accomplished—these are said to be the three kinds of *Vyasanas* attending the performance of acts.

26. Lust, want of forgiveness and forbearance, too much tenderness (of feeling), bashfulness, crookedness, and want of straight-forwardness, arrogance, self-conceit, excessive piousness, poorness of the army and its dishonoring,

27. Malice, terror, negligence, and carelessness, incapability of enduring the inclemeneies of the weather, hot, cold, and rainy,—these (causes) favored by the advantages of the season, are sure to hinder the achievement of success.

28. The wise say that there are seven kinds of party—*vis*—that which is the kings own, that which is of the allies, that which has sought the kings protection, that which has been created by some act or other, that which arises out of some relationship, that which was a party before, and that which has been weaned over by various services and display of politeness and courtesy.

29. A loyal party is to be recognised by his ready obediennce, his singing in praise of the (king's) merits, his not putting up with the insults and blame offered to the king, his efforts to fill up the holes (*i.e.*, redeem the weaknesses) of the king, and by his conversations regarding the richness, energy and courage of the monarch.

30. One of high lineage, straight-forward, learned in the *Shastras*, polite, high in rank and position, firm in his allegiance,* grateful, and endowed with power, intelligence, and wisdom,—such a one should be recognised as a faithful and well-behaved party.

31. Energy, an accurate remembrance, contentment,

* Lit. 'never intending to forsake the king.'

courage, truthfulness, liberality, kindliness, firmness, dignity, self-control, endurance, bashfulness, and eloquence (or boldness in speech)—these are said to be the qualities of the (king's) self.

32. Its management according to the commendable rules of polity, is said to be the power of counsel. The solvency and the efficiency of the treasury and the army respectively, are said to be the power of the king, and strong and powerful exertion is said to be the power of energy ; the possessor of these three kinds of powers becomes the victor.

33. Expeditiousness, skilfulness, courage in seasons of adversity and coolness in prosperity, an infallible, matured and social wisdom resulting from close study of the *Shastras*,

34. Energy, boldness, perseverance, exertions, resoluteness and manliness in the performance of acts, healthiness, the ability for the achievement of the ends of action, a favorable fortune and cheerfulness—these are qualities worthy of a king.*

35. Laying hold of the enemie's treasury by sowing dissension among his partisans, a king should march upon the foe disunited from his supporters. Always acting in this way, (*i. e.*, undertaking such expeditions only), a king obtains the dominion of) the earth washed by the waves of the ocean (*i. e.*, rules over the whole length and breadth of the earth surrounded by the ocean).

36. The best season for the marching out of the elephants is when the sky is overspread with masses of rain-clouds ; seasons other than this, is suitable for the march of the horses ; and the proper season (for military expedition), is that which is neither too hot nor too cold, nor rainy nor dry, and when the earth is covered with corn.

---

* These two Slokas are hopelessly elliptical—having no connection with those preceeding or following them. The last portion must be supposed to be understood.

37. At night, the owl kills, the crow; and the crow kills the owl when night passes away. Therefore a king should set out on an expedition marking well the (advantages or disadvantages of the) seasons. It is in proper season that attempts are crowned with success.

38. A dog can overpower a crocodile when it is on land, and the crocodile can overpower the dog when it is in water. Therefore one (a king) exerting with the advantages of the place in his favour, enjoys the fruition ot his acts.

39. On horses on even tracts, and on elephants on watery (marshy) lands and countries abounding in trees and covered with rocks, and united with the army of his partisans and reviewing his own strength, a king should march out, for the conquest of countries.*

40. On desert tracts when the rain falls, in Summer through countries abounding in water, and mixed up with allied troops, a king should march, as it pleases him, for the conquest of countries.†

41. Following a route on which there is not too much water or which is not totally destitute of water, which abounds in corn and fire-woods, and where plenty of carpenters are to be found, a king should proceed towards the enemy by easy marches.

42. That portion only of the enemy's country should be marched into, where there would be no difficulty for the supply of food and for the support of the allies; which would abound in water, and whose watery expanses would be

---

* The last portion is understood. This and the following sloka may be taken together; but then their construction will be still more clumsy.

† We confess we have not been able to make out any very good construction of this and the preceeding sloka—what we have embodied in the translation is a clumsy and forced one, but it is calculated to give the reader some idea of the author's meaning.

free from sharks &c., and crossed over by faithful followers; and whence the sick and wounded wood not shrink back.

43. Those incorrigible fools who without much deliberation, rashly enter into the enemy's territory which is long way off, soon feel the touch of the edge of the enemy's sword.

44. Posting sentries on the route and in the camp, arranging duly for his safety, and with brave warriors lying by his side ready for action, a king should enjoy a balmy sleep undisturbed by dreams.

45. When from the enemy's camp the neigh of moving horses and the roar of a elephants proceed, and when the sound of bells reaches his ears, he (the king) should then even in his sleep, call out saying—'what brave hero keeps watch there.'*

46. Then awaking, he should purify himself and offer adoration to the gods; cheerful and dressed in beautiful garments, he should then be duly paid homage to by the prime-ministers, priests, allies and friends.

47. Then deciding with their help as to what should be done, that possessor of beautiful conveyances, should march out riding on a (first-classs) vehicle, and surrounded by foot-soldiers of noble extraction who are equal to himself (in prowess).

48. The king should himself look after the tending of the horses and elephants and the repairing of the chariots, and the comforts of the detachments and the soldiers severally. He should see that the favorite horses and the leader elephants are supplied with *Bidhána*.†

49. The king should be accessible to all and his speech

* The text is vicious—the translation is free. The author means that even during sleep the king should be watchful so that at the slightest alarm he may be ready for self-defence.

† *Bidhána* is the food given to horses and elephants in order to intoxicate them.

should invariably he preceded by smiles. He should speak sweet kind words, and pay (the soldiers) more than their wages. Won over by sweet words and liberal payment, the troops will gladly lay down their lives for their lord.

50. By constant practice, one becomes quite competent to ride upon chariots, horses, elephants and boats, and attains great mastery in bowmanship; constant practice bestows on the intelligent ability for performing even most difficult acts.

51. Riding on a huge elephant duly equipped and with followers and soldiers accoutred in mail, and with the ranks of the army teeming with brave heroes, a monarch should march forward, having at first held consultation with the ambassadors of the feudatory kings.

52. He should bring to light the latches of the foe through the agency of his highly intelligent and liberal-mind-spies. A ruler of earth abondoned by his spies, becomes like a man deprived of his sight.

53. The ally of the enemy should be own over by tempting offers or by the giving of some trifling thing; that portion of the enemy's party that may be bought off, should be bought off by the payment of a proper price.*

54. If the foe is not unwilling to enter into a treaty, a king should establish peace with him by deputing his ambassadors, and finish what he has undertaken as desirable, as soon as possible. On the other hand—(if the foe is unwilling to enter into a treaty), he should sow dissension among his partizans and thereby help his own advancement.

55. A king should wean over to his side by gifts, conciliation &c. the foresters, and frontier tribes and commanders of castles, whom he may come across on his route. In difficult and intricate tracts and when one is confined within them, these become the guides, and point the way out.

* We have not been able to make out any plausible meaning of this sloka. The text is hopelessly vicious; what is given above is only a rational conjecture.

56. Of any person who for some reason or without it, has gone over to the enemy's side forsaking his former allegiance, the movements should be watched, when he comes near armed with weapons.

57. One possessed of the power of counsel and desiring his own advancement, should at first hold deliberate counsels (and then undertake any act). Power of counsel is of greater importance than that of the arms (*i.e.* brute force). Indra conquered the Asuras through the power of his better counsel.

58. A wise monarch conversant with the principles of polity should in the proper season undertake an act, being guided by his keen and pure intelligence, and putting forward evey effort for a successful termination. It is in proper season only that success can be achieved.

59. The divine majesty of the powerful and high-souled monarchs, who are possessed of knowledge and heroism, and who walk on the duly lighted path, is said to hang on their own arms resembling serpents in length.

60. When the earth would be adorned with plenty of corn and filled with prosperity and cheerful men, when there would be no rain and consequent muddiness of the soil, and when the woods would seem to blaze forth with the beauty of the blossoming mango trees,—in such a season putting forth his endeavours, a king should march out for conquering the enemy's territories.

61. Thus with his best efforts and his mind totally concentrated on the attack, a monarch should fall upon his foe. A foe whose possssions have been snatched away, gets back his territory if he serves the victor faithfully.

Thus ends the fifteenth section, the dissertation on military expedition, in the Nitisara of Kamandaki.

---

* That is the power of counsel and of wealth are better means for subjugating the foe than the strength of the army.

SECTION XVI.

1. MARCHING into the vicinity of the enemy's town, a king acquainted with the ways of encamping, should pitch his camps on grounds recommended by the wise.

2. The camp should be quadrangular, with four entrances; it should not be either too spacious or too narrow, and should be surrounded on all sides with highways, bulworks and intrenchments.

3. The pavillions inside the camp should be made square* crescent-shaped, circular or long, according to the advantages and measure of the ground (on which they are erected).

4. Decorated with broad, disjointed and several tops, adorned with tents, having a secret chamber, and easy outlets on all sides,

5. Possessing a treasure-chamber inside, and capable of imparting a sense of cheerfulness and comfort, the king's pavillion should be erected there, and be protected by mighty and veteran troops.

6. Having received them with welcome, a king should place near his own pavillion, the old soldiers serving the royal line for generations, the rank and file, the troops of the allies and of the enemies weaned over, and classes of foresters, in successive order.

7. On the outskirts of the camp, numerous formidable hunters of wicked deeds who have been handsomely paid and won over, should be placed in circular array.

8. Elephants of celebrated names and horses fleet as the glances of the mind, both under the management of faith-

---

* *Sringátam* lit: means a crossing or where four roads cut one another. Hence the signification embodied above. It may also mean elevated.

ful dependants, should mount guard at the vicinity of the monarch's pavillion.

9. For his own safety a king should day and night remain armed with weapons and prepared for action, being ever on his guard, and with the interior of his pavillion cleared of soldiers.*

10. An elephant with huge tusks, trained in the modes of warfare, duly equipped and ridden by a brave guide, and a fleet steed, should ever be kept ready at the entrance of the king's pavillion.

11. With a portion of his own troops and with those of the allies, and placing the commander-in-chief in his front and accoutred in mail, a monarch should at night fall upon the enemy out-side his own encampment, (in order to take them by surprise).

12. Swift horsemen capable of running to distant boundaries and border-lands, and of great fleetness, should ascertain the movements of the enemy's troops.

13. Strict watch should be made to be kept by faithful troops at the entrances decorated with flags, flag-staffs, and porches adorned with garlands of flowers.

14. Every body should go out and come in keenly watched. The enemy's spies should dance attendance upon the king, ready to receive his commands.

15. Prevented from drinking, gambling and useless noise-making, the men should stand prepared for all acts, ready with all accessories and instruments.

16. Leaving grounds spacious enough for the drill and exercise of his own good swordsmen, a king should destroy all other lands outside his own intrenchments, for the purpose of destroying the enemy's troops.

17. The ground around the camp should be pervaded, at

---

* This word may have another signification *viz*, guarded by self-controlled soldiers.

places with thorny branches of trees, at places with iron-pointed pegs (caltrops), and at places with secret holes and crevices.

18. Every day the drilling of the soldiers should be performed, with various appliances and on grounds cleared of trees, shrubs, stones, trunks, earthen mounds and water.

19. The place where desirable grounds for the drill of the king's own troops can be obtained and where all the disadvantages will be on the enemy's side—such a place is said to be the best (for encamping purposes).

20. Where grounds equally advantageous for the drill of one's own troops and those of the enemy can be found—that place is said by persons interpreting the *Shâstras*, to be of middling merit.

21. Where there are spacious grounds for the drilling of the enemy's troops and where the reverse is the case with regard to a king's own troops,—that place is said to be the worst of all places.

22. Always wish to have the best encamping ground; in its absence, try to get a middling one; but never, for the sake of success, use the worst place, which is no better than a place of imprisonment.

23. A camp—which seems to be within the clutches of some body, where numerous diseases prevail, where suddenly hostilities spring up, and heavy frosts fall,

24. Which is blown over by unfavourable winds, where suddenly dusts begin to fall, where each tries to injure another and where the drums do not sound (well),

25. Where there are constant alarm and frght, where pealing thunders roar and where meteors fall, where the (king's) Parasol appears to be on fire and emits smoke and where yelping of jackals is heard from the left side,

26. Which is infested by flocks of crows, vultures and other such birds of ominous note, where great heat is suddenly felt and showers of blood fall,

27. Where the *Raj-nakshatra** is seen to be surrounded on all sides, by other baneful portentuous planets, and whence headless trunks are seen in the sun, and where the vehicles and draught animals are suddenly stupified,

28. And where the ichor exuding from the temples of elephants in rut, suddenly dries up,—a camp where these and such other kinds of omens ill do prevail, is a very bad one (is not commended by the wise).

29. A camp—where the inmates, men and women, are all cheerful, where the drums and kettle-drums sound aloud where horses neigh deeply and elephants duly equipped roar tremendously,

30. Which rings with music of the Vedic chaunts and the saying of *Punyaha*,† where melodious harmony of songs and dances rise up in wave after wave, where there is no cause of alarm and great excitement prevail, and where the expected victory is indicated by good signs,

31. Where there is no dust-storm but excessive rain falls, where the *Grahas* are seen to be on the right ride, and no unusually portentuous phenomena, either heavenly or earthly, are viewed,

32. Where favourable winds sing auspiciousness by their blowing, where the troops are well-fed and cheerful, and where incenses are burnt on blazing flames,

33. Where the elephants are mad without having drunk intoxicating liquors and where the *Asáras* are in highly prosperous state,—a camp where these auspicious sings prevail, is praised by the wise.

---

* *Fajnakshatra*—may mean the moon ; but we are not sure. The allusion is to the belief that when certain star are seen in certain positions it portends evil and no act is to be undertakens while their influence lasts.

† *Punyahas* mean auspicious days—here it means the prayer for an auspicious day.—May this be an auspicious day, the Hindus rise from their beds with this prayer on their lips.

34. When good and auspicious signs are seen in the camp, the foe is sure to be routed, and when they are bad and inauspicious, reverses are to be suffered by the king. It is omens that indicate good or bad results.

35. For these reasons, a monarch versed in the *Shastras* should mark all the omens. When the augeries are good and the king exerts with a pure heart, he leads to success the commendable works undertaken by him.

36. Victory is of him, who possesses allies, wealth, knowledge, prowess, favourable fortune, perseverance and manly efforts.

37. The king is called the *Skandha* inasmuchas he is said to be the root (of the prosperity)of the people. The functions of the ministers, the army and other members of a government are said to be *Abâra*.

38. When for the advancement and prosperity of the people the *Skandha* or the king is supported or helped forward by the great *Abâras* or ministers, armies &c, it is said to be *Skandhâbâra*.

39. The destructions of the privillions, the clothing, the drinking water and the food grains, and of the supporting troops of the allies,—these are said to be the deaths of the *Skandhâbâra*;—these therefore should be carefully guarded against.

40. Thus the army should be carefully encamped and its good or bad state viewed; this (good or bad condition) should also be carefully watched with regard to the enemy's army. When no evil omens would be seen, a king should begin (action).

Thus ends the sixteenth section, the desseration on encamping, in the Nitisâra of Kamandaki.

SECTION XVII.

—o—

1. POSSESSED of a keen intelligence and armed with manliness and a favorable fortune, a monarch with proper endeavours and perseverance, should bring to bear against the enemy, the expedients for subjugating them.

2. A solvent treasury and a good counsel, fight better than an army consisting of the four kinds of forces. Therefore a king of sound political knowledge—should conquer his enemies by the power of counsel and treasures.

3. Conciliation, gift (or bribery), display of military power, and domestic discord, these four, and deceit, neglect and conjuring—these, seven in all, are said to be the means of success against an enemy.

4. The enumeration of the good services done mutually, the extolling of the merits, the establishment of some relationship, display of majesty,

5. And to say in sweet and smooth words—"I am yours" &c,—these are said to be the five kinds of concilation, by those who know how to apply it (conciliation).

6. To give away acquired wealth in good, bad or middling manner, to give in return for what is obtained, to suffer to be taken what has been taken away,

7. To give away some wonderful thing, and the remmission of what is due—these are said to be the five kinds of gift.

8. To cause affection and love to wither away, to generate rivalry, and to threaten, these are the three modes of sowing domestic discord.

9. To kill, to plunder wealth, and to inflict loss and distress, these are said to the three kinds of display of military power, by those who know how to use it (military power).

10. *Danda* (or infliction of punishment), is said to be of two kinds *viz.*, open and secret. The enemies (of the state) and those who are disliked by the people should be openly dealt with.

11. Those who cause anxiety to the people, those who are the kings favorites, and those who stand very much in the way of the material prosperity of the state should be dealt with secretly (*i. e.* secret punishment should be inflicted on them).

12. By poisoning, by the help of mystic ceremonies (*e. g. Márana* &c.) by assasination, (lit. by weapon) and by throwing down,*—by these methods, secret punishments should be so meted out that no body could come to know of them.

13. On Brāhmanas, or on any other caste, on pious people and on low and mean classes of men, an intellegent king, should not—for the advancement of his material (spiritual) welfare, inflict the capital punishment.

14. Those against whom secret punishment is recommended, may also be done away with by neglect. But a prudent person should avoid to show this neglect out-wardly (or in a prominent manner so as to attract attention).

15. Thoroughly scanning, reviewing and studying their hearts and speaking sweet words and thereby appearing to be shedding nectar—a king should employ conciliation as an expedient against the foe.

16. Sweet and melliflous speech is said to be conciliation itself. Euloguim, truth, sweet speech, these are synonymous with conciliation.

17. Appearing to view the undertaking of the enemy in the light of his own, a king should enter into his heart (lit. penetrate him) unperceived, like water penetrating into the mountain.

---

* The other reading found in same books, means by the throwing of water &c.

18. The immortals and the Danavas succeeded in churning the ocean of milk and obtained desirable results only through conciliation.* The sons of Dhritarastra who were against the policy of conciliation, were soon slain by (the sons of Pandu).†

19. An intelligent and wise king should pacify a threatening foe by means of gift or (bribery). When intent on ruining Indra, Sukra was pacified through gift.‡

20. When Bhrigu's son was enraged in consequence of the fault of Sarmistha(Vrishaparva's daughter), Vrishaparavan the lord of the Dānavas made himself happy by giving her over (to Sukra so that she may serve this one's daughter.)§

21. One desirous of peace should, even approaching the powerful king uninvited, give away things to him for pleasing

---

* An eternal hostility exists between the gods and the *Dānavas* (the demons) who always fight with each other. But when it was decided to churn the ocean of milk, they were reconciled, but for which no churning could have been accomplished. It is by the policy of conciliation that the gods won the *Dānavas* over and persuaded them to help in the matter.

† The sons of Pandu were ever for peace and conciliation. But the sons of Dhritarastra stubbornly refused all overtures—so much so, that they declined to give even five villages only to the five Pandava brothers. They were completely ruined and slain in the battle that followed—the great battle of Kurukshetra.

‡ The allusion is obscure. Sukra was the preceptor of the Demons and consequently the enemy of Indra.

§ Sukras daughter Devayani and Vrishaparvan's daughter Sarmistha were fast friends. Once upon a time Devayani and Sarmistha went to bathe keeping their clothes on the shore. But the god Wind changed their clothes—and when they were dressed they began to quarrel about the change—until Sarmistha so far forgot herself that she slapped her companion on the cheek—and threw her into a well. There she remained until she was seen and rescued by Yayati who married her with the consent of father; and Sarmistha was ordered to be her servant as a recompense for the insulting conduct she offered to Devayani.

him; the sons of Gāndhari* refusing to give (to the Pandavas a portion of the kingdom) met with their complete destruction.

22. Alluring by mighty hopes, but fulfilling little of them, a king should wean over the four kinds of alienable parties, knowing them through spies.†

23. The greedy who have been deprived of their dues, the honorable persons who have been dishonoured, the irritable persons who have been angered, and those who have been extremely abused,

24. These are the four kinds of alienable parties, who should be won over, each by the fulfilment of his particular desire. But to establish peace in his own party as well as in the party of the foe—is a better policy.

25. With all efforts and carefulness a king should effect the alienation of the ministers, counsellors, and priests; and when these have been alienated, the highly powerful princes should be tried.

26. The prime-minister and the crown prince are said to be the two arms of a lord of earth; the former is also said to be the king's eye,—and the alienation of this one cannot be compared to the alienation of any body else.

27. An intelligent king should with all endeavours try to vitiate (alienate) one of his rival monarch's own family; such a one when vitiated destroys his own dynasty like fire destroying the fuel which produces it.

28. One highly disaffected at heart is equal to one of the rival monarch's own dynasty, (so far as the facility of alienation is concerned). Therefore a king should wean

* Gandhari was the wife of Dhritarastra and the mother Duryodhāna and his brothers. They refused to give to the Pandavas even five villages only—see Supra.

† *Ubhaya-betana* means one receiving wages from both masters—hence treacherous spies.

him over in any way and maintain peace and conciliation among his own ranks.

29. Secret overtures should be made only to one who is capable, of doing good or bad.* But with keen and scrutinising intelligence it should be at first ascertained whether he is a straight-forward or a hypocrete person.

30. A straight-forward person should try to fulfill his words to the best of his power. But a hypocrete, in consequence of his longing for wealth, would betray both parties.

31. *Quandom* commanders, mean-minded persons, those who serve the king only to pass the time any how or other,† those who have been punished without rhyme or reason, those who long for (personal) prosperity, those who are invited and then neglected (or dishonored),

32. One of the king's own family (dynasty) who is jealous of (hostile to) him, he that is found fault with by the monarch, those who have given up their business (idlers), and those on whom heavy taxes have been levied,

35. Those who love to fight, those who are rashly bold, those who are self-conceited, those who are severed from virtue, wealth and desire,‡ those who are of a excitable nature, the honorable persons who have been dishonored,

34. Those who are cowards, those who live in constant fear (of being punished) for their offences, those who have created enemies through want of kind treatment,§ those who love the company of those inferior to them, and who drive away their equals,

---

* The original word lit: translated would mean—one who is capable of showing wrath or mercy; hence "having much influence."

† These people do not feel for the king, and may be weaned over by the offer of petty advantages. The word may mean also—those who are procrastinating.

‡ That is, whose existence have been blasted and who have no love for life.

§ The text is vicious, the translation is free.

35. Those who are imprisoned without cause and who have been specially favoured for some reason or other, those who have been apprehended without reason, those worthy and worshipful persons who are disregarded,

36. Those whose family and possessions have been plundered (*i.e.* confiscated), those who are inflamed by a strong desire for enjoyment, those who have been ruined,* those who are friends outwardly, those whose goods and chattels have been taken off,† and those who have been driven out,

37. These are said to be the alienable parties. When any of these is found with the foe, he should be weaned over. Those who come over to the king's side (*i.e.* are won over) should be honored by (the present of) those things they may desire to have; in this way also, a king should maintain unity and concord among his own partizans.‡

38. To find out what is coveted by both (the king and the alienable party), and to see what both fear and are apprehensive of, and chiefly, bribing (giving presents) and honoring—these are said to be the means for effecting alienation.

39. Assailed by a powerful enemy, an intelligent king, should try to effect alienation among the former's party. The powerful Sanda and Amarka,§ alienated from each other, were vanquished by the gods.

40. Causing disunion in the united army of the foe, a king should annihilate it by open attack. Disunited, it is

---

* It may mean bankerupts.

† *Bahirbandhu* and *Bahirdravya* may mean—those who have got friends outside, and one whose property lies outside the dominions of the particular king, respectively.

‡ The translation is free in the latter portion.

§ The allusion is obscure; probably they were two demon brothers, the gods finding them united, applied the policy of alienation against them, and afterwards slew them.

destroyed like a piece of wood which is set fire to with dried grass.

41. Supported by faithful allies and favored by the advantages of the soil and the season, and inflamed with energy, a king should drive his enemy to destruction by open attack, even like king Yudhisthira himself.

42. Reviewing the measure of his own strength, a monarch should regulate his attacks (lit. lead his army to battle). In the days of yore, Rama* possessed of strength and energy, slew the *Kshatriyas* single handed.

43. Those who are idle, those who have lost all power those who have exhausted their efforts in an undertaking, those who are suffering from extensive destruction and loss, those who are routed,

44. And cowards, fools, women, boys, pious men, and wicked and brute-like persons, as also those of a friendly nature and of a peaceful turn of mind—these should be won over by conciliatory measures.

45. The greedy and the poor should be brought under subjugation by being honoured with gifts, so also those wicked ones who are disunited being afraid of one another and through fear of the punishments inflicted on them.

---

* The allusion is to the story of Parasurama son of Jamadagni. This Brahman is said to have been the sixth incarnation of Vishnu. While young he cut off with his axe the head of his mother *Renukà* at the command of his father, when none of his brothers was willing to do so. Some time after this, king Kartaviryya went to the hermitage of his father and carried off his cow. But Parasurama when he returned home fought with the king and killed him. The sons of the Kartaviryya hearing of the fate of their father, came to Parasurama's hermitage and shot his father dead in his absence. Thereupon Parasurama made the dreadful vow of exterminating the whole Kshatriya race. He succeeded in ridding the earth twenty one times of the warrior race. He is said to have penetrated through the Krouncha mountain. He is one of those who will never die—and is believed at present to be engaged in austerities on the Mohendra mountain.

46. Sons, brothers, and friends, should be won over by persuasive words (or wealth), for, who can be equal to them, although they may be made distant by the enemy?

47. If per chance these (sons, &c.,) fall off from their allegiance, conciliation should be employed against them. Indeed, sometimes they are incorrigibly vitiated through pride and boastfulness.

48. They in whom nobility of birth, good conduct, charity, kindness, piety, truthfulness, gratefulness and harmlessness are to be found, are said to be *Acharyyas*.

49. A king conversant with the policy of gift and alienation and knowing the ways of inflicting punishment, should win over the citizens and the people and the leaders of the army by gift and alienation.

50. Offended friends should be reconciled by honouring and gifts and kind words; others should be won over by the proper employment of the policy of alienation or bribery or gift.

51—52. Men hidden inside the images of gods, pillars, and holes, men dressed in the clothes of women, and assuming terrible appearances at night and appearing in the semblance of *Pisáchas* (demons), and gods,—in this way do persons practise the policy of deceit and this is known as *Máyá*.

53. To assume different appearances at will, to shower down weapons, iron balls and water, and to be hidden in darkness, these also are the artifices practised by men.

54. Bhima killed Kichaka by being disguised as a woman.*

---

* While Droupadi in the guise of Sairindri was residing at the court of king Viráta, his brother-in-law Kichaka saw her and her beauty excited wicked passions in his heart. He became enamoured of her and through his royal sister, tried to violate her modesty. Droupadi complained of his unmannerly conduct to the king, but he declinedto in fere; she then sought her husband Bhima's assistauce, who told her to show herself favourable to Kichaka's advances. An appointment was then

The god of fire also remained hidden for a long time by practising divine *Máyá*.*

55. Not to prevent one from wrong, from war and from danger—these are said to be the three kinds of *Upekshá* or deplomatic neglect, by those who are conversant with its nature and use.

56. Intent on the performance of an misdeed and blinded by lust, Kichaka was neglected by Virata and allowed to be slain (by Bhima).

57. Afraid of the unfulfilment of her own desire, Hidimva, although seeing Bhimasena ready for the combat, allowed her own brother to be slain and thus neglected him.†

58. The exhibition of clouds, darkness, rain, fire, mountain and other strange shapes, and of troops which are at a distance marching with flowing banners,

59. And the exhibition of cut off, severed and slaughtered troops, and of highly efficient armies—all these kinds of conjuring should be resorted to for inspiring terror into the enemy's host.

60. These are said to be the expedients that serve various purposes of the monarchs; of these, a king conversant with the nature of conciliation, should employ it whenever it pleases him.

61. At first the policy of gift (or bribery) should be employed and then conciliation and alienation. But these latter two when united with the former, are sure to bring about success.

---

made between Kichaka and Draupadi that they should meet in the dancing hall of the palace at night; pursuant to this appointment Bhima disguised as Draupadi went there and when Kichaka tried to embrace him taking him for Draupadi—he was crushed to death.

* This allusion is obscure.

† Hidimva was a demoness; she became enamoured of Bhima—and to satisfy her lust she induced Bhima to slew her brother Hidimva. The story is contained in the Mahabharata.

62. The policy of conciliation without the support of the policy of gift seldom brings success in an undertaking. Conciliation without the help of gift cannot produce the desired effect even when it is employed against one's own wife.

63. These expedients, a king conversant with the science of polity, should skilfully bring to bear against the enemy's troops or in his own forces. A king exerting without employing these expedients, proceeds towards his end like a blind man.

64. Prosperity is sure to come into the possession of those wise persons (kings) who employ these expedients; nay it swells (every day). When properly managed with the help of these expedient efforts of kings bear fruit.

Thus ends the seventeenth section, the use and employment of the expedients, in the Nitisara of Kamandaki.

SECTION XVIII.

1. THE three policies of conciliation, gift and alienation having failed, a king conversant with the principles of polity and the ways of punishing, should lead his army against those who deserve punishment.

2. Having worshipped the gods and the twice-born Brahmanas and with the planets and the stars shining propitious, a king should march towards the foe, with his six kinds of troops arrayed in due order.

3. The *Moula* the mercenary, the *Sreni* the allied, those belonging to the enemy weaned over and the forest tribes, these are the six kinds of forces; each preceding is of greater importance than each following; so also is their *Vyasana*.

4. For their respect and love for the king, for the fact of their helping in the removal of the dangers that may happen to him and for their being inspired with the same thoughts and sentiment, the *Moula* troops are more reliable than the mercenary.

5. The mercenary troops again are more reliable than the *Sreni* troops, for the former depend on the king for their livelihood.

6. The *Sreni* troops are again more reliable than the troops of the allies, for these latter do not enjoy a share of the king's victory, whereas the former participate in his joy and grief, and moreover live in the same country with the king.

7. The allied troops again are more reliable than the troops of the enemy weaned over, inasmuch as the former persue the same object with the king, and their country and time of action are known, whereas the latter often differ in opinion.

8. The low forest tribes, are by nature faithless, greedy, and sinful; for this reason, the weaned over troops of the enemy are better than they, who are wild and undisciplined.

9. Both the forest tribes and the weaned over troops of the enemy, follow the king waiting for the moment when to accomplish his ruin; so, when all chances of their causing any difficulty will be over,—victory is sure to embrace the king.

10. A king has great cause of apprehension from these two (the forest-tribes and the weaned over troops of the enemy), for secret overtures may be directed towards them

by the foe. From his own side also, a king should commence intriguing, for intrigue is ever sure to give victory.*

11. An enemy highly powerful in consequence of his being possessed of *Moula* troops swelling with energy and faithful in allegiance, should be encountered with the same kind of troops capable of enduring loss and destruction.†

12. When the march would be long, or the campaign will be a protracted one, a king should proceed with the *Moulas* duly protected. The *Moulas* being of long standing are capable of bearing up against loss and destruction.

13. In these matters (*i.e.* in protracted marches and campaigns and the like) an intelligent king should not depend much upon (lit: leave off), the mercenary and other kinds of troops; for when they are worn out with the toils of the protracted march or campaign, their alienation (by the foe) may be apprehended.

14. When the troops of the enemy are numerous, when the fatigue and toil are excessive and protracted, and when the army is always sent abroad and put to difficult tasks—its alienation (by the enemy) follows as a matter of course.

15. A king is virtually powerless when his mercenary troops are numerous, and *Moula* troops are small in number. So also, an enemy is powerless, when his *Moula* troops are small in number or are disaffected.‡

16. Battles should be fought more often with the help of the power of counsel—for then victory is obtained with little difficulty. When again the soil and the season are unfavorable, the destruction and loss become immense.

17. When the enemy's troops give up their efforts in the direction of alienation and become trustworthy, the merce-

* The Sloka as given in the text is unintelligble. It is after comparing several readings, that we could make out the meaning embodied above.

† What the another means is this that when the enemy leads out *Moula* troops the king should meet with his own *Moula* troops.

‡ The translation is free.

nary troops defy them saying:—"They are of base mettle and should be slain."

18. Three kinds of troops (*viz.*, the forest-tribes, the troops of the enemy weaned over and the *Sreni*) may be induced to excessive drinking and thus rendered incapable of service. With his own troops who have been duly drilled and who have not stayed in foreign lands for a long time (for then they would have been worn out), a king should fall upon the foe.

19. A king whose resources for battle are small may by his power of counsel make the allied troops like his own; and thus his strength may be increased.

20. Acts in which the king and the allied monarch are both equally interested, acts whose success depends on the ally, and acts in which clemency and cleverness are to be displayed, such acts should be undertaken in conjunction with the ally.

21. Supported by a large host of the enemy's troops weaned over, a king should march against a powerful enemy. Then like a dog waiting to kill a boar, he should bring into action conciliation or other kinds of policy.

22. The troops of the enemy that have been weaned over should be employed in, and oppressed with the task of rooting out the thorns of the difficult paths; for otherwise, there is danger of their being morbidly irritated.

23. The foresters also should be employed in similar tasks; and when entering into the territory of another, a learned king should always place them in the front.

24. These are the six kinds of troops and these constitute a complete army together with the cavalry, infantry, car-warriors and elephants. Such an army supported by the power of counsel and a solvent treasury constitutes a *Sadanga vala* or an army of six members.

25. A powerful monarch arranging these six kinds of

troops without the least defect, should proceed to encounter an army stronger than his own.

26. By his power of counsel, &c., a king should know its (his army's) connections and he should also apprise himself of what his generals do or do not.

27. One of high extraction, belonging to the king's own country (*i. e.*, the king's own subject), conversant with the rules of counsel and acting in conformity with them, a careful student of the science of *Dandaniti* and its administrator,

28. One possessed of the qualities of energy, heroism, forgiveness, patience, amiableness and richness, one endowed with power and manliness and who is depended upon by his followers for their support (*i. e.*, one who has got followers and dependants),

29. One who has got numerous friends and whose relations and cognates are many, whose countenance reflects genersosity, and who is large-hearted and a thoroughly practical man mixing freely with the people,

30. Who never cultivates other's ill-will or enmity without any reason, whose number of foes is very limited and who is of pure character, and is a profound scholar of the *Shastras*, and acts according their precepts,

31. One who is healthy, stout, brave, forbearing and acquainted with the opportuneness of season, and is possessed of a noble appearance, and has full reliance on his own power,

32. One who knows how to tend horses and elephants, and repair chariots, and is indifatigable, and skilful in fighting and duelling with swords, and can move with agility,

33. Who knows the divisions of the field of battle, and whose power remains unperceived till the time of action like that of the lion, and who is not procrastinating and is watchful humble and self-controlled,

34. Who knows the marks (good or bad) of horses, elephants, chariots, and weapons and is fully acquainted with the

aticons and movements of the spies and scouts, and is grateful and conversant with all alternatives (of acts),

35. One who observes all pious ceremonies and is skilful and followed by skilful dependants, who is expert in all modes of warfare and is competent to manage the army,

36. One who having been naturally gifted with the power of reading others' heart, can perceive what the men, horses and elephants want, who also knows their designation and can supply them their food,

37. One who knows all countries, languages and human characters, and can decipher all writings and is possessed of a retentive memory; one who is thorougly competent to lead nocturnal attacks and who can ascertain by his keen intelligence what should be done,

38. One who knows the times of sunset and sunrise, and the position of the stars and planets and their consequent influences, and who is fully acquainted with the routes, the directions, and the countries (though which the army is to pass,)

39. One who is neither frightened nor fatigued by the pangs of hunger and thirst and the inclemencies of the weather, hot, cold, and rainy, who can bear up against alarms and weariness and who gives asurances of safety to the good,

40. One who can create breaches in the army of the foe, and who can undertake difficult acts, and can detect and remove the cause of alarm of his own troops,

41. One who can protect the camp, and is capable of bringing into light any (underhand) act of the troops, one who fully knows the disguises and the pretences put forward by the spies and messengers, and who reaps success by his great exertion,

42. One who always accomplishes successfully acts undertaken by him, and enjoys their fruition, and who is disregardful of near or remote consequences, but is only anxious about the material prosperity of the kingdom,—

43. One possessed of these characteristics should be made the leader of an army. The army should always, day, night, be carefully protected (from evil influence).

44. Wherever in rivers, mountains, forests and difficult regions there will be any chance of danger, the general should proceed there with his army arranged in due order.

45. The guides supported by a detachment of heroic troops should march in the van; the king and his camp, and the treasury solvent or insolvent, should be in the middle.

46. The horses should march in both the flanks and they should be flanked by the chariot warriors; these last again should be flanked by elephants whom the forest tribes should flank.

47. The accomplished general thus having placed every body in the front should march slowly in the rear, arranging the host of troops, and breathing comfort to the wounded and the weak.

48. When there should be danger in the van, the troops should be disposed of in the Makara (crocodile-shaped), or in the two-winged *Syena* or (hawk-shaped), or in the *Suchi* (needle-shaped) array and then marched forward.

49. When there would be danger in the rear, the *Sakata* (or chariot-shaped) array should be formed; when the danger would be in the flanks, the array called *Vajra* should be formed; and in all situation the array known as *Sarvato-bhadra* that frighten the enemy, should be formed.

50. When the troops are fatigued in consequnce of protracted marches through long routes and over hills dales forests and narrow woody defiles and through rivers and river-beds, when they are afflicted with hunger, thirst, and cold,

51. When they are harassed with raids of robbers and distressed with diseases, want of food and pestilence and oppression, when on the route of march they get muddy

unclean water for drink, and when they become separated or huddled together,

52. When they fall deeply asleep and become busy in preparing their meal, when they are not in the proper ground and are not prepared for attack; when they are afflicted with the fear of thieves and fire, and when they are overtaken by rain and storm,

53. When all these calamities overtake his army, a king should protect it; but when the hostile troops are overtaken by them, he should fall upon them and annihilate them.

54. Having effected an alienation between the foe and his *Prakritis* and with the advantages of the season and the soil in his favour, a king should fight a pitched battle; otherwise he should fight in underhand ways.

55. In unfair warfare, the foe when busy in pitching tents on unfavourable grounds, should be slain by the king who is on favorable grounds; when a king is on his own grounds he is said to be on favourable grounds.

56. A king who is cheerless in consequence of his *Prakritis* being separated from him should be slain through secret agents, foresters, and brave soldiers, who should employ against him gift or bribery or alienation.

57. Displaying himself in the front and thence having ascertained the mark, a king should slay his enemies from behind, falling upon him with agile and heroic troops.

58. He may also placing the greater part of the army in the enemy's back (where consequently his attention will be drawn), slay this latter from the front, falling upon him with the best part of his troops. In this way the flanks also may be assailed in unfair warfare.

59. If the ground in the front be unfavourable, a swift-moving king should (change position and) slay the foe from behind. A king should slay his foe going over to his side who foolishly believes that he has conquered him.

60. Alluring the troops of the enemy out of their camps,

villages and castles into pastures, a cool-headed king should slay them.

61. Concealing the inefficient portion of the army, and with the rest of it supported by the allies, a king should crush the foe falling upon him even like a lion.

62. Remaining hidden, a king should slay his foes when he is engaged in hunting; or he may slay him enticing him away by the hope of plunder and then blockading his route of return.

63. The troops that could not sleep through fear of being attacked in the night and that have been worn out through the toils of night-keeping should be assaulted and annihilated on the day following.

64. A king knowing the rules of nocturnal attack, should lead out a night-attack with the fourth part of his army, against the foe unsuspectingly locked in the arms of sleep.

65. With agile swordsmen inflamed with wrath, a king should slay the foe whose eyes are blinded in consequence of the sun's rays falling on them or the wind blowing against them.

66. In this way, a king possessed of agility should slay his foes.

67. Mist, darkness, herds of kine, pits, hillocks, underwoods, and river-beds—these indicate the foe, for they are the seven kinds of hiding places.

68. A persevering sovereign exerting in the right manner, should slay his foes by the different kinds of warfare, knowing their movements through the agency of his spies.

69. Thus always a king should slay his foes by unfair-war. The slaughter of foes by deceitful measures is not detrimental to one's righteousness. The son of Drona with his sharp weapon slew the troops of the Pandavas when

they were unsuspectingly locked in the arms of sleep at night.*

Thus end the eighteenth section, the modes of warfare, the movements of the generals, surprises &c., in the Nitsara of Kamandaki.

SECTION XIX.

1. To go in front in all marches, to first enter into forests and difficult tracts, to create roads and passages where there are none,

2. To descend into and swim over watery expanses, to conquer the body-guards (consitituting a part of the enemy's army), to break through united ranks, and to gather to their own side the routed troops,

3 To ward off sources of danger, to break down walls and gates, to protect the treasury and the uniform adherence to the policy from all dangers, these are the functions of the elephants.

4. To investigate the woods, the different directions, and the routes, to protect the supplies of food and the supporting troops, to effect with promptitude the acts of pursuit and retreat,

5. To approach and help the distressed portion of the

* The son of Drona promised to Duryodhana to slay the sons of Pandu. One night he went to their camp and instead of slaying the Pandava brothers slew the five sons of Draupadi and brought their heads to Duryodhana. This upset Duryodhana and he died soon after.

army, the *Kotee* and the *Jaghana*,* these are the functions of the horse. Of infantry the functions are always to be armed with weapons,

6. To purify† the pits and the passages, the roads and the tents, and to know the stock of fodder and food and everything like Viswakarma‡ himself.

7. High lineage, youthful age, the tact of knowing other creature's heart, prowess, skilfulness, promptitude resoluteness and the inclination for the performauce of good acts,

8. These are the qualifications of infantry, cavalry car-warriors and horses, who posses good marks and follow all rules of conduct; the possessor of all these qualifications only should be employed in action.

9. A ground free from stakes and thorms and of which the trees and copses have been cut down and the mounds levelled and which possesses outlets of retreat such a ground is thought advantageous for the movements of the infantry.

10 Grounds with small number of trees and stone, having no pits, creepers and caves and which is steady, and free from gravel or mud and possess outlets for retreat, such gronuds are said to be cavalry-grounds.

11. Devoid of sandy soils, mud, earthen mound gravels and stones, and free from marshes, creepers, pits, trees, copses, and such like things,

12. Where there are no gardens and chasms, which are capable of bearing the tread of hoofs, and are steady and can bear the wheels, such grounds are said to be chariot-grounds (*i. e.*, where chariots may be driven with safety).

---

* *Kotee* and *Jaghana* are certain parts of the *Vyuha* or array. *Jaghana* has a speacial meaning viz., the rear guard or the reserved portion of the army.

† The word 'purify' is here used in a metaphorical way, it means "to clear of the foe."

‡ Viswakarma is the divine architect; probably he is also gifted with a keen observation.

13. The grounds for the chariots, the horses and the elephants should be steady and hard. The wise should not consider that the grounds for the horses are not for elephants.

14. Grounds where are there trees to be crushed (*i. e.*, delicate trees which the elephants may eat up) and creepers to be rooted out, which is free from mire, and is fertile and rough, where there are accessible hillocks, such are grounds for the elephants.

15. An intelligent monarch desirous of victory should never hazard a fight without good cause (or his rear well-protected). In case of sheer necessity he may fight being surrounded by numerous troops.

16. Placed on elephants and guarded by lighter troops, the treasures should be carried where the king goes; for royalty depends on treasures.

17. After the completion of a difficult work, praised and held in respect, a king should (liberally) remunerate the warriors; for who does not fight for a liberal-handed king?

18. A king should cheerfully give ten millions of *Barnas* to the slayer of his royal antagonist; half the amount should be given while this latter's son or his general is slain.

19. When a chief of a brave detachment of heroes is slain, ten thousand *Barnas* should be given.

20. When an elephant or a car is destroyed half of this amount should be given; and a thousand *Barnas* should be given, when an archer or a foremost foot soldier is slain.

21. A score of cows or any other object of enjoyment or gold or any other base metal—these belong to them who conquer them.

22. The king should cheerfully remunerate the soldiers according to the things they bring; then he should place the powerful in battle array.

23. The number of horses should be three times the number of cars and elephants, and five and five should be

employed together. Foot-soldiers should be employed with them at the interval of one and horses at the interval of three.

24. Elephants and cars should be placed at the interval of five. This kind of division is commended by all masters of polity.

25. The horses, men and car-warriors and elephants should fight in such a way that their efforts in case of retreat may be unobstructed.

26. When dangerous irregular fight ensues it should be fought with mixed troops. In fierce wars, the mighty and noble dynasties should be sought shelter with.

27. Three men should always be made antagonists and an elephant should alway be opposed by five horses.

28. Fifteen men and four horses, these are said to be capable of withstanding an elephant or a chariot.

29. The weakness of a force is said to be *Panchachâpa* by those who are conversant with the forming of arrays and are accomplished in the art of war-fare.

30. The *Uras*, the two *Kakshas*, the two wings, the centre, the back, the rear and the *Kotee*—these are the seven limbs of the *Vyuha* or array mentioned by those conversant with their nature.

31. According to our preceptor the *Vyuha* has the *Uras*, the *Kaksha* and the wings and the rear parts only; according to Sukra it is devoid of the *Kakshas*.

32. Unalienable, nobly-born, pure-hearted, accomplished in smiting, sure of aim, and competent to fight with resoluteness, such men should be made leaders of divisions.

33. Surrounded by these heroic and brave persons a king should stay on the field and should fight unseperably and protecting one another.

34. The flower of the troops should be placed in the centre of the array and the fighting materials should be placed in the *Jaghana*.

35. The fiercest of the forces accomplished in war should be employed in the fight. A good general is said to be the soul of the battle, and it is lost if there is no general.

36. The *Vyuha* that infantry, cavalry, chariots and elephants constitute, one at the back of another, is said to be *Achala*; that formed by elephants, horses, cavalry, and infantry is in-capable of being withstood.

37. The cavalry in the centre, the chariots in the two *kakshas*, the elephants in the flanks,—such an array is said to be *Antavid*.

38. In place of chariots horses may be posted and in place of horses foot-soldiers may be posted; and in the absence of chariots, an intelligent king should arrange the elephants.

39. The foot-soldiers, the horse, the chariots and the elephants should be thrown in the middle in divisions. The elephants surrounded by the infantry, cavalry, and cars should be placed in the centre.

(Slokas 40—57 contain descriptions and names of the several kinds of array and the ways of using them),

58. Where the enemy's troops are weak, separated, led by vicious persons, there it should be assailed—and thus a king's own strength should be added to.

59. The enemy should be pressed by doubly strong forces,—and he should be oppoesd when united together, by furious detachments of elephants.

60. Unconquerable elephants (of the enemy) should be slain by elephants besmeared with the fat of lions or by groups of elephants ridden by brave guides.

61. The troops of the enemy should be slain by foremost of elephants duly equipped, furious, caparisoned with iron net-works, ridden by brave warriors, and irisistible in consequence of being in rut.

62. A leader elephant in rut and possessed of courage, can slay detachments of the enemy's troops. The victory of

the rulers of earth depends on the number of the elephants. Therefore the armies of the kings should teem with elephants.

Thus ends the ninteenth Section—the arraying of troops, the functions of elephants, horses &c, in the Nitisara of Kamandaki.

FINIS.